لجائزة العالمية للرواية العربية
INTERNATIONAL PRIZE FOR ARABIC FICTION

EXCERPTS FROM
THE 2016 SHORTLIST OF THE
INTERNATIONAL PRIZE FOR ARABIC FICTION

Tareq Bakari

Rabai al-Madhoun

Mohamed Rabie

Mahmoud Shukair

Shahla Ujayli

George Yaraq

Go to page 161 to read an extract from each shortlisted novel
Check out the winner from 26 April 2016 on

www.arabicfiction.org

GINGKO LIBRARY

On Literature and Philosophy
The Non-fiction Writing
of Naguib Mahfouz: Volume I

Between May 2016 and May 2018,
Gingko Library are to bring the complete
non-fiction writings of Naguib Mahfouz
into English for the first time. This first of
four volumes offers a rare glimpse into
Mahfouz's early, formative years as a
writer and journalist. Included are essays
on a number of philosophical themes as
well as on authors from Anton Chekhov
to his own Arab contemporaries such as
Taha Hussein.

INTRODUCTION BY **Rasheed El-Enany**   £28 | 176pp
TRANSLATED BY **Aran Byrne**   9781909942776 | May 2016

THE NEW DIVAN | *AN EAST-WEST CONVERSATION*

In the spirit of the great German poet Johann Wolfgang von Goethe,
The Gingko Library is proud to announce the preparation of
The New Divan to be published in September 2019 to mark the
200th anniversary of the first publication of Goethe's
original *West–östlicher Divan* (West-Eastern Divan).

The New Divan will contain 12 poems by living poets writing in the languages
of the East (including Arabic, Persian, Turkish) and 12 living poets writing in
languages of the West (including French, German, Italian and Spanish).

The 24 poems will be translated into English and published facing their original
language texts. In addition, there will be essays and commentary by historians
and experts in the field.

harback 9781909942-96-7 | paperrback 9781909942-96-7 | ebook 9781909942-97-4

 @gingkolibrary   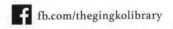 fb.com/thegingkolibrary    gingkolibrary.com

PUBLISHER: Margaret Obank

EDITOR: Samuel Shimon

CONTRIBUTING EDITORS
Fadhil al-Azzawi, Issa J Boullata, Peter Clark,
Raphael Cohen, Bassam Frangieh, Camilo Gómez-Rivas,
Marilyn Hacker, William M Hutchins, Imad Khachan,
Khaled Mattawa, Anton Shammas, Paul Starkey,
Mona Zaki

CONSULTING EDITORS
Etel Adnan, Roger Allen, Mohammed Bennis,
Isabella Camera d'Afflitto, Humphrey Davies,
Hartmut Fähndrich, Herbert Mason,
Saif al-Rahbi, Naomi Shihab Nye,
Yasir Suleiman, Susannah Tarbush, Stephen Watts

EDITORIAL ASSISTANTS:
Annamaria Basile, Valentina Viene, Charlotte Collins

LAYOUT: Banipal Publishing

CONTACTS:

WEBSITE: www.banipal.co.uk

EDITOR: editor@banipal.co.uk

PUBLISHER: margaret@banipal.co.uk

INQUIRIES: info@banipal.co.uk

SUBSCRIPTIONS: subscribe@banipal.co.uk

ADDRESS: 1 Gough Square, London EC4A 3DE

PRINTED BY Short Run Press Ltd
Bittern Road, Sowton Ind. Est. EXETER EX2 7LW

Photographs not accredited have been donated,
photographers unknown.

BANIPAL, ISSN 1461-5363, is published three times a year
by Banipal Publishing, 1 Gough Square, London EC4A 3DE

Banipal, founded in 1998, takes its
name from Ashurbanipal, last
great king of Assyria and patron of
the arts, whose outstanding
achievement was to assemble in
Nineveh, from all over his empire,
the first systematically organised
library in the ancient Middle East.
The thousands of clay tablets of
Sumerian, Babylonian and Assyr-
ian writings included the famous
Mesopotamian epics of the Cre-
ation, the Flood, and Gilgamesh,
many folk tales, fables, proverbs,
prayers and omen texts.
Source: *Encyclopaedia Britannica*

Supported using public funding by
ARTS COUNCIL
ENGLAND
LOTTERY FUNDED

Leila Aboulela

Najlaa Osman Eltom

Hammour Ziada

Ahmad Al Malik

Hamed el-Nazir

BANIPAL 55
Magazine of Modern Arab Literature

Sudanese
Literature Today

Ahmad Al Malik, Najlaa Osman Eltom,
Jamal Mahjoub, Hammour Ziada,
Leila Aboulela, Tarek Eltayeb,
Stella Gaitano, Mansour El Souwaim,
Nur al-Huda Mohammad Nur al-Huda,
Emad Blake, Rania Mamoun,
Abdel Ghani Karamallah,
Mohammad Jamil Ahmad,
Hamid el-Nazir, Amir Tag Elsir,
Abdelaziz Baraka Sakin

PLUS Excerpts from the
2016 Shortlist of the
International Prize
for Arabic Fiction

6   **EDITORIAL**

        SUDANESE LITERATURE TODAY

8   Ahmad Al Malik: *A Short Introduction to the Sudanese
        Literary Scene*

10   Hammour Ziada: *The Wad Azrag District*, a short story
        translated by Jonathan Wright

26   Ahmad Al Malik: *Lovers don't Steal*, a short story
        translated by Robin Moger

33   Mohammad Jamil Ahmad: Seven Poems, translated
        by Basil Samara

36   Leila Aboulela: *Amulet and Feathers*, a short story

44   Abdel Ghani Karamallah: *The Jealous Star*, a short
        story translated by John Peate

54   Najlaa Osman Eltom: Two Poems, translated by
        Maysoon Elnigoumi, Raphael Cohen and Ann
        Harrison

58   Hamed El-Nazir: An excerpt from his novel *The
        Waterman's Prophecy*, translated by Adil Babikir

68   Jamal Mahjoub: *The Ghost of Dr John Garang*

74   Emad Blake: An excerpt from his novel Shawarma,
        translated by John Peate

88   Rania Mamoun: A short story, *Passing*, translated by
        William M Hutchins

92   Tarek Eltayeb: *Helmy Abu Regileh*, a short story
        translated by Sally Gomaa

104   Stella Gaitano: *Testimony of a Sudanese Writer*,
        translated by Adil Babikir

116   Mansour El Souwaim: An except from his novel *A Rogue's Memory*, translated by William M Hutchins

136   Emad Blake: *The New Novel in Sudan*, translated by Rosie Maxton

144   Nur Al-Huda Mohammad Nur Al-Huda. Interview by Azza Rashad, translated by Becki Maddock
      SUDANESE BOOK REVIEWS

154   Volker Kaminski: *Der Messias von Darfur* by Abdelaziz Baraka Sakin

155   Olivia Snaije: *Nouvelles du Soudan*

157   Clare Roberts: *Ebola '76* and *French Perfume* by Amir Tag Elsir

161   **INTERNATIONAL PRIZE FOR ARABIC FICTION THE 2016 SHORTLIST**

162   Tareq Bakari: Excerpt from *Numedia*, translated by William M Hutchins

168   Rabai Al-Madhoun: Excerpt from *Destinies: Concerto of the Holocaust and the Nakba*, translated by Paul Starkey

175   Mohamed Rabie: Excerpt from *Mercury*, translated by Robin Moger

182   Mahmoud Shukair: Excerpt from *Praise for the Women of the Family*, translated by Jonathan Wright

189   Shahla Ujayli: Excerpt from *A Sky Close to our House*, translated by Nancy Roberts

196   George Yaraq: Excerpt from *Guardian of the Dead*, translated by Raphael Cohen

      BOOK REVIEWS

204   Gretchen McCullough: *A Portal of Space* by Mahmoud Saeed

209   Laura Ferreri: *The Dust of Promises* by Ahlam Mosteghanemi

      TRIBUTE

212   Fatema Mernissi (1940–2015)
      The Sindbad of Fes travels against the Cowboy by Khaled Hroub

      EVENT

218   The 2015 Saif Ghobash Banipal Prize for Arabic Literary Translation. Report, and online interview with Youssef Rakha, by Valentina Viene

222   **CONTRIBUTORS**

Stella Gaitano

Jamal Mahjoub

Mansour El Souwaim

Rania Mamoun

Emad Blake

EDITORIAL

We start Banipal's nineteenth year of publication with a sharp eye on the essential character of the contemporary Arab literary scene. While much of the Arab world is plunged into chaos with wars and devastation, sectarian divisions, repression and censorship, the Arab literary side of life is essentially modernist, secular, progressive and enlightened, speaking out for the marginalised – and needing to be heard across the world. In response to this, for the first time in our history, almost the entire issue has been given over to voices of writers from Sudan, with further translations and articles available online on our website, and more to be continued in the Summer issue.

Long months of preparatory work, volumes of emails, Skype conversations, working with authors and translators, locating umpteen works – novels, short stories, and poetry – have led to this issue on *Sudanese Literature Today*. Like our earlier features on the little known literatures of Yemen, Tunisia and Libya, we look forward to Sudanese literature in translation finding new audiences around the world, particularly through the encouragement and promotion this issue gives. Over the last few years Sudanese writers have been crowding onto the Arab literary scene in increasing numbers, making headway in several pan-Arab literary projects and prizes. With the majority of them living out of the country in the Arab Gulf or in Europe, they are creating almost a virtual Sudanese literary scene, one that cannot be silenced or censored.

We open with a short introduction by **Ahmad Al Malik** that immediately focuses attention on the fact that writers are finding new openings for sharing their work "despite the formidable hurdles", which include routine "confiscation of books and newspapers" and the closure of most cultural venues. **Emad Blake** writes for the feature on "The New Novel in Sudan", looking back at its pioneering writers of the mid-20th century, with Tayeb Salih's now classic novel *Season of Migration to the North*, then to the particularly slim period of the 1970s to 1990s, and on to the millennium, when the Sudanese novel has "flourished in a spirit of openness and true revolution", even though many are writing from outside the country. That spirit is certainly present in the fiction and poetry of the following pages.

Hammour Ziada has an intriguing story about how a village learns tolerance and living with difference after Bedouin incomers arrive at the town, to the initial consternation of the village sheikhs. Ziada has the knack of creating suspense and atmosphere, allowing the story to unfold with small incidents building a picture that is visual and dramatic. There is more suspense, or surprising twists in the tail, in a short story by **Ahmad Al Malik**, whose central character, an old policeman, finds an unusual place to hide a stash of money from a thief. In a story by **Leila Aboulela**, her character Maryam is rightly happy, in the end, to be thwarted in her plan to violently avenge her father's death. Both these stories look at weaknesses of human nature and ways of counterbalancing them.

There are a few works whose main characters are children, and one written for children, that we had to include, which is a salute to science and the natural world, "The Jealous Star" by **Abdel Ghani Karamallah**, in which a star complains of the attention the moon gets and convinces all the stars to leave the night and go to daylight – with unexpected consequences! **Tarek Eltayeb**'s short story about young disabled Helmy Abu Regileh and his football-mad friends, who find ways of playing truant, but who fear their mums' clever questioning as to their whereabouts, has a wonderful mixture of panicky schoolboy bravado between the boys and politeness towards the mums. The chapter from **Emad Blake**'s novel *Shawarma* is a tantalising glimpse into the tale of a young boy, run away from home, whom we first meet perched on the roof of a railway carriage, along with dozens and dozens of others, the whole length of the train, clanking its way to Khartoum through the vast and varied countryside with its rich cargo of characters on top. **Rania Mamoun** is an experienced storyteller and her story "Passing" is an elegy to the loss of a dear father, as the protagonist daughter is struck by memories and taken vividly back to the very moment of her father's passing.

There are but two poets in the feature: **Najlaa Osman Eltom**, who transports the reader into Maryam's aching sorrows and a moment's walking in a crowded, hot street; and **Mohammad Jamil Ahmad**, who in a series of short poems presents stark images of silence, the absolute, secrets untold and ancient whispers.

The chapter from **Hamed el-Nazir**'s historical novel *The Waterman's Prophecy* recounts how a community of maligned and abused former slaves works to break away from their slave-owning families and establish an independent community in the village as good neighbours. Their leader, the waterman, explains that "only love is capable of defeating injustice, disparities and grudges".

Jamal Mahjoub brings readers back to reality with the disturbing account of how Dr John Garang, inaugurated as Vice-President in Sudan's 2005 Government of National Unity, met an untimely death in a helicopter crash, ending the hopes of many for a single unified country. **Stella Gaitano** was born in Khartoum, studied pharmacy at the University and became a writer; it used to annoy her that people always introduced her as "the Southern writer who writes in Arabic", when she was just a writer. She writes about her struggle to deal with Sudan's warring sides and her forced move to South Sudan when the country partitioned, ending with the question we can all ask: "Aren't we in the throes of an insane drowning?"

The anti-hero of **Mansour El Souwaim**'s novel *A Rogue's Memory* is more than a misfit, he's wickedness itself, symbolically bad from birth with legs withered and inert; Adam Kusahi learns hard and fast, charms the hookers and deceives the superstitious for easy money, but also feels great compassion, friendship and love. In this chapter he relives his early life with his solvent-sucking mother, her gruesome death, begging with street girls, learning to read and write, and begging for coins on a traffic island at a busy junction – they called him Kusahi the King.

One of the obstacles for Sudanese writers is the state of publishing in the country. In an exclusive interview, the major Sudanese publisher **Nur al-Huda Mohammad Nur al-Huda**, head of Azza Publishing, explains candidly how the problems he faces of high costs, lack of modernisation in the printing industry, random banning of books by the government, alongside lack of libraries and "worsening illiteracy and poverty", are compounded by Sudan being "the greatest consumer of counterfeit books", which are "sold for half or even one third" their prices. He laments the fact that from the governnment there "is no real will to develop people through knowledge acquisition", but also says that the Sudanese reader is changing and that "the novel has jumped to first place and become the most read genre".

MARGARET OBANK

AHMAD AL MALIK

A Short Introduction to the Sudanese Literary Scene

Literature and art in Sudan are making significant headway despite formidable hurdles and complications besetting the country's cultural scene today. Many Sudanese works of fiction have recently made their way onto literary award platforms across the Arab world. This has happened despite the fact that the Sudanese authorities look suspiciously at all literary and cultural activities, which they see as camouflage for a subversive act in the making.

It prompts them to reach for their "guns". They recently banned a recycled book fair that a youth group organize periodically to facilitate exchanges of books and to provide a forum for dialogue about new releases and literary issues.

That fair was a innovative attempt to circumvent an increasingly choking environment. Due to high taxes, book prices have soared beyond the reasonable means of the majority. Besides, confiscation of books and newspapers has become a daily routine. In the past few years, the authorities closed down most of the cultural centers that had served as venues for cultural events and as cultural catalysts. One of those was the Sudanese Studies Center, which had published scores of literary and cultural books and periodicals, and had hosted cultural programs geared towards guaranteeing freedom of thought and innovation.

Despite all these hurdles, the new generations of creative writers always find new openings for sharing their work. One of these is the internet, although the service is not widespread enough to make it a viable substitute to print. Another of the latest initiatives is *Albaeed*, an online magazine that provides a publishing platform for a new generation striving for a space in the world of literature. A major emphasis of the magazine is on publishing critical articles by young writers, in a bid to redress the yawning gap between literary criticism and literary fiction.

There is another magazine called *Sardiyat* (Narratives), published by a group of young enthusiasts who are battling against the odds to keep it running, depending on their own sources and the help of some activists.

In the past few years, three Sudanese writers have made it on to the International Prize for Arabic Fiction (Arab Booker) long and short lists. And, last year, two Sudanese writers won two literary awards, in Qatar and in Egypt. However, in the absence of any support from the state, access to publishing remains the main obstacle.

In 2002, the Abdel Karim Mirghani Cultural Center organized a special event in tribute to Tayeb Salih. At that event, the Center decided to establish an annual award in the name of the international novelist that would recognize outstanding works of fiction from Sudan. Since then, the award has created significant momentum in the Sudanese cultural scene, bring-  ing to light some of the best literary works, and organizing cultural programs as part of the annual award ceremony.

But like all community-driven initiatives, the award was met with considerable obstacles from the authorities. Meanwhile, a major telecommunication company launched a similar award, also in the name of Tayeb Salih, and opened a competition for writers from across the Arab world. This second award, which is enjoying unprecedented governmental support, is widely believed to have some hidden agenda (exploiting the award for commercial purposes, and to build an image of the Government as a supporter of art and culture). The Abdel Karim Mirghani award, on the other hand, derives its merits from the fact that its patron is a respected cultural foundation. Although its resources are very limited compared to the other one (sponsored by Zain Telecommunications), it remains an important initiative that has a significant impact on the cultural scene.

Translated by Adil Babikir

HAMMOUR ZIADA

The Wad Azrag District

A SHORT STORY
TRANSLATED BY JONATHAN WRIGHT

Photo by Kheridine Mabrouk/IPAF

T he Wad Azrag district went through several phases before it acquired wholly equal status as one part of the village of Hajar Narti. You could say that it grew as gradually as the beard of an adolescent boy. It didn't emerge suddenly and it didn't come about as a result of any planning. It arose haphazardly and laid down roots like a shadow creeping across the ground. Between the time Ahmed Wad Azrag laid the first mud brick and the time mains water reached the houses, the neighbourhood showed no interest in hurrying to bridge the gap between a parasitic existence and an existence by right, but it did manage its opportunities well and take advantage of events.

It was a scorching summer's day and a hot simoom was blowing when Ahmed Wad Azrag arrived In Hajar Narti with his family. At the time there were only three parts to the village: the mosque district, the Awlad Mustafa district and the upper district. There was nothing strange about the arrival of Ahmed Wad Azrag and his family and he drew no attention. They were a small family, led by the thin nomad with skin the colour of wheat burnt by the desert sun and with a massive moustache, a skinny wife who looked like a threadbare garment, dragging behind her two children who looked like mangy young donkeys.

He made his camel kneel behind one of the houses, and unpacked some of his shabby old saddlebags. Then, while his wife, struggling to cope with meagre resources and two naked children, carried out the traditional duties of a Bedouin wife, Ahmed Wad Azraq went into the village seeking work. He presented himself outside the shop, but the men sitting there were bad-tempered in the summer heat. They ran rings around him with questions, but considered his answers carefully. They saw how thin he was and they tried to read his eyes, which were as dead as the deserts from which he had emerged. When he had allayed their suspicions, they tried to discourage the idea that they were in fact interested in case he persuaded them to give him a promise of work. But his many travels and mixing with village people only made Wad Azrag more insistent. So he ignored their reservations, and pleaded for work. He pleaded and pleaded with such persistence that they must have thought he was one of those pesky flies that keep landing on your face when it's sweaty. Impatient to put an end to his pleading, Sheikh Abdel Aal said, "I'll give you some date palms to pollinate."

But Wad Azrag made it clear he knew nothing about pollinating date palms.

"If you want, you could help me dig the mayor's well," butted in Abdel Bayyin, a slave who had long enjoyed the honour of sitting with the masters.

But Wad Azrag brought his wisdom to bear on those sitting around.

"Now, you good folks, a job that takes me far from the face of the earth, either upwards or downwards, is not what I'm looking for."

They laughed at him, and then Sheikh Abdel Aal agreed to give Ahmed Wad Azrag and his camel a job hauling the palm trunks he wanted as roof beams for a new room in his house.

So, by the time the groaning camel carried its load off towards Sheikh Abdel Aal's house, the village had accepted Ahmed Wad Azrag as one of its landmarks. For years he plied this trade with the camel he had come with and then with another camel he bought when that first one died, and the wasteland behind Hajj Hamad Nasser's house became his home in winter and in summer. When there was a sudden downpour he took shelter in Hajj Hamad Nasser's enclosure, which protected him from the flow of water. He and his wife and his two sons took refuge there and watched the rain anxiously, praising God at every flash of lightning and trembling at every clap of thunder.

The years came and went. Ahmed's sons, Mahdi and Kheir, grew up and were replaced as infants by their baby brother, Abdel Aal, named in honour of the sheikh, who had passed away suddenly, shortly before noon on the day of the Eid al-Fitr feast that marks the end of Ramadan. Few people spoke about or showed interest in his birth, and few people in the village heard about him until months later. The same day he was born his mother resumed work plaiting palm fronds to make baskets and bowls. Like his brothers, at first he was free to roam across the large expanse of wasteland, but he had hardly taken the first unsteady steps of childhood before walls made of straw grew up around him to make the first house in what was destined to become the Wad Azrag district some years later. Mahdi and Kheir joined their father in his work, touring the village with him looking for jobs. The village impressed its character on them as they grew up and they were not afraid of pollinating date palms or digging wells. They earned their living from the surface of the earth and from its depths. They grew accustomed to eating watermelon in people's houses and, unlike Ahmed Wad Azrag, they didn't complain that it made them sick. Ahmed always said he would rather consume vegetable oil than watermelon.

Mahdi faced his first problem with living in the village when he had grown into a strong young man, more like the trunk of a well-watered date palm than the mangy young donkey he had been the day his parents brought him to the village. Because of his work he could go into some houses whenever he wanted looking for jobs to do. The women didn't cover themselves up when he went in, and so he could have a good look at them. Harira, the daughter of Hamad Nasser, made a particular impression on him. She was the most beautiful girl in the village, with a firm brown body and ample breasts that swung like ripe oranges on a precarious bough shaken by the wind. Mahdi went into their house one afternoon and found her coming out of the bathroom, her plaits glistening with the remains of the water as she flirted in the courtyard singing. The young man was on fire inside and his ardour did not abate. Unattainable desires coursed through his bloodstream. He became obsessed with Hajj Hamad Nasser's house and contrived opportunities to pass by whenever possible on the chance of seeing her. On the day that Harira married, Mahdi went away. He stayed away for months, then came back to the village, with one of his paternal cousins in tow. He had married her in the desert.

The village accepted his newly arrived wife as it had accepted Wad Azrag's family. The only effect that her presence had was that a new room made of straw matting was built alongside the first room. The village found out about his marriage only by chance, and Bakhita, the bride, wasted no time in becoming a new source of income for the family and an extra channel for interaction with the village, because she went from house to house washing clothes and helping the women with their housework.

Seven months later Umm Baleena joined the family.

Umm Baleena was a relative of Bakhita on her mother's side. She was said to have scandalised her family and to have misbehaved in a way that could not be ignored, so her family decided to send her somewhere far away and out of sight, to Wad Azrag's family in Hajar

Narti. She arrived from the town market at midday one Thursday on a market cart carrying shoppers, drawing attention to the house of the thin nomad.

The young men gossiped about her and told stories about how pretty she was. When she turned up in front of the shop buying things for the family, some of the men gasped in admiration and several harboured evil intentions.

Within weeks several village boys were trying to court her. The effect was evident in the way she walked and laughed and in the wily looks she gave those around her.

Kheir's blood seethed. He spied on her at night and caught her in a compromising position with one of her lovers. He beat him up until he was almost dead. But, in line with Bedouin tradition, he didn't touch her. He merely dragged her off to the straw enclosure and soundly insulted her. He then handed her over to his mother, who consoled her and made her promise to behave properly in future.

The storm didn't end that night. The family of the lover that Kheir had beaten up in his anger gathered together and threatened to do harm to Wad Azrag, since his son had assaulted their son for no good reason.

Wad Azrag hurried to Hajj Hamad Nasser his neighbour to ask for his help. After long negotiations and many threats Kheir was forced to leave the village and go into exile in the wilderness.

Things calmed down a little, but the incident generated a suppressed anger throughout the village towards Wad Azrag and his family. There was much talk about the Bedouin and how untrustworthy they were. Some people blamed the family for everything that went wrong, starting with the flirtatious girl who lived in Wad Azrag's household and ending with the attack on the local boy.

The village elders said that Bedouin brought bad luck to any village where they settled.

The incident didn't keep Umm Baleena away from her lovers or keep them away from her. But her admirers were the scum of the village – young men who had moved on to Umm Baleena from having intercourse in secret with young donkeys in the animal pens. They were men who didn't wash and who were so covered in sweat that it was like a second skin. The rites of manhood included calling on Umm Baleena as a half-way stage between donkeys and other

women. This became a well-established ritual in the life of the vil-
lage. Umm Baleena performed some chores for the family. And with
her body she covered the cost of batteries and various other things
that Mahdi couldn't afford to buy from the shop.

Then the Nile flood suddenly arrived, and a new phase began for
the family.

The village lost its harvest, several houses were destroyed and the
floodwaters drove Wad Azrag and his family out of their base behind
Hajj Hamad Nasser's house. But Wad Azrag's gallantry in aiding the
needy and helping people evacuate the livestock working on the
waterwheels a few hours before the flooding began earned him
gratitude and appreciation.

As a result of that effort and the village's appreciation of him,
after the flood had receded and he had brought his family back to
their base behind Hajj Hamad Nasser's house, Wad Azrag dared to
build a room with low walls built of dried mud. This was a giant
step that would never have come about without him saving the cow
and calf of the village sheikh, Sheikh Merghani, from the flood.
When Abdel Bayyin stormed off angrily and complained to Sheikh
Merghani about the Bedouin's affrontery, he found that the sheikh
felt indebted to Wad Azrag and was full of praise for him. Anxious
to reward the valuable service that Wad Azrag had provided, Sheikh
Merghani ignored his offence in daring to build a permanent struc-
ture. Wad Azrag's only comment was to say that he hadn't built full
walls but only half ones and that the upper part of the walls was
made of straw. His purpose was to protect the house from water
damage and from crawling insects.

As he laid the first mud brick, Wad Azrag never imagined he was
founding a new section of the village, which was still reeling from
the shock of the recent flood. The flood brought other benefits for
the family. Mahdi had been pollinating date palms for several farm-
ers, and the flood had brought about a fall in the harvest and dam-
aged the interests of the landowners in a variety of ways. Abdel
Shakour, the headmaster at the village school, who didn't have time
to farm, brought Mahdi in as a partner in ten date palms so that he
wouldn't need to pay to have them watered and cleaned. Under the
partnership arrangement Mahdi was assigned half the trees in return
for looking after all of them.

Mahdi was energetic in the new partnership. He looked after the trees well, kept them clean and irrigated them whenever they needed it. His energy caught the attention of a number of landowners, who gave up farming their land and handed it over to Mahdi, to take advantage of his energy and to irritate the other farmers in the village. Mahdi agreed to partnerships in whatever form they were offered, and was not interested in arguing or bargaining. He thought that being a partner was in itself a gain for him. Within two years of the flood Mahdi was a partner in sixty-seven date palms and was owed four acres of land and fifteen basins that he was cultivating.

Some people were worried about these partnerships but well-informed people said with confidence that the Bedouin were lazy and didn't have aspirations to justify such concern.

Closer contacts with the rest of the village didn't change Mahdi's character, but they led Kheir astray when he came back.

Kheir returned on the afternoon of a gloomy winter's day. He headed to Sheikh Merghani's house before going home. He filled the water jars, sprinkled water on the floor of the sheikh's permanent reception area to keep the dust down and put the chairs in place. He impressed the village elders with his energy and they asked those who were angry with him to forgive him. By the time Kheir went into his parents' half-mud room after evening prayers, he had obtained a pardon.

Kheir joined Mahdi in farming as his helper. But unlike his brother and his father he was proud of the new relationships that the partnerships provided for his family. On accounting day Mahdi made sure he visited each partner at home and sat at a respectful distance. He was polite and acted as if he owed them a debt of gratitude. He went over the accounts with such servility that it looked like the landowner had done him a favour. But Kheir changed all that. He made sure he went to do the accounts at sunset. He sat on a chair facing the landowner, drank tea with him and talked to him at length about the affairs and problems of the village. Then he began on the accounts by talking about all the expenses, in such an alarming manner that the landowner had the impression he had ended the season without any profit. After saying how much work he had done and how much he had spent, Kheir then began to reassure the landowner by gradually revealing the profits they had made.

Kheir loved to see the landowner's face scowling and sullen in

worry at the large costs he was hearing about. He watched the grad-
ual change to relief, then complete acceptance and then gratitude
when he found out how much money he had made. In this way, by
the time Kheir left, his partner was gratefully singing his praises.
Kheir inspired in them a sense of respect that was not easily dis-
pelled.

The brothers' style gave them a special status in the village and a
place in many hearts.

But the big event was what Kheir did one date harvest season.

That season Kheir brought groups of relatives from the desert to
do the date picking. Kheir took over the process, which had previ-
ously been the work of the village poor, some of the farmers' rela-
tives, the remaining slaves and individual Bedouin who came to do
it without any coordination.

Kheir brought more than thirty relatives on his father's side and
they dispersed like desert locusts throughout the village. The new-
comers behaved with matchless integrity and asked for wages that
were significantly lower than anyone else. Whereas it had been cus-
tomary for the pickers to get paid by the sack, the newcomers were
content to be paid by the day, at a rate that was in effect about half
what the owners of the trees were accustomed to paying.

The fact that Kheir pocketed half of the pickers' wages didn't
bother anyone. But what was remarkable was that not all of those
who had come left at the end of the season. About ten men stayed
on, and it emerged that one of them had married Umm Baleena.

Those who stayed were bold enough to build straw enclosures
around the rooms where Wad Azrag and his sons lived. In the
evening people in the shop made jokes about this building boom,
but they didn't make too much of it but rather accepted it for all its
faults, especially when the experts said that this used to happen in
the past in several villages. The Bedouin would later pick up their
straw and their livestock and depart, answering the call of the desert
from which they could not bear to be parted.

When did the women join their husbands? No one noticed them
arriving, but the women suddenly made their way into the village
houses and every newcomer had customers who wanted them to
wash and to clean.

Where Wad Azrag had once had one camel, there were now five
– three females and two males – at work transporting things in the

village. The big migration came after the year of the drought and it was too big to ignore.

In the year of the drought the sky refused to rain and the Nile fell until it was just a pathetic trickle of water in the middle of the broad riverbed. The long-distance trucks brought news that the famine had struck across the country. Food shortages and the desert locusts attacking in swarms that blocked out the sun made it another year of devastation.

That year relatives of Ahmed Wad Azrag on his father's side arrived by the dozens. They did not come one by one but as complete families. They all encamped around the dwellings built by Wad Azrag and the other Bedouin who had come earlier.

Sheikh Merghani was unable to ignore this influx, as he had the earlier ones.

Accompanied by Abdel Bayyin and others, he visited the encampment of the new arrivals. He was shocked by how dirty they were and by the dry snot under the noses of their children. When we saw their womenfolk he was surprised how thin they were and by the filth that covered their clothes.

Sheikh Merghani thought the families that had spread out to the west of Hajj Ahmed Nasser's house looked like a painful skin rash. He decided to rid the village of them, even if he was forced to take drastic measures.

How did these Bedouin manage to negotiate with Sheikh Merghani and persuade him to let them stay?

No one knows exactly. Some people say that Sheikh Merghani was provided with services that satisfied his vulgar taste in women, and others put it about that the sheikh, who was easily tempted, received a bribe in the form of a half of whatever the Bedouin earned from their work.

The truth is still unclear and no one believed the sheikh's version – that he felt sorry for the Bedouin when he sat down with them and saw how poor they were and how they were suffering.

But insiders said that the village had been lucky because with the arrival of the Bedouin there was plenty of cheap labour.

Then, in the year of the elections, the great leap forwards took place.

Kheir showed an intelligence that none of the original inhabitants of the village had yet shown.

In the rural constituency the government chose as its candidate a man who had won its approval through services to the security agencies in cases that had led to several of the local men being sentenced to long prison terms. His opponent was a well-established local man who had been a leader of an old political party and had a loyal following among the local people because of his Sufi connections.

Although most of the people in Hajar Narti were members of the government party because that served the interests of the village and filled the gaps in local government, they could not abandon old allegiances. So they gave their support to the old party candidate in opposition to the government informer.

Government circles in the nearby country town were annoyed when they saw their candidate struggling in the face of the villagers' loyalty to their sheikhs and to their old party, which had been suppressed two decades earlier. It looked as if the election campaign was going to end badly and delegations arrived from the capital, rebuking the government's local supporters for failing to ensure that their candidate was well placed to win election to parliament in spite of the large amounts of money expended. Just when defeat seemed such a strong possibility that some thought of cancelling the election, Kheir came to them with good news.

From deep in the countryside he came and, with the instinctive cunning of a Bedouin, brought a neat solution that would relieve the concerns of those who were worried, save their candidate and all the money they had spent on the election campaign, and stave off imminent disaster.

Kheir bin Ahmed Wad Azrag proposed to the city masters sitting in their offices that they register his Bedouin relatives as voters in the constituency to make up the difference that the government candidate needed. In return for a sum of money for each voter, Kheir would make sure the Bedouin voted in the way they were told.

On polling day, when the opposition candidate had slaughtered a bull in front of the polling station to celebrate the victory he seemed likely to achieve once the seals on one or two ballot boxes had been broken, Kheir turned up with hundreds of Bedouin behind him to turn the balance in the constituency head over heels.

The Bedouin, who could hardly read or write, none of whom had identity papers and most of whom did not know who the current president of the country was, arrived shouting "Allahu Akbar" and cheering, carrying big cloth banners with slogans insulting America, threatening it with dire consequences and supporting the Islamist agenda and its candidate.

> *Proudly and with tireless patience the village of Hajar Narti warns*
>   *America for the second and last time*
> *A million martyrs are pledged to reunification*
> (the signwriter had in fact written pledjed instead of pledged)
> *Islam will prevail*

Supporters of the government party shouted "Allahu Akbar" and cheered for the troops that cunning and the storehouses of the land had given them and, although they despised the Bedouin, this time saw them as succour from God, troops through whom God had made the truth triumph, along with his chosen followers.

The election campaign filled Kheir's pocket with plenty of money, some of it his share of the bribes paid to the Bedouin and some of it in the form of legitimate donations made by the town dignitaries out of gratitude for his loyalty and his faithful support. The campaign also earned him a membership card in the youth wing of the ruling party, which he took out proudly whenever he sat with a group of people. He contrived in every way possible to talk about his visits to the local administrator and his meeting with the provincial governor on the trips that the ruling party organised to the provincial capital every now and then to ensure that the masses remained loyal and to receive instructions on how to confront the challenges of the new stages, which never ceased to arise.

After that how could Sheikh Merghani, the village sheikh, object when Kheir bin Ahmed Wad Azrag, his fellow party member, embarked on building an extension to his house in baked brick, along with a large reception area where he could receive the guests he expected? The insiders said that the state was trying to replace the local people with Bedouin, but that it wouldn't succeed.

Kheir's success with his extension tempted many of his relatives to start building their own dwellings out of dried mud bricks and some of them even dared to install permanent roofs made from palm tree trunks, just as in the houses of the local people.

Within four months the mud-brick rooms were well established and the area took on the name "the Bedouin district" — a grudging form of recognition extracted from the people of Hajar Narti. The local people reluctantly commended the Bedouin for building only single-room dwellings rather than complete houses with walls around a courtyard, but that would not last long.

The walled courtyards appeared at the same time as the new name of the district — the Wad Azrag district. That came about with the rising of the star of Hamad al-Arabi. Hamad, who had come to the village as part of the influx in the year of the drought, had previously worked in a coffee shop used by travellers on the road to Omdurman and had experience in running shops and buying and selling. From his work harvesting dates and his role in the election campaign he had earned enough money to make himself the cornerstone of a partnership with several of his relatives. The partnership built a structure on the edge of the Bedouin district, fixed shelves to the walls and hung a sign outside with the words Happiness Grocery, written in an unsteady hand.

The new shop was a matter of identity for the Bedouin and they resisted all attempts to close it down. They teamed up with their relatives and told their womenfolk not to buy from the shops owned by the Dongola people, as they called the original inhabitants of Hajar Narti. Hamad al-Arabi put three low benches in front of the shop for people to sit on in the afternoon to exchange news and keep each other company. He bought a cassette player on which he played the latest music to draw more customers.

When Kheir was late in visiting his farming partners to settle their accounts, the former masters had to step down from the elevated heights of their poverty and make their way to the Bedouin district to get their share of earnings from their wily partner. Since Kheir liked to sit outside Hamad al-Arabi's shop in the afternoon, the Dongolans had to sit down with him. When they had been sitting there several times they started to notice the shop stocked little things that their households needed but that they couldn't remember buying from the village shops that were closer. It didn't occur to any of them that the Bedouin, who had access to their domestic secrets through their work, were quick to tell Hamad al-Arabi what each house needed. The shopkeeper would then quickly put such items in a prominent place whenever one of the original villagers came to visit him.

In this way the Dongolans found themselves contracting small loans from Hamad al-Arabi's shop, which forced some of them to shift all their purchases to him to avoid confusion through having a multiplicity of creditors.

The villagers' constant visits to the Bedouin district resulted in two things. First, when they went home they took with them the new name that the Bedouin used in their presence: the Wad Azrag district. At first they tried to ignore the new name and implicitly agreed among themselves to keep calling it the Bedouin district. But they did not hold out for long against the wiles of the Bedouin, who repeated the new name in their hearing and feigned complete ignorance of any place in the village called the Bedouin district.

Although Sheikh Wad Azrag, now stooped and doddery from old age, had said in public several times that he rejected the name, he so enjoyed sitting with the old men on a rickety wooden bench outside Ahmed's shop that in the end he became more receptive towards the name and the honour that the other Bedouin conferred on him by naming it after him.

The second thing was that some of the Bedouin set about building walls for their makeshift houses on the grounds that they needed to protect their womenfolk from the eyes of strangers visiting the shop. Everyone made the most of this excuse, even al-Taher al-Arabi, who lived at the far end of the district and whose house was overlooked only by some remote date palms and a livestock pen that he managed in partnership with Abdel Bayyin. He too set about building a brick wall around his house, though he never completed it.

Seventeen years had now passed since Sheikh Ahmed Wad Azrag and his wife had arrived.

The Bedouin had proliferated and their influence, presence and relationships had expanded. But the village insisted on seeing them as merely an appendage – one that couldn't be excised and that it might be useful to accept to some extent. They thought that the district both existed and didn't exist. Their view was the people who lived there weren't interested in the village's problems or in deciding its future, so it was up to the original villagers to make such decisions, and the Bedouin should just accept the results of those decisions submissively, adapt to them and take advantage of them as well as they could.

But this assumption proved to be mistaken when a technical problem arose with the village's water cistern and a campaign began to collect contributions to buy a new pump and do maintenance work on the water distribution system.

The campaign organised by the village and by villagers living in the capital and abroad failed to raise the amount that the government was seeking in order to carry out the maintenance work and to sell them a new generator to pump water up to the cistern. In fact the government had already received generators as aid from European countries that the people of Hajar Narti had never heard of.

The shortfall wasn't large but the village would only be able to raise it if it was given more time. The engineer in charge told them that time wasn't in their favour, because if they didn't make up the difference immediately the rest of their region's water allocation would be transferred to the west of the country to meet the needs of people there.

The villagers appealed through intermediaries and contacted people with influence but the only result was that time continued to run out. The whole village was mortified that it couldn't raise the money when, after a year and a half of deprivation, they were so close to succeeding.

Was the solution the idea of Ahmed Wad Azrag or of his wily son Kheir?

Nobody knows exactly, but those who presented the proposal were Ahmed Wad Azrag and his son Mahdi, who had good relationships in the village.

The village didn't believe that the offer came from the frugal Bedouin, but couldn't find any clear evidence that Kheir was involved, especially as he openly opposed the idea and said it would be a waste of Bedouin money to spend it on the Dongolans.

Ahmed Wad Azrag's suggestion was that the Bedouin contribute to the cost of restoring the water supply to the village and, on top of that, pay for a new pipe bringing water from the cistern to the Bedouins' houses in the same way as the other parts of the village received water.

So it was a choice between going thirsty and recognising that the Bedouin had a right to exist — a hard choice that the village would take only when its back was up against the wall.

It was very humiliating for the village to plead with Kheir when he stood outside the shop and announced that he rejected the proposal for a very logical reason – that the Bedouin didn't consume enough water to need a pipe to bring it to their houses. Their donkeys and young men brought plenty of water to the district from the cistern, from the river and from wells as part of a harmonious social system that did not need to be disrupted by piping water into the houses. The project would add to the financial burdens on the Bedouin and give young people so much free time that no one knew how they might use it.

The village begged Kheir not to oppose the plan and let the whole village enjoy the blessings of piped water. Some of the people of Hajar Narti found devious ways to remind Kheir of the brotherhood and common history of the whole village and of the mutual love and affection between all its districts.

After much pleading Kheir agreed to take part, grumbling angrily all the while that it was a trick the Dongolans were playing on the poor Bedouin. When he announced he would agree, the women trilled and the men applauded. So quickly that it suggested prior planning, the Bedouin handed over the money to the contributions committee.

And piped water came to the houses of the Wad Azrag district.

The district deserved to be a part of the village on an equal footing with the Mosque district, the upper district and the Awlad Mustafa district. The village accepted it and set aside all its old fears. Abdel Shakour agreed to enrol the Bedouin children in the school to keep them busy studying and fill the time they now had spare with water always available at home.

Yes, there are still some people who ask anxiously if the time will come when the Bedouin will dare to ask to marry their daughters. But the Dongolans who are in the know assert that that is very improbable.

AHMAD AL MALIK

Lovers don't steal

A SHORT STORY

TRANSLATED BY ROBIN MOGER

Sergeant Abdel Jabbar was the first to arrive. A tentative stirring in a world still sleeping on the brink of chaos . Threads of morning light crept across the vast square in the heart of the city and with it the rising din of engines as vehicles started to arrive, mixed in with the cries of cockerels and donkeys' brays and the singing of a few drunkards who were unable to sleep from hunger (among other complaints) and so preferred to stick around and watch the travellers.

It was the second time Sergeant Abdel Jabbar had made the monthly trip to the capital to collect the wages of the policemen in his district. Some months ago the venerable commander of the village police station, Sergeant Awadh Al-Karim, had passed away and he, Abdel Jabbar, had become chief. Death wasn't always a bad thing, he had thought as he'd been handed the letter of appointment but he did feel that the task of collecting the wages was beneath someone with his long record of service during which he had made a name for himself as a highly disciplined member of the force and a former warrior who had fought in the Second World War. At the same time it was a chance to visit the capital at the government's expense, an opportunity he used to visit a sister who lived and worked with her husband in the clinic of a famous ophthalmologist, and every time he was in town this sister would take him to the doctor for a free check-up. Once, the doctor had replaced his old glasses without asking him for a penny, giving him a new pair that lent him what his colleagues assured him was the air of a senior officer.

Sergeant Abdel Jabbar carried a large paper envelope containing the policemen's wages. On his first trip he had been fortunate. Not a single thief among the other passengers. Most of them had been pilgrims returning from the Holy Land and hadn't seemed to be in any rush to commit fresh sins, especially since the price of washing them out had risen with the growing costs of the trip to Mecca. On that occasion he had placed the bundle of notes beneath his head and slept deeply. The journey lasted a single night, the bus travelling through the desert and reaching its final destination early the next morning.

The other passengers started to arrive. With a sixth sense formed over long years dealing with criminals, Sergeant Abdel Jabbar knew there was a thief among them.

Disaster! You couldn't keep a secret in this world. News that he was holding the wages must have got out and someone had had their appetite whetted by the thought of easy pickings from the government pot, which some people regarded as quite acceptable to plunder, being public money which belonged to the people, to everyone their share.

Happily, there was a law that disbarred thieves from being members of the people.

He realised that he would most likely be unable to indulge his favourite pastime: sleeping in a moving vehicle. Just like a child, he got tired these days, and due to age and other considerations he would find it difficult to remain awake all night. He tried singling out the thief from among the passengers sitting on the goods, which had been loaded onto the bus roof the day before. A young man holding a lyre. With the aid of his sixth sense he could tell that despite the sadness in his face the young man was kind. Then it occurred to him that the young man was a lover. His extensive experience of thieves told him that lovers don't steal. There had been that one occasion when a lover had made off with the chief of police's sandals while he prayed in the village mosque but it later emerged that he was not a true lover but rather a money-lender who had come to the village for one stated reason, love, and one reason unstated, waiting to marry the woman he had run into on the train and who, he had learnt, was due to inherit a lot of land and thousands of palm and citrus trees from her deceased father.

The lover did not steal, Abdel Jabbar said to himself, then turned his gaze to another passenger, a bearded man with prayer beads in his hand. As he stared at him a popular saying popped into his mind, that he who lets his beard run wild lets other things run wild, too. That beard might be cover for greed.

His eyes wandered away from the old fellow and lighted on an elderly woman sitting away from the men. Women hardly ever stole. They might sometimes give their men a beating when the men had drunk so much they couldn't get home at the end of the night and someone had to help them make it. A scandal for which a beating was a satisfactory solution. There was no law against teaching a foolish old man a lesson. A woman had once stolen a dress from the market for her little girl. The stall owner had caught her with the stolen dress in her possession, but Sergeant Abdel Jabbar had not written up a report. Sergeant Abdel Nabi had sorted it all out by paying the stall owner for the dress out of his own pocket, because the woman had been so very poor and had been trying to assuage the tears of her little girl who had so wanted to wear a new dress for Eid Al-Fitr. If I'd been in her place I would have done the same thing, Abdel Jabbar had said to himself. The poor had nothing but waiting. Waiting for deliverance. He was poor himself. His wage scarcely covered one small part of his modest expenditure and in winter he was forced to cultivate a small field he owned so he wouldn't have to buy wheat.

As they passed him, working away in his field, some would say, "Who's protecting us from the thieves so you've got time to farm?"

He liked his little joke. No problem, he would answer, there's only one thief in the village and he's standing next to me. So long as you're right here, he would chuckle, then I can do my job as a policeman and farm at the same time!

A villager had once become angry at the sergeant's teasing insinuation that he was a thief and had threatened to report him to his superiors for having a second job and neglecting his duties as a police officer. He had laughed at the man: "And who told you there's any duty about it? When I work a second job, I'm a farmer, and that way I slow the rate at which the police wastes its money. Other officers use their free time to take power. They become mayors and headmen. They issue orders in the name of the republic and everyone has to do what they say. Cops and civilians at one and the same time!"

"But there's never been a cop involved in a coup, has there?" the man had replied.

Sergeant Abdel Jabbar checked that the bundle of notes was still tucked beneath his arm, then went back to surveying the passengers. He saw two young women sitting off to one side near the old woman. Almost certainly on their way back to the village after a trip into the city to see relatives. He knew one of them. A good-hearted girl with a soft spot for stray dogs. She would feed them and care for them, clearing the paths of thorns and stones. Though poor and always busy tending her flocks outside the village, she always found time to care for the stray dogs, or stay up late talking to Lame Hammad who spent his days sitting beneath the sycamores or chasing dogs away. He had once hit a dog with a stone and some of its teeth had shattered. The young girl had helped it. She had pulled the stone out from between its jaws.

Hammad wasn't a bad man, despite his poverty and his persecution of the dogs, but boredom and his loathing of the sycamore figs on which he lived sometimes made him vicious. In any case there was no law that forbad stoning strays.

It must be him then, thought Abdel Jabbar, gazing at a heavily moustachioed man sitting at distance from the main group and doing his best to seem indifferent to his surroundings even as he gave everything a most careful inspection. It was Al-Safi. No one in the village knew what he did for a living but his clothes were always

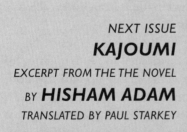

NEXT ISSUE
KAJOUMI
EXCERPT FROM THE THE NOVEL
BY **HISHAM ADAM**
TRANSLATED BY PAUL STARKEY

new, he did as he pleased, and he owned a tape player from which the sound of songs rose up at night, the young boys gathering near his house to listen to the voices backed by lyres. He travelled a lot and some said he went to the city to gamble, that he loved betting and that his luck was amazing, since everyone he played with would sink into poverty while he, slowly but surely, became better and better off.

The compass needle of his sixth sense swung round towards Al-Safi, but Abdel Jabbar did not fail to notice another passenger, someone he did not recognize. Presumably one of those who came to the village and the surrounding area for the date harvesting season, to collect their share of the fruit and take it back to the city.

The journey began. Time dragged by as the unwieldy vehicle made its way through the dunes. It was very hot indeed but the breeze produced by the motion of the bus kept it bearable. Sergeant Abdel Jabbar gave the passengers another once-over from where he sat behind a sack of rubber sandals. Al-Safi, he saw, was watching him. Disaster! He must be thinking of a way to steal the money that night! If he managed it Abdel Jabbar would lose his job for sure and might be forced to work every day for the rest of his life just to pay back the government its money.

The old woman fell asleep followed shortly afterwards by the two girls. The light dust covering their hair and faces made it seem as though sitting next to the old woman had suddenly aged them.

The bus stopped at a roadside café so the passengers could get something to eat. The sun had begun its descent and as they clambered down to eat and rest and relieve themselves the passengers felt completely shattered. On the pretext of searching for something in his bag, Abdel Jabbar stayed behind, waiting until they had all disembarked and either gone inside or wandered into the desert to do their business. Abdel Jabbar knew that he was so tired he would be unable to prevent himself from going to sleep but that if he did drop off, even for instant, the money was bound to be stolen. He thought of somewhere to put it. He could stash it in the sacks of wares they sat on, or hide it somewhere in the vehicle's chassis. He could put it in the box where the driver and his assistants kept their food. A short while later Abdel Jabbar climbed down from the bus, having hidden the money in the place he believed would be safest.

Darkness had descended and a beautiful crescent moon risen between the dunes by the time the bus resumed its journey. No sooner had the moon risen, in fact, than the young man began plucking his lyre and singing with the voice of an angel, as though in response to the moon's unspoken command. The sound acted on the Sergeant's heart like a spell and he fell instantly asleep.

No sooner had the crescent moon passed the halfway mark of its arc across the sky and its light dimmed, as the snores of the passengers swelled and the melodies of the now-sleeping boy's lyre became whispered memory, Al-Safi went to work. Cautiously and expertly he went over every inch of the bus and its contents. Abdel Jabbar even felt him checking his sandals, but he ignored it and went back to sleep. The driver's assistants were sitting on top of the box of food at the front of the bus, chatting and dozing fitfully, their slumbers interrupted by the driver who would shout at the from time to time. Al Safi hunted round them without them sensing a thing. He searched through the luggage of all the passengers comprehensively and patiently. He came across rubber sandals and the locally-made cowhide sandals the passengers were bringing as presents for their families. He found small sums of money which he left untouched, cheap plastic children's watches and dirty underwear. But he couldn't find what he was looking for.

The next morning the sun dawned over the dusty bus. Al-Safi was the only one asleep, exhausted after his night spent searching. A short while later they drew up at their final stop.

Sergant Abdel Jabbar woke Al-Safi then pointed at the man's bag and asked him, Does that belong to you?

A tired Al-Safi answered that it was.

Open it up, the policeman ordered.

The thief opened his bag and the sergeant reached in and pulled the envelope of cash from beneath the carefully ironed and folded clothes: "I couldn't think of anywhere safer to keep my money than in your bag."

MOHAMMAD JAMIL AHMAD

SEVEN POEMS

TRANSLATED BY BASIL SAMARA

SILENCE

There is no one chasing after me to frighten me, dear loneliness
I am the isolation of words,
the breeze that blows through the slopes' shade,
the whisper from alleyways and caskets
the one who gifts the echoes the remains of his life
and voices their ring.
I am: the silence
descending the alleyways and waving with whispers

MOHAMMAD JAMIL AHMAD

THE ABSOLUTE

You are an absolute.
Alone, you are the one who treads the days' low tides.
who crosses the wilderness
with the dregs of white temples.
Who, alone, sees the evening mail.
Who cries: "The past of days"
to his mirrors in existence
where darkness reigns.
You are an absolute.

Riyadh, March 2015

THE EPOCHS OF JOY

In the small shadows
You see what looks like a passerby
While the one who passes through you to emptiness
who fails to pluck your soul's strings
A fragrance that rots in the ruined moulds
and echoes that do not return
Beginnings are tender sparrows for time's nightmares
. . . When you touch the void
the epochs of joy dissolve

THE PINNACLE OF MERCY

In the white inundation with joys
The sky immersed me
In illuminated grasses
That my soul extinguished
In a marshy land!
Oh, sky,
I have lost my secrets

MOHAMMAD JAMIL AHMAD

HOLDERLIN'S SUNSET

Dear Holderlin
You, blade of grass of lost innocence,
you left your secrets behind with an eye open
Set on another sunset
Where secrets that no one knows blossom
while the mask remains as marble
in the minds of passersby.

THE CLOUDS' PRAYER

In the highlands
Light rain shines rays of water
And mirrors polished by mirages
Oh, flower of the clouds
Rain the senses' passion
to turn the kingdom flesh green

ETERNITY'S WAILING WOMAN

My wailing spirit
I heard her ancient whisper
in the Pharaohs' caskets
and the cities' flowers
Ah … if only my soul were of marble
and not be pierced by this wailing

Yanbu al-Bahr, July 2007

LEILA ABOULELA

Amulet and Feathers

A SHORT STORY

Today I set out to avenge my father's death. I took his dagger, the one with the two points and I filled a pouch with poisonous leaves. I put on my brother's clothes and his turban so I would not be recognized. I hid the shells, feathers and cowries deep in my pocket – I would only need them when I arrived in Gobir. I looped my amulet on a cord and tied it round my neck. I did not feel afraid.

My mother was alone in her room. She would mourn my father for months not scenting her body or wearing gold. From outside, I heard her praying. She wanted to dream of him, to see how he was in his new life. But he had not yet visited any of us in a dream. I did not go into her room to say good-bye. She would stop me. She would say a young girl had no business travelling beyond the outskirts of town.

In our courtyard, I looked at everything – at one of our goats heavy with child, our water pots with their reddish brown colour and the coop where the pigeons fluttered and cooed. I looked at the ashy remains of yesterday's cooking fire. I picked up my little cat. She knew who I was, she was not fooled. I kissed her and said: "I will not play with you today or give you milk. Even tomorrow I will still be away."

In the market place, I pulled down the sash that was wrapped around my turban and covered my mouth. I walked fast so that no one would recognize me. I bumped into my friend Aysha, her hair in corn rows. I almost cried out: "Aysha, you have plaited your hair at last!" But she brushed passed me and did not notice who I was.

Bello was buying guava from a seller but he happened to glance my way. Unlike Aysha, he stopped and looked again. He started to

Photo by Ekko von schwichow. Berlin

follow me and I pretended not to hear him. "Maryam," he said: "It's you, isn't it, Maryam?" He looked like the village idiot, gaping and shadowing me.

At last I said: "Bello, go away and don't tell my family that you have seen me."

He started to ask one question after the other. "Where are you going? Why are you dressed like that?"

We had left the market place by now and were at the outskirts of the town. There was hardly anyone around. I stopped under a tree and we sat down. I moved the wrapper from my mouth and said: "I am going to Gobir to avenge my father's death."

"But he has already been avenged. The man who killed him was stabbed immediately by your father's men."

"I know all this," I said and started to remember the worst day of all, when my heart hurt so much that I couldn't breathe, that bad bad day when my father's body was carried back from the mosque, his robes wet with blood.

I said to Bello: "Do you know the name of the man who killed my father?"

"Yes, Ibra. He killed your father because in a land dispute your father ruled against him."

"No," I said: "Ibra was sent by someone else."

"Maryam, you can't know this. You have never set eyes on Ibra or spoken to him."

"I saw him after he was killed. I went especially to see him."

"Why?" Bello's eyes were wide.

I did not answer his question because he would not understand. Only my father would have understood because he was the Shehu and a Shehu could see inside people, he was blessed. People came from far away to consult him because he could answer any question put to him. Sometimes my father made decisions that others didn't understand but because they had faith in him, they accepted his judgement. When he betrothed me to Bello, my mother wasn't happy – she complained to her friends: "He teaches his daughter how to read and write. He takes her with him to the mosque. He says she is the best girl among the Fulani and then he gives her to Bello!" There was nothing special about Bello. His family were neither skilled, nor high in position. I too was surprised at my father's choice because I had thought my future bridegroom would be a grown man and that I would be in awe of him. Instead Bello was a boy my age.

Now I brushed away his question. "It does not matter why I wanted to see Ibra's face. What matters is that he told me he was sent by someone else."

"Oh," said Bello: "He woke up from the dead and spoke to you! Maryam, you are not making sense. No one gave Ibra a chance to speak."

"Don't mock me. Ibra came to me in a dream. He said Hind from the tribe of Gobir sent him to kill the Shehu."

"Why would she do that?"

"I don't know but tomorrow I will reach her and find out. And tomorrow I will avenge my father's death."

It was not easy to get rid of Bello. He wanted to come with me but at the end I threatened him that I would break off our engagement. He didn't argue with me. He knew it was my right. This was the dowry my father had decided upon – that Bello would give me freedom to do whatever I wanted. "He is giving you away for free," my mother grumbled. But my father was patient and explained. He said: "Ambitious, proud men mould women and shape them as they wish. But no man could mould my daughter, he would break her if he tried. She needs someone modest and solid, someone who would encircle her but not come too close." I understood my father's words but my mother didn't.

At night I camped near a stream. The moon was yellow and bright. The wind was pleasant and nothing was still, not the grass, not the djinns, nor the tigers and hyenas who breathed and listened. I was not afraid because my amulet with the sacred verses protected me. But I could smell the animals' hunger. The djinns twisted and bounced around me, their breath warm against my face. Because they were so many I felt lonely and small. I missed my father. He was my mentor and I shall never have that again. An ant bit my foot and I guessed it was a viper which the amulet had reduced into an ant. "We can never be fully protected," my father used to say: "we belong to this earth and we live by its rules. But prayers and amulets can make a calamity small and soften the blows that fall on us." So instead of a deadly viper's bite, I had an ant's bite to scratch. Instead of hyenas and vultures, I only heard frogs and bats. All because of my amulet.

When I entered Gobir, I was dressed like a fortune-teller. A wandering child-witch with shells, cowries and ribbons. I walked about the market place, calling out that I had fortunes for sale. People looked at me because I was a stranger and they smiled their welcome. I found a tent where two hairstylists were plaiting women's hair. While their hair was being pulled and twisted, I tossed shells and read their fortunes in the sand. Soon a lot of women gathered around, pleased with what I was saying. I pretended to study the position of the shells when they fell, how they clustered or separated and which side they lay on – but I was really studying my client and using my thinking. I could guess at a woman's personality by looking into her eyes.. I could feel her anxieties and wishes by the way she sat and the payment she promised. I tossed my shells on the ground and all the time my ears were ready to hear the name Hind. I was in Gobir so she could not be far now. I had already spat on the poison herbs, kneaded a paste and smeared it onto the blades of my father's dagger.

Noon came and went but no one mentioned Hind. I could not accept the Gobir's hospitality. I could not swallow their food and their water tasted sour. My mind hurt from making up lies and from the effort of guessing. I sat cross-legged on the ground, encircled by three young girls my age. They giggled as I told their fortune one after the other. They were only interested in who they were going to marry. I touched the shells on the ground and said: "You will marry one of three brothers – see how these shells are close together – one, two, three." I made up stories about their future. The silent, beautiful one would travel with her husband across the sea. The strong, fat one would prosper in the market place. The one who had a rough voice and was as restless as a boy would one day give birth to many sons. Now she said, grinning: "There's Hind! Hind, come and have your fortune told."

I looked up and saw the white light of the sun and the flutter of a large fan made of ostrich feathers. Hind was the most beautiful girl I had ever seen. I praised the Almighty for creating her and she smiled her thanks, her voice low and pleasant. She looked like she was older than me, her skin was clear, her hair plaited with gold beads. It was when her friends made room for her and she moved to sit down, that I noticed her slanting wary eyes, her nervous manners. Her movements were not smooth. Her head dripped forward like she was an awkward bird, like she was ill. I had expected her to be strong and smooth and that was how she first looked, but now I saw that deep inside her was a kind of weakness that couldn't tell right from wrong. She sat hiding her mouth behind her fan, it made her eyes look bigger. Her turn now to have her fortune told. I shook the shells in my hands and tossed them onto the ground. They didn't cluster together, they broke apart.

"You have blood on your hands," I said and my voice didn't break. "You sent a man named Ibra, south to Soketo, to kill the Shehu."

There was a hush in the gathering. None of the girls contradicted me. They were in awe of what they imagined to be my magical powers. Hind didn't stop fanning herself. I looked at the sway of the black and white ostrich feathers, smooth and pretty. I looked into her eyes and there was nothing, no guilt or sadness, just nothing.

My head throbbed and I felt hot and sweaty. I blinked but everything seemed blurred. I saw a vision of that day, when I lost the one I loved most. I saw how it had all happened. There was my father in the mosque just as he was about to lead the prayer. He turned first like he always did, tall and smiling, saying: "Straighten your lines and stand close. Don't leave gaps for Satan to come between you." Then Ibra, who was standing in the very front row stepped forward and stabbed him in the neck

I heard my voice, careful and soft: "Tell me, Hind, why you wanted to kill the Shehu."

She stopped fanning herself and instead held the fan in her lap, stroking each feather. Her voice was almost flirty and her eyes shone with mischief and pleasure. "Ibra was courting me. He asked me to set a sum for my bride-price. He was ready to give me everything." She laughed and her friends looked at her with admiration. I could imagine Ibra under her spell, wanting her at any cost. She went on: "But I already had wealth, I told him, give me something more precious than wealth, give me life, not any life but a mighty life, a life of a chief or a saint or a warrior. Ibra was meant to escape, I didn't want him captured or hurt but he was stupid. He asked me, "Who should I kill?" I could think of five big men but I couldn't choose which one. So I gave each a colour ..." She giggled and shrugged. She was like a little girl describing a game.

"I dyed three of my feathers. I dyed one green and one red and one blue. I left one naturally black and one white. So I had five altogether, five men, five feathers. I put them all in a sack and closed my eyes. I put my hand in the sack and took out one feather. It was the green one – green for the Shehu."

I stood up and said: "I am Maryam and I am here to avenge my father's death." Her mouth fell open but she didn't scream like the others. I reached into my pocket. Hind raised her fan and arms as if to protect herself. The dagger was too light, something was wrong. I raised it and because it was too light my hand jerked forward. Hind lowered her arms and sighed. I looked at my hand but instead of a dagger, I was holding a feather. It was as if sunset had come because I couldn't see very well and the cry that came from me didn't sound my voice. I dropped the feather and ran.

I ran from Gobir, leaving my bag, my shells, even my brother's turban. I cried and kept running. Around me the light was purple and sleepy. I kept running until I reached a forest. I leaned against a tree and vomited, which made my head throb more. Why did my dagger turn into a feather? How could it when Hind was the one to blame? I heard someone calling my name. It sounded like Bello but I wasn't sure. I started running again and now it was completely dark. Now the bats came out and the owls. My feet caught on something and I tripped. I fell face forward. There was a pain in my foot but it was good to lie on the ground. I was ashamed that I had got so close to Hind, heard her confess and then, just like a weak girl, done nothing. I pressed my face into the dark sand.

I saw my father in his room at home and knew I was dreaming. But still I felt relieved that he was standing up, tall, smiling, looking only at me. This was what my mother had prayed for – that my father would visit one of us in a dream. And he had chosen me. I wanted to tell him how sad I'd been but I was so happy to see him. Here he was young in his new world. He was comfortable and laughing. I could hug him and we could sit on the rug in his room and like old times, I would ask him one question after the other. "Why did the dagger turn into a feather?"

"Because of your amulet," he said.

"My amulet protected Hind?"

"No," he laughed: "It protected you from the consequences of hurting her. Besides it was my dagger and a Shehu's dagger mustn't be used for revenge."

I sat very quiet, knowing this was a dream and I shouldn't wake up. I must make it last as long as I could. He said: "Why did you go to look at Ibra after he died?"

"Because I wanted to see the face of someone who was going to Hell. But he looked ordinary, just like anyone else."

"And when you went looking for Hind," he asked: "what did you want to see?"

"Evil: "I said: "I wanted to see the face of evil and I saw a beautiful girl."

He paused and then said: "You will always want to know and learn. This is a good thing. But it is an eye for an eye and a life for a life and my death has already been matched by another's."

"This is what Bello said. But it is not fair, Hind – how could she! She must be punished."

"She would have been, if my friends had questioned Ibra instead of silencing him forever."

"They were angry," I said, defending them. No one had ever criticised them and now he, of all people, was!

"Well," he went on: "Is anger a good thing?"

"No, because it does not make us see clearly."

He smiled and his voice became gentle again. "I don't want you to be angry Maryam. When we are born, our day of death is already decided and nothing can change it. Every day we live, we are walking towards it. Listen good!

My foot hurt but I made myself listen good. He went on: "If it wasn't Hind and Ibra, it would have been someone or something else. I am well and happy and I want you to be happy for me."

I woke up in my room. My mother was looking over me. She smiled and kissed me. My foot was wrapped in a bandage. It hurt when I tried to move it. "You broke your toe," my mother said: "don't worry, it will heal. Bello found you near the stream and carried you all the way here. He had been following you all along to keep an eye on you."

She would start to like him after this. Now she wanted me to drink warm milk with honey. Now she wanted me to speak. I told her how I went to Gobir and how I saw Hind. I told her how I did not, after all, avenge my father's death and how I dreamt of him. How well he looked in my dream and all the things that he said.

ABDEL GHANI KARAMALLAH

The Jealous Star

A STORY FOR CHILDREN
TRANSLATED BY JOHN PEATE

ILLUSTRATIONS BY THE AUTHOR

"Hahahahahahahahahahahahaha!" The cynical old star cried, laughing and twinkling: "When I was a little girl, not even six billion years old, I was too scared to sleep on my own. I used to lie clinging to my grandma, only a million miles between us as I snuggled up next to her. She only used to be thirty million miles away. There was no moon in the sky because it hadn't been born yet. So how come all these humans jump for joy every night when the moon rises?"

The stars and planets didn't twinkle and shine by themselves in the old days. They just reflected light, like the moon does now. Even so, they adorned the night like thousands of glittering, golden beads on a black dress, sparkling in gorgeous, outlandish, heavenly patterns. Yet still they were jealous of the moon's neat little radiant beauty. They felt like a hulking great mass by comparison.

"How come there are a thousand million and one of us and nobody even knows our names? There's only one little moon spinning round the earth, yet every human knows and loves it. And how come we're so far away from the earth, where all the people and cities could see us better? That's where the poets and the praise and

the glory come from!"

No-one praises stars like they do the moon. And stars like compliments, you know. They have often heard the folks down on Earth professing their love for and singing their praises to the moon. It makes the stars jealous and angry, sulking up there in the night sky.

"The moon is beautiful," an old man whispers.

"Isn't it amazing?" a little girl declares to her dad, pointing up at the moon lighting up the night.

"Why doesn't down here look like the moon?" cries an envious youth.

"The beauty of your face is like the moon, my love," says a man to his darling wife.

And there are so many stars out there! So abundant! So diverse! So brilliant! Always, always there (for no star ever forgets to show up at night)! Yet no-one cares about the stars! Every night they never fail, however small or dim, to light up the entire sky in their millions, yet no-one cares!

That's how the stars and planets felt about it, so they all got together: The Pleiades or Seven Sisters, Saturn, Mars, and Venus;

every star in the Milky Way; every constellation in fact, even those that none of Adam's tribe yet know, that no telescope has spied. The stars all came together to deliberate on why they were so neglected and what to do.

One aged star said, addressing that huge multitude in a whisper, in case the moon heard what they were scheming: "Sister stars, I was born a million million years before the moon, and, if you compare his size to mine, it's like comparing a grape seed to a watermelon. I'm always there, every night, never late lighting up the skies, even by a single second. On time, every time, there I am! But the moon goes missing for a fortnight every month. I don't know where he disappears to! He's lazy, not grafters like we are. And another thing: my light takes nine million years to reach the Earth, never tiring for a second, never breaking into a sweat either. The light of the moon takes less than two seconds! Two seconds!! Ha! Ha! Ha!" she laughed sarcastically.

Breathing out light which filled all creation with its beauty, she went on: "And yet this moon seems to enchant them so much more than I do. When my light first left me, there were only a few thousand people under the skies of Africa, that's all. But by the time it arrived, there were billions of humans in every corner of the globe. Oh! All that hard work! All that time and effort I take to bathe the Earth in beautiful light and to nourish it, and this is how I'm treated!"

The star next to her, proudly glowing in the heart of the night, added: "And our light is really good for them, and really powerful too. It can travel through rocks, bodies, anything! Our rays can penetrate mountains, the very earth itself, just as through transparent glass. Nothing can stop us, but it's still only goodness they get from our beams! As for our speed: ha, ha, ha! Who could match us for that? Winds, space rockets, satellites: they're all like old tortoises compared to us!"

The heavens were filled with cheers and applause. The stars were all so happy to get their frustration and feelings of injustice off their chest. They felt good about themselves again. Even the clouds were amazed at the thunder cracking loudly above them that no lightning had forewarned them about.

Jupiter said: "I am bigger than the moon, and older too, and I've always looked the same. I've always been the same shape, but the

Abdel Ghani Karamallah at a story-telling session

moon starts every month looking like a banana! Then it turns into a sickle, and then it ends up looking like a gold shilling! And it disappears so quickly too. And yet have you heard of the month of Saturn? Or Jupiter? No! But everyone on Earth knows about the lunar month. The whole world watches the moon on tenterhooks for Ramadan to start. Our light's so much greater than his measly beams, but still these gullible humans say: 'It's a beautiful moonlit night.' We never hear anything about a beautiful starlit night, do we? The moon's the one that gets all the praise and the glory. He's the one who seems to bring them joy."

A little star that loved telescopes and gazing out into the vastness of space, sneered: "I've seen human footprints on the moon. Men have walked all over it. You can see metal debris all over it. You can see the countless scars and craters they've made all over it as well. Oh! If only humans knew what the moon was really like!"

They all gathered around this little scientist star, and she showed them the true face of the moon through the telescope: there were little children sliding up and down its crescent, because trips to the moon had become like any other holiday on Earth.

The stars all laughed at the moon, as though it were a donkey. Yet that's not to say that there wasn't a little jealousy deep inside them, too, that spoiled the joke a little.

After this stormy meeting, the stars decided to scatter and disappear. They headed off for the edge of daylight, like birds migrating from one valley to another, deep in the dead of night. They fled in an angry band, with only the littlest, weakest, laziest stars trailing behind in the night sky.

One star had turned up late because she came from far away: way, way, way away. From right over there! No, even further! Much, much further! Further than you could ever imagine! Does space go on forever, do you think?

Anyway, she said, sarcastically: "The moon is hanging around the Earth because it's petrified of the big, scary universe."

She was from a billion billion billion billion light years away, or more. A number with oodles of zeroes is how far from Earth she was. Ooooooooooodles of zeroes!

When she arrived, she shouted to them: "And my neighbour is still on the way!"

Even the stars were amazed at the vast expanse of space. "Oh! Lord. This is going to take too long, and there's not much of night left!" they cried at the top of their voices.

The still faraway star said, panting away: "I can't go any faster! I can't! I can only move at 186,000 miles a second! That's just how it is. The universe is just soooooooooo vast! Really, really, really vast! Ginoooormous! No star has ever seen the end of it. It's gigantic, full of life of all kinds, all trying to find a place to live!"

The little star shook its head, wishing it could speed up, or even slow down. What would that be like? Would we see light move like clouds with darkness in front and behind?

She mocked the moon's laziness, but another star scolded her, saying: "No, our speed is one thing, but you don't need to exaggerate because of jealousy! Just tell the truth, whether it works for or against us!"

So the stars all fled the night, leaving the moon alone in the night sky.

* * *

So there they were, a convoy of stars fleeing the night and the moon, and heading for the daylight.

One of them said: "Think about this! It takes humans four days to get to the moon, and the moonlight one second to get to the Earth! Imagine how long it would take for humans to reach my beautiful sunlit surface!" Her light took a million years to reach Earth.

She was secretly worried, though, what the humans would think about it all, yet she worked it out in her head and crowed that it took a million million million million million million years for their light to arrive, and the children of Adam died from old age at eighty. Humans only live a single hour of some stars' days. They are born, grow, marry and die all in a single hour. Ha ha ha!

One wily, witty star said: "They could put three pregnant women in one spacecraft. They'd give birth on board, then the children could carry on with the flight, get married to one another, and then their grandkids could take the helm. That would just show the craftiness and curiosity of mankind. They are curious, clever, intrepid, unbelievably creative!" Yet the star also fretted that one day humans would end up scraping away at her surface, and digging mines and tunnels into her belly.

Eventually, the last lazy star arrived at the daylight, leaving no other hanging in the dome of the heavens. Many hands make light work, as they all said together, and one more was always welcome.

* * *

The people were shocked at the stars' disappearance. The poets cried over their absence. Ships lost their way to the harbour. "I won't be home to see the children tonight!" sighed the captain. "Where are the stars? Where are my guides in the darkling night? It's my lovely daughter's birthday today!"

The astronomers sighed too. The seasons were thrown out of sync, telescopes went blind, and the children in the villages cried because they used to love counting the stars every night.

Even the fish in the rivers and seas wept bitterly, because they used to love the stars' reflection on the beautiful face of the waters, letting the fish play in the depths under their light.

So many people came out to demand the return of the stars, unfurling their slogans written on their banners. Crowds of all kinds of people came marching: doctors, peasants, shepherds and herders.

The Doctor's Union: Where's the starlight? We need it to treat eyes and make diagnoses!

The Shepherds' Guild: Where is the star Canopus to guide us to the green pastures in the North?

The Farmers' Union: How do we know when we can sow the melon seeds and harvest the grapes? How do we know when to plant our palm trees, if the stars don't appear, sounding the bell to begin?

There were dozens of slogans expressing how dearly the stars

were missed. Doctors warned that starlight was needed for the good of little children's bodies. Poets wrote: "Where has our beautiful inspiration vanished to?" One lamenting voice arose from a lake whose dark-night surface had once reflected the stars, making it seem a beautiful dress studded with gold. The starlight had danced on its rippling waters, leaping from wave to wave and making it look like liquid gold.

Many caravans in the depths of the deserts lost their way, as the stars had always been their steadfast guide, leading them and their marvellous merchandise through the pitch-black darkness to their homes. The caravan leader cried out: "Where are our beloved compasses, the East and West Stars that guide us to the warmth of our family's encampments and back among our tribes? Where are our stars that show us the way to the markets of the Levant, Najd, and Yemen, to India and Africa even?"

The children cried because the caravans had lost their way, and their family had not returned on the day they were expected. "Why is this happening? Why is Daddy late?" cried a child. "Daddy knows how to find his way by those lovely stars, but where have they gone?"

His sister heard his sad complaint rising up from tents deep in the desert, his wife impatiently awaited her husband, and the merchant awaited his goods.

The people were sad all those exquisite stars that had magically studded the sky had vanished. It was now just an ugly dark dress with the little dimly twinkling moon for a brooch. "How strange the moon is without the stars. It's an apple without its sweetness, a river without its flow, a life with no memory, a mother without her children," the people sighed to one another.

And when the sun rose, the people were all stunned by its daaaaaaaaaaaaaazzzzling light, so bright they couldn't see, and they cried out things like:

"What is this blinding light shining in our faces?"

"I can't even see the end of my nose . . . what is it?"

"It's a fiery ball burning our eyes!"

"It's roasting our faces!"

"We've all been thoughtless how we've treated the stars!"

Fierce arguments broke out among the stars, and a wise one yelled that they shouldn't have run away to the daylight: "We don't know what's out there in the daytime, so we shouldn't have taken the risk!"

They all laughed at her and called her arguments cowardly.

She yelled back: "But, it's the sun!"

The others all replied: "The sun?"

"Yes, the sun is the mother of the moon, and the earth. It's the sun."

The sun had made all the stars disappear, like a beautiful poem rubbed from a blackboard. The sun had rubbed them from the face of the day. They lost their light, even their existence.

The stars all started crying. There was no escaping the fact. "The moon is the king of the night, and the sun the queen of the day! And who are we, after all? Who are we?" they cried.

The stars were so astonished to find they could not be seen from earth during the daytime. They could not even see their neighbour stars, or even themselves. They could hear their sisters' cries, but could not see them.

"What has happened to us? Why can no-one see us? Why can't we see each other?"

The stars listened in on the humans talking about their disappearance from the night sky. Newspapers talked about it, too. People held seminars on it. Poets cried. Lakes were bereft, inconsolable. The schoolkids blubbed: "We're going to fail in maths, because we used to use them to count with."

The stars heard the people, all talking: the sailors and astrologers, the children and the lovers, the lakes and the fish. Then the stars felt the importance of their role, the necessity of their being, their existence.

"We're here! We're here!" the stars all shouted. But nobody could see them for the dazzling sun.

The stars were amazed, too, by how close the moon was to the earth, and realized its surface did not shine by itself, but just reflected the sun, unlike them. The moon had once been part of the earth, and the two were still inseparable, like mother and child. Astronaut humans had even walked on the moon, it was so close.

But one puffed-up little star said: "The moon? It's not like us. No human has ever set foot on us, nor any other creature. Look at the moon! Spacecrafts probe it, and children slide up and down it. They have field trips from schools and universities every month these days! There's a probe of theirs on Mars, too, called "Curiosity", exploring it, and scraping away at its surface." Mars sensed her malicious joy at the moon's misfortune and was angry.

* * *

The following night, the people were astonished to find the sky embroidered with stars again. "They've come back! They've come back!"

And ever since that day, the stars have twinkled and shone, and each star has been honoured by people's words, and their gazes, and their drawings, and attempts to count them. The whole world was so happy they had come back. And the stars were no longer jealous of the moon, because they now understood how important they were to humankind, to the heavens, and to the night.

So everyone was free once more to bask in heaven's beauty. People everywhere: in villages and cities; inland dwellers and coastal dwellers alike. Half the world gazed upward every night at the beauty of the stars shining and gleaming. And the more stars there were to be seen, the more admirers of the moon there were. But the stars were no longer jealous. In fact, they loved the moon, because they now understood the beauty it brought to the magical dome of the heavens, just like they did.

They mimicked what the humans had said before, when they had disappeared that time:

"How strange the moon would be without the stars: like an apple without its sweetness, a river without its flow, a life with no memory, a mother without her children!"

So the stars shine on happily, joyful now, each and every one of them. And the happiest were the children, beside their parents in the heart of the desert, celebrating the safe return of their father, their cousins, and who, from the bottom of their hearts, thanked the kind stars for their radiating light over the desert dunes.

NAJLAA OSMAN ELTOM

Two Poems

MARYAM

TRANSLATED BY

MAYSOON ELNIGOUMI AND RAPHAEL COHEN

Unwrapping the gift of death, I remembered
that you were my gift.
I remembered your hands:
cruel-fingered keys to bliss.
Bliss my birds: abundant pale modest
seated on a train.

Festivals are over
virtue is over
to dare is over.
In my hands, keys forgotten by doors
to unlock blankness
as your guards along the walls raise moonlight banners
dimming shimmering dimming shimmering.

On the throne of Heaven you sit, my lord,
but in the garden your voice blasphemes:
"Just once stop following me.
In your dream annunciation that's not me.
Look at your face.

Do you look like a prophetess?
Do I look like a miracle going sour?
Your neighbours wail in vain
I did not bring them good news
and your son I never was.
I am here
in the dream that terrified you just now,
and you stoppered in a copper phial.
I am that promiscuous bloom."

March,
over your flock in the valley
cross the river to the woods and split the labyrinthine sun
into a pair of mirrors
and once you have seized your momentum
gaze deeply into them
to where resurrection despairs of the dead
and immortality is transfixed.

Beneath the gates of abandonment
where no one is called
where names are immolated in numbered caves
and bodies steeped in motherhood
I, black deaf amnesiac,
am calling you.

Pluck me from the trenches
pluck your body the child
from the flower of the cross
shroud it with bushes, drape it in plagues.
Pluck me from oblivion
I am your infatuated arrogance sobbing penitently over the
    calamity

NEXT ISSUE

**FOUR POEMS
BY NASSAR EL-HAJ**

TRANSLATED BY BASIL SAMARA

a glorious frog
buried and always forgotten.

UNDER THE COLONIAL ARCADES

TRANSLATED BY ANN HARRISON

I don't know why I remember her face,
the tea-seller
very young
boiling the water,
with her thin hand
some milk, with national sugar.
Hey, Girl!
Under our relentless sun
patient, sweating a little,
you are the carnation of this stinking street
teeming with men
wisely following your bold dress
and grumbling
about the heat
under the colonial arcades.

Khartoum, 1998

HAMED EL-NAZIR

The Waterman's Prophecy

AN EXCERPT FROM THE NOVEL,
TRANSLATED BY ADIL BABIKIR

"Sons of the bondmaid!" That morning, Uncle Abu Ali was grunting like an aged camel. After over a thousand years of servitude, some of the slave families decided to break away from the yokes of their masters. They announced their intention to establish an independent community, and requested that the Government approve the nomination of "Faraj the waterman" as their chief.

The news reached every corner of Ajayeb and the surrounding villages, and people from both sides of the issue poured into the central square. By sunrise, huge crowds were thronging the area.

"You can call us the Ahfaad, the Grandsons," Faraj the waterman declared in a confident tone, as he stood in the middle of the crowd, leaning on his stick and looking up at the horizon. A mix of cheers and shouts was building up, and the whole place consumed by chaos. Uncle Abu Ali strode towards the centre of the great circle of people. Although he could hardly stand on his feet, he stretched out his humped back and gestured to the crowd with his hooked stick for everyone, including Chief Mohammed, to let him lead the debate.

"The grandsons of whom?

"Just Grandsons!

"Grandsons must have ancestors. Do people just spring out of nowhere?

"That's none of your business. If you don't respect our wish, the Government will force you to do so."

"Then you need to find yourself a land other than this."

"It is our land just as it is yours."

The thing that annoyed Uncle Abu Ali the most and sent him raving was the defiant tone that he had not experienced before. It was as if all that he had seen during his long ninety years was mere fancy.

The Awtaad tribe behaved as if it was all a surprise to them. But it was not. Meetings had been taking place for months, in view of the village and behind its back. Meticulous arrangements had been made and every single detail had been accounted for.

The Grandsons had been waiting for this moment for many centuries past. Their ancestors had dreamt of it, and shared their dream with their sons and grandsons but it had never materialized. They had continued to live on the margin of life, without identity, waiting for the moment of salvation.

But the saviour had not till then appeared. When signs of him coming began to show, they realized that such a leap would not take place at the time of their choosing. It could only happen naturally of its own accord – like a legend or a miracle – once only in history!

* * *

A spacious room, with a high ceiling like a temple, and filled with antique furniture. It had small ventilation windows that were around the height of one and a half men from the ground, and a small door opening on to the other side of the house, the women's section.

Ismael took off his shoes and entered. Exactly in the centre of the room stood a large rectangular table. It was clean and tidy and covered with a light blue cloth. On it books were neatly stacked, and inside each one was a small finger-sized piece of paper that protruded from one side. In the middle was an oil lamp, papers and pens.

Ismael advanced cautiously and, without asking for permission, sat on the only wooden stool, which was covered with a soft silk mat. He picked up an open book and held it in his hands. Inside it was a paper on which some remarks were written in pencil in clear and neat handwriting. He closed the book and read its title. It was a book in political sociology by an author who was apparently French as the name suggested. From where he sat, he observed the books in front of him. They were arranged in such a way that their titles were perfectly visible to anyone sitting on the stool.

He ran his eyes quickly over the catchy titles and the names of their authors. No time for elaborate reading. Perhaps he could do that later on. He didn't want to waste the short time he had on something already known to him. There must be other secrets behind this man Faraj. He moved around to examine the other parts of the room. It was neither a library nor a museum. Perhaps a combination of both. Three of its walls were covered with wide mahogany cabinets about the height of a tall man. They had shelves of equal size, packed with books on history, politics, heritage, biography, and literature – each subject area occupying a separate section. Above the cabinets, and on all the walls were numerous framed photographs, black and white, and coloured, old and new. Photographs of herdsmen, peasants, construction workers, and watermen – barefoot, bareheaded, with naked backs, and exhausted faces. He could easily figure out that they were photographs of "The Grandsons". On the wall behind the stool, there were oil paintings and some maps marked with signs and lines.

Ismael was overwhelmed by surprise as he continued to examine a place he had never expected to see in Ajayeb. He was examining the portraits and reading the captions, while the waterman followed behind him without uttering a word. He stopped at a strange photo: five or six dead bodies, bloated and stacked one on top of the other. Standing on tiptoe, he reached up and took down the picture. He dusted it off.

"These are of 'The Grandsons'. They didn't drown in a river. They didn't die in battle. Their master threw them down a well as punishment because some of his sheep had been killed by hyenas."

Ismael examined the picture more closely. There were some lines written in English in small font: "Slave herdsmen who died in the 'Dig' water well on the Eritrean coast. It is believed that their master threw them in as punishment for their negligence. From the British Archives, Eritrea, 1946."

Another photograph attracted Ismael's attention. It featured bare-chested young girls, smiling at the camera. They were pretty, with long soft tresses flowing down to their chests. Their facial features were captivating: wide, sad eyes; fleshy lips; and straight, slim noses. Although the photo was not in colour, their shining beauty was still vividly clear. Without taking his eyes off it, the waterman said:

"Those young girls are from 'The Grandsons'. One is my grandmother. Can you believe that? Another is my mother's aunt, but I don't know which one. They were bondmaids of one of those lords. Personal property, as they say. This photograph dates back to the colonial era. It was taken during a visit by an Italian friend who had a great passion for photography. We brought the photo from Rome!"

Another black and white photo, which Ismael immediately recognised. It showed charred bodies, some on the floor, others lying on the ginning and weaving machinery. Beside them was a row of cone-shaped bobbins of cotton thread, but they had not been affected by the fire. A caption written in Amharic under the photo read "Fire in the textile factory, Ajayeb, 1931".

Ismael grew even more astonished when the waterman told him it had taken them more than 20 years to collect these photos from the archives of Asmara and Addis Ababa and from other sources.

"They were collected by young people like yourself. That gives some consolation to people like me, and an assurance that our efforts will not be in vain."

He looked nervous, his face sweaty and discoloured, like a land over which a cloud had passed, leaving some parts dry and others wet. After a brief pause, he continued:

"All this spacious land once belonged to the Grandsons, who were solidly united except for a few who always allied themselves with the colonial powers. Then history had its say, sending some people up the scale and lowering others to the bottom. We lost our unity to a successive series of famines, wars, and tyrannies, which gave birth to other classes of neo-slavery. These included soldiers, employees, prisoners. All this land around us is the Grandsons' land. Look more closely. You will see what I mean!"

The waterman returned the photo to its original position and showed him others that he held in a special folder. Most of these had been taken in recent years, in Ajayeb and elsewhere. A recent one showed Faraj with his water skin and white donkey in front of a house. Another one showed him smiling to something behind the camera.

"Forgive my curiosity," Ismael said, "but may I ask why you stuck so long with this job when you are far more talented than the others?"

The waterman smiled but his face quickly regained its stern outlook. "Because I didn't want to forget. That is crucial for people like me. Besides, I don't believe in an easy life: a paid job, a senior position, or even the presidency. All that is lifeless – an illusion. The body is the most powerful aspect of life and it's only when the body works at full gear that life and man's role in it become meaningful. I would have loved to go around and deliver water to every house, but the majority of the Grandsons were against this. I might do that again one day. I still have my donkey in front of the house.

Patting Ismael's shoulder affectionately, he added: "Nothing is more rewarding than quenching someone's thirst."

Ismael nodded politely. He was highly impressed by the man's knowledge and good-heartedness and he grew more eager to decode the mystery behind him.

He headed towards the corner to the right of one of the ventilation windows. There he found an old box on which a *jubba* had been laid. It was new, red in colour with golden embroidery on the edges. It was carefully folded and above it on the wall there was an old whip hanging on a nail. The waterman approached the box and opened it after moving the *jubba* to a nearby table. Inside the box, he found three old yellow manuscripts in leather covers. Beside them was a pair of dried-out leather shoes, thin at the back and broad at the front, like a cow's tongue. There was also a wrinkled water-skin secured on both sides with a thin rope – and another garment, threadbare, with a faded colour that suggested it had originally been red. Ismael noticed that it was like the first *jubba* in terms of its wide collar and fine golden embroidery. When the waterman placed them beside each other, they looked identical despite the age difference.

"These things – the *jubba*, the pair of shoes, the whip, and the water skin – belong to a grandfather of mine. He was a highly compassionate person and was nicknamed 'Gamboos', which means 'a person in kneeling position', because he spent a good part of his time on his knees pouring water for thirsty people and cattle across this desert. Unfortunately, we have no idea what his real name was. Perhaps he was a leader of 'the Grandsons' some time back. Perhaps I inherited his passion for delivering water but I didn't inherit the other great attributes of his that I had heard a lot about."

After a brief laugh, he continued:

"Gamboos dug plenty of wells in the desert. Each year, at the beginning of summer, he would hold a special ritual and would order his people to make offerings to the river so that it would not cut its supply. I have no accurate account about that early period hundreds of years back, but according to Bakhiet and other old men, the Grandsons had ruled these territories for a long time until some people from the Ethiopian mountains invaded and drove them out. Those who could not run away were taken as slaves and assigned hard jobs like fetching water, herding and milking, while the women and young boys were taken as domestic servants. The invaders would make fun of them, calling them the watermen, in reference to their grandfather Gamboos. They apparently misread his compassion as weakness because such values had no place in the cruel life of the desert people."

Ismael gently lifted one of the three manuscripts and cautiously flipped through its pages. They were full of drawings. Predators – lions, cheetahs, and elephants. Warriors with finely braided hair and pretty faces, who looked closer in appearance to the Grandsons than to the Abyssinians, even closer to the people of Himyar, in ancient Yemen, in facial features, with their round heads and broad foreheads, and deep grief that, ironically, exposed the beauty of their eyes.

He leafed through some maps and obscure figures. The letters in the three manuscripts belonged to the old Ge'ez language, which is still in use throughout the entire area of historical Abyssinia. Although Ismael was familiar with the language, that particular text was of little help to him as it contained very few words that were still in use.

Feeling embarrassed at having spent too long there, he put everything back in the box and returned with his host to the external part of the living area. They sat in their original places. The waterman wiped his face with his palms, and with an affectionate smile, said:

"I hope it will never occur to you that we are doing what we are doing in order to bring history back to life. That would be foolish. We are not trying to show off, either, or avenge our past. What we want is to see love reign; to see this whole horizon lined with parallel crack-free mirrors. Only love is capable of defeating injustice, disparities, and grudges. To be honest with you, I don't believe in superstition, although Fatima's marriage has opened the door wide to superstition: about the one person who can sacrifice his life to save his people. When we started this endeavor, Fatima had not yet been born. But she blossomed and was perfectly ripe at harvest time. That's simply what has happened."

Those words hit Ismael hard. He let out a deep breath as the image of his friend Mahmoud rolled across his mind like a film. Silently, he listened to sounds carried from afar through the utter silence. Sounds of cars far away, the breathing of the waterman's donkey next door, barking of dogs. Those sounds now mixed with clamorous sounds from history with animated images of troops and elephants, the image of Gamboos and other obscure symbols that he had seen in the manuscript. Then came images of Fatima, Mahmoud and the elders of Ajayeb. Gatherings building up and dispersing. Noise. Then suddenly it was quiet again, as if someone had switched the sounds off with a single push on a button. The waterman's voice brought him back to his senses:

"All that was a small fact encapsulated in grand illusions. If the Awtaad tribe had been closer to the real picture they would have realized that human blood is in all cases like red water and has a neutral yeast smell. It is neither cheap nor expensive. For this reason, sir, we call it a revolution or an uprising – because we are a nation, not a tribe. The Grandsons are not alone on this land. Under each mountain of tyranny are rocks, dissolving and cracking, now running below ground and coming together beneath everything. One day you will see this, in one shape or multiple shapes – it doesn't matter. The important thing is that it is going to happen. I have no doubt about that. Tell your students that the Grandsons are nothing but them and us and you and all the others – in varying degrees. Perhaps you know this better than I do, so don't forget to pass it on to our children."

After a brief pause, he took a deep breath and then continued:

"I won't ask you to be neutral. You can't. You are our memory. History is memory, sir, and memory is us. We, after all, are humans. You all belonged to Adam, who was made of earth."

* * *

The waterman stayed awake for the rest of that night until dawn. That day marked the end of an era and the beginning of a very new one. He had to be alert and to account for everything as every moment in that day – which had not been seen for centuries – had its own importance. Every hour that passed drove away the old era and brought closer the new one. The events of that day were running vividly in his mind like a stunning panorama.

He left the Grandsons' meeting and headed to the nearby river. He walked leisurely through the onion and clover fields that bordered the riverbank. The farmers had opened the irrigation sluices onto them just before the break of dawn, and with the faint dawn light that now painted the sky's dome, the fields were turned into mirrors that reflected the waterman's shadow as he passed until he climbed a barrier on the riverbank.

He looked down at the houses of Ajayeb. They looked as lifeless as ruins inhabited only by ghosts. However, the roaring of the river water by his feet gave him a different feeling. It filled his ears with the sound of life, so vigorous, as if life itself emanated from that very place where water and clay met.

He took a deep breath and sat down, looking at the river and the dark thick trees on the opposite bank. It looked as if an army had landed there under cover of darkness and was lurking there, ready to choke to death a day tethered to the rope of history. He looked up at the faint light coming out of the womb of darkness just as pure milk came from between excretion and blood. He felt relieved.

By sunrise, the spacious open square in front of the Chief's house thronged with people. The house itself looked like a dilapidated temple and the chief an ancient god as he sat facing the gathering. The workers from the textile factory, in their dark blue uniform and white masks, which now looked clean, had come early. They were carrying sky-blue flags and pictures of the waterman.

Faraj the waterman read out his first announcement in a confident tone. It was an eloquent speech, full of wisdom and lessons from history. He was ready for this day, which was a thousand years overdue. He had been viewing things from on high, but captured the right moment to descend to the foot of the mountain and change course, once and for all.

Uncle Abu Ali arrived, seething with rage. Once he had heard the news that the tribes had gathered in the square, he had thrown his blanket to the floor and threatened his wives, who were sitting around his bed, with divorce if they didn't allow him to go. He strode off furiously, one leg beating against the other until he reached the middle of the square. But things didn't develop as he wished. The square trembled with both joy and rage, with pride and loathing.

"This place cannot be led by two heads. That is impossible," Uncle Abu Ali said in a desperate tone, amid the rising dust and din. The waterman was still on his platform, his hands on his stick, his eyes and heart on the future.

"We are not seeking to become heads, or tails. What we want is far more modest."

"What is it you want?" asked Uncle Abu Ali.

Looking at the gathering, the waterman said:

"Simply, we don't want anyone to exercise any authority on us against our wishes. We want to have our names separated from the names of your families. We want you, from now on, to call us the Grandsons, the name we have chosen for ourselves. You should not deny us our legal rights. We need to share water and bread and living space, fairly and respectfully, and to live as good neighbours."

Uncle Abu Ali moved around the centre of the now silent crowd that had gathered since sunrise to watch the confrontation. Heat and thirst had taken its toll on the gathering, and the smell of sweat and now scorching sun filled the air.

Uncle Abu Ali finally spoke. He dismissed the waterman's demands as contrary to the will and the order established by the Creator, who had created people in different classes. But the waterman kept reiterating that human beings were born equal.

Uncle Abu Ali never tired of talking as he spun round and round like a bull on a waterwheel. It was now almost noon and the waterman had not even moved his position. For almost three hours, the chief also had not uttered a single word as he sat there on his seat, looking down. Occasionally, however, he would grumble. Sometimes he would hit the ground with his stick. At others, he would make drawings in the sand. The other tribal heads were silent too, while the Government messenger wrote and wrote, filling dozens of sheets of paper. Sweat, ink and words intermingled with each other.

Perhaps the waterman wanted to exhaust them by allowing the hopeless confrontation to drag on until everyone grew too tired to let even one word escape their lips and so would leave before the battle came to an end.

Uncle Abu Ali finally became exhausted, his parched throat finally letting him down. He gestured to those around him to bring him water. Someone handed him a jug of water that must have been hot by that time. He collapsed on his emaciated backside to the ground and emptied the contents of the jug down his throat in one draught. He started choking and coughing profusely before vomiting over the ground. He tried to stand up but his strength failed him as he felt the ground trembling under his feet. Those around him rushed to his rescue and sprinkled water on his face, but it was too much for him and he drifted away, taking with him the follies of history.

As everyone stood watching old Abu Ali, the waterman stepped down from his platform and went directly to where the tribal heads were sitting. He shook hands with them one by one, looking them politely in the eye in such a way as to miraculously win from them a combination of admiration, shyness, and recognition.

Translated from *Nabuat al-Saqqa*, The Waterman's Prophecy, published by Dar Al-Tanweer, Beirut, Lebanon, 2015

JAMAL MAHJOUB

The Ghost of Doctor John

EXCERPT FROM A WORK-IN-PROGRESS

At around 5pm on the 30th July, 2005, a Russian-made Kazan Mi-172 helicopter took off from Entebbe airport in Uganda. Aboard was the first Vice-President of the newly enstated interim Government of National Unity (GNU) and President of the Government of South Sudan (GOSS), John Garang de Mabior. Altogether, including crew and entourage, there were thirteen people aboard the aircraft. It was late in the day to be setting out. Light was already fading and weather conditions were not good. The flight to the SPLM headquarters at New Site on the Ugandan border should have taken just over two hours. They never arrived. The helicopter went down in the Zulia Mountains only a short distance from their destination. Everyone on board was killed.

A commission of investigation was launched in both Sudan and Uganda. The helicopter belonged to Ugandan President Museveni. Both the flight data recorder and cockpit voice recorder boxes were the property of the Ugandan government. The investigating commission included members from both North and South Sudan as well as a US Homeland Security officer; ballistics and explosives specialists; pathologists, police officers and aviation experts. The commission travelled to Moscow to question the technical staff at the International Aviation Centre as well as the makers of the Kazan. They visited the site of the crash, they interviewed eyewitnesses and people connected to the flight and the First Vice President. Satellite images of the crash were requested through the Ministry of Defense. They put together a reconstruction of what had most probably happened.

According to the report it was raining that evening and the sky was overcast. The helicopter which had recently been overhauled and updated in Moscow, had been back in operation for little over a week, clocking only twenty hours flying time before the crash. The Ugandan pilot and co-pilot were experienced and well-trained. The explosives and ballistics team concluded that no firearms or explosives were involved. At the nearby SPLA camp of New Cush, a commander reported hearing the sound of a helicopter and wondered why anyone should be flying in such bad weather. He was relieved when he heard the helicopter veer right, away from the clouds. Later on, he saw a light in the distance but it wasn't until the next morning that a search party found the wreckage of the helicopter, still burning.

The flight data recorder was damaged by fire, but on the cockpit voice recorder the co-pilot can be heard urging the pilot to climb higher as the helicopter lost altitude. They were facing mountains that were two thousand metres high. Shortly after that it would appear that the machine started to become unstable in the bad weather and there ensued a discussion about diverting to another destination. Up to nine minutes before the crash the helicopter was still on course. Seven minutes later, with less than two minutes to live, the crew appear to have decided to descend, thinking to fly under the cloud. At this point there is some indication of error. A discrepancy was later found between the two GPS devices on board, indicating that at least one of them had been set to the wrong altitude at the start of the flight. Was this simply a mistake on the part of one of the pilots, or something more sinister? Resetting a GPS to an incorrect altimeter reading is not that difficult. As a method of bringing down the aircraft, however, it hardly seems reliable, even factoring in the bad weather. The cockpit recordings gave no indication that the crash was intentional, that it was a suicidal plunge by either pilot. The report suggests the simplest conclusion of all, that the most likely cause of the accident was a combination of bad weather and pilot error.

Despite the apparent rigour of the investigation and the lack of any obvious signs of foul play many people will never accept that it was a simple accident. There was too much at stake, at that precise moment in history, after two decades of war and the victory heralded by the 2005 Comprehensive Peace Agreement. It was the dawn of a new age, and Garang was the man who had brought it about. Sudan was united and he was there at the top, just as he had promised he would be. Even among rational, informed people it is clear the crash was not a simple accident. To one such man, who had been close to Garang, there was no doubt, it was just a matter of time: "It hasn't been proved yet."

Certainly there was no doubt in the minds of the thousands who ran riot through the streets of Khartoum when news of his death was announced. The disturbances lasted three days. Officially, the number of people who died was put at twenty-four, unofficially 130, but others say there were many more casualties. Damage to property, to shops, homes and cars was considerable.

The fates could not have conspired to time Garang's death more poignantly. It has all the air of a Greek tragedy. The exiled king returns to take his rightful seat on the throne only for death to intervene, snatching him away in his hour of triumph. Garang had finally attained the pinnacle of power in the country he had fought for over two decades to liberate from tyranny. Over a million people turned out to greet him when he arrived in Khartoum to be officially instated as Vice-President of the interim Government of National Unity, after twenty-one years of war. Twenty-one days later he was dead.

John Garang was a complex figure. To some he was a messiah, to

Dr John Garang

others an authoritarian who would not abide dissent. This intransigence led, in the early 1990s, to a major fracture within the SPLA and one of the bloodiest episodes in the civil war. A number of commanders broke away, deciding they could no longer serve a man who refused to listen. More than a politician or rebel leader Garang was seen by many in the South as a larger-than-life father figure, a beacon of hope that promised freedom and dignity.

In the wake of Garang's death, a process of beatification began. 'It is the body that has gone,' his wife declared tearfully on the radio in an attempt to calm the anger. 'His spirit, his vision, his program – we're going to implement them.' It was a claim that proved to be short-lived. Garang had been in pursuit of a myth, that of becoming the first Southern president of a united Sudan. Along with unity went the aim of liberating the country from the oppressive centralist and sectarian politics that had dominated the arena for so long.

By all accounts Garang was no saint, but his absence will long haunt the country as the embodiment of possibility. Unity had been his goal right from the moment he took up arms against Khartoum back in the 1980s. It was the cause of his strife with many of his Southern commanders in the 1990s. In spirit at least, Garang represented the potential to overcome the sectarianism that has dominated Sudanese politics. In his concept of a New Sudan, Garang envisioned a country in which discrimination on the basis of race, religion or ethnic identity were a thing of the past. A country whose history belonged to all its citizens, a syncretic blend of elements that reflected the unique sequence of events and influences that came together to create this nation. Whether he would ever have been able to achieve such an ambitious aim will never be known, but what is certain is that with him that possibility essentially died.

With Garang out of the way the slide towards separation was inevitable. The South was left to embark on a new life as an independent state, and the North free to continue its idle dream of a puritanical Islamist state, surviving on the petrol fumes of an exhausted economy. Neither course offers a solution to the country's problems. Secession may have divided the territory but it did not solve the internal conflicts that have dogged the country since independence. The elite profits, and the vast majority of the population are left to fend for themselves. Whatever our view of him, of whether he was murdered, all hopes of national reconciliation died with John Garang.

Born in the town of Wanglei, in Eastern Twic, part of the Jonglei region, Garang was a Dinka. His parents were simple farmers with no education. They had seven children of whom John was the second youngest. He attended secondary school in Rumbek but never finished. Instead he went off to fight, joining the small Anyanya rebel army, which had been fighting for secession since 1955. It was a short-lived war. When the Addis Ababa Accords brought an end to the First Civil War in 1972, Garang had only been a captain for six months, four of which were spent in training. He never experienced battle, nor the hardships of life in the bush. Indeed, he remained

NEXT ISSUE
RETURN OF GRANDMA
A SHORT STORY BY
KAMAL AL-JAZOULI
TRANSLATED BY ADIL BABIKIR

opposed to the peace agreement at first, claiming that the time was not ripe for peace. It was an argument that found no real support within the Anyanya movement, but it was only when he realised he was in a minority that he accepted it.

With the end of the war, the Anyanya forces were absorbed into the national army. Garang moved swiftly through the ranks, going on to Fort Benning in Texas for advanced training. Described as a studious young man, always with his head in a book, his mind filled with big ideas, he graduated from Iowa State University in 1981 with a PhD in agriculture, a subject that remained a lifelong interest. Farming, he believed, would transform his homelands. He even taught for a spell at Khartoum University's Agricultural College in Shambat.

By 1983, Nimeiri was busy deconstructing all the good work he had achieved with the Addis Abeba Accords. Desperate to get his hands on the rich oil fields in the South, he made the decision to replace Southern troops in the Bentiu area with Northerners. The result was mutiny. Nimeiri compounded his error by sending Garang to deal with the problem. Garang went to Bor, listened to the grievances of the soldiers and decided to throw in his lot with them. Nimeiri, used to dealing with the grumblings of the increasingly toothless old Anyanya leadership, had been lulled into a false sense of security. In May 1983, the Southern People's Liberation Army was born and the Second Civil War began.

The SPLA headquarters at New Site lies right on the Ugandan border. The Kazan helicopter struck the ground at an altitude of approximately 1650 metres at a position of 04 degrees North. The symbolism is striking: The dark forces conspiring to prevent the returning exile entry to his new kingdom. There he was, on the edge of a new era, flying along the front line of a vast country that stretched all the way up to 22° North, a full eighteen degrees of latitude, rich in diversity and variety, which until now had been entangled in internecine conflict, fracticide, unending suffering and oppression. To Garang, as he floated down over those misty green hills, it must have seemed as though everything was finally in his grasp, as if he were poised on the threshold of infinite possibility.

EMAD BLAKE

A ride on the roof

CHAPTER ONE OF THE NOVEL *SHAWARMA*,
TRANSLATED BY JOHN PEATE

I will tell you a tale, my son, and you're going to like it very much. It's the tale of your father's lifelong struggle, of which you are the fruit. I will tell you everything when the time is right, and all I ask is that you listen well. I know you will, because nobody can tell you better than me what happened. That said, if this true tale were ever to be written down, there is no-one better than your aunt to do it, and she'll do it just as faithfully and accurately as she has promised me she will. You'll find out who exactly she is when the time is right, too, because she is not, strictly speaking, your aunt. After all, she is Turkish and you're Sudanese. Even so, she's still your aunt because she deserves to be.

Anyway, there was the boy – he being me – sitting on top of a railway carriage, gazing off into the distance, dreaming his faraway dreams as if, one day, he was going to be somebody important. One day, in spite of everything, the whole world would open its doors to him. He felt it to the very core of his being. Nothing else inspired him at that moment except gazing at the clouds racing past the train in the opposite direction, hanging up there in the sky, while he was squatted down there on the earth. Well, to be more precise, he was sitting on the roof of a railway carriage, dodging a fare he couldn't afford. Where would a poor boy like him find ten guinay? Anyway, he wasn't doing anything wrong, it seemed, because there were many like him, even old folks, doing the same thing, riding the train car roofs and paying nothing to the train company bosses.

"It's the state that owns this train, my lad," an elderly man sitting right in front of me said, the cold February wind blowing through

his bones. He was better off than me, though, as he had a cotton scarf to wrap around his face. In fact, you could barely see his face because of it. Just two tiny eyes, a tinier nose, and the outline of two little cheeks. He lit a cheap Abu Nakhla cigarette and said nothing else for a while. You could see on the side of the packet a little palm tree – the Nakhla in question – with its four orangey fronds above. They were just like the ones my father used to smoke when he came home drunk in the middle of the night and set about my mother with his fists, loud enough to wake the whole neighbourhood.

The man sitting in front of me started speaking again:

"Travelling on the roof of the train is great fun, my lad. And, even better, it's free. What's your name, young man?"

I told him in a low voice. It seemed he couldn't make out what I said, either because of the noise of the wind or the advanced age of his ears. He leaned the right one up close to me, trailing his cigarette smoke unintentionally into my face, and repeated his question. I told him again, yelling this time so he could hear. As much as I raised my voice, the chill winter wind rushed in to swallow my words whole and carry them off and away. I wondered where the wind took people's words. How could the wind swallow up all the shrieking and guffawing of the passengers on the roof like that? Where did it take it?

There were dozens of us up there, along the full length of the train, as far as the eye could see, eating, laughing, gossiping, smoking, doing all kinds of things in our own little neighbourhood suspended between earth and sky. Once he'd learned my name, the old man turned around, evidently deciding to teach me a few things, as I strained to hear what he said: "The state's money is halal, my boy, and this train was bought with the people's money." That set him off on a long monologue of no interest to me, and one I couldn't understand anyway. His words were carried off by the ever-rising wind, but I made out words like "president", "ministers", "peasants", and "merchants". He talked about theft and corruption, and about confidence tricks, injustices, and dark conspiracies.

That last phrase reminded me of my father coming home late at night – when night was murkiest – with no electricity in our house, or almost anywhere else in the village. Back in those days, there was neither lamplight in the house, nor in the street. That is, except for in one house, which sat near the river in the gap between the broad bean and white bean fields on the one hand and the local government offices where my father worked as a driver on the other. It was a large, fancy, two-storey house and was the only one in the village lit up day and night. Lit up night and day it was, and, in the middle of the night, you could hear the sound of its generator rumbling as clearly as anything, when all else in the village was quiet. Well, quiet except for the shouting and screaming coming from our house after Dad came home and handed out his daily lesson, scaring us all out of our sleep.

Anyway, the old man kept rambling on, his voice ebbing and flowing on my ears while I shivered in the perishing cold. My trousers and thin shirt were all I had to keep the cold out. Nothing underneath. I really thought the old man might have been kind enough to lend me his scarf, like adults normally do for children, but he didn't. Not an ounce of sympathy for me, except for in his words – those I could catch every now and then, anyway – about the strange disease that had struck the people of this country down, one he sometimes called envy, and, at other times, selfishness. He rounded his soliloquy off with: "It's a lack of faith, my boy. A lack of true faith."

He repeated himself. He testified to this astonishing revelation that had been bestowed on him. It all explained, for him, the misfortunes of the obscure idea he called "the people", that both he and I were part of, from what I could gather from his wind-swallowed words.

I would have died of cold, if God had not been kind. A boy just like me came wandering along the carriage tops, serving passengers from his tea kettle and slipping their coins into his pocket. He had a large pocket sewn onto a dirty piece of cloth strapped to his shoulders by a coarse kind of belt. I knew that tea would take the edge off the cold. My mother would make it for us to warm our little bodies as we sat indoors in the winter holidays from early morning until dusk, or until Father got home for a hasty breakfast and to wreak havoc on us all at the same time.

My son, I hadn't the money, like I said, to buy a ticket and travel inside the train. Unlike my hateful and domineering father, I liked to look after myself. As luck would have it, I found a tiny little coin I had forgotten about till then nestled deep in my pocket. It was enough to buy two cups of tea: one for me, and one for the old man. He thanked me very much, though I didn't know if he had had any money himself and could have done the honours, rather than me. Anyway, he raised his hand high up to the sky and stammered out some words I didn't quite hear, but guessed were a prayer to God for me. As he did so, his scarf slipped onto his shoulders a little, partly revealing his pure white head of hair, over which that you could clearly see lice crawling. He soon worked out I had spotted the little black creatures weaving in and out of his locks, and, staring back at me as he lit another cigarette, said: "It's a home for them, my boy, and I won't be the one to evict them."

My own hair had been lice-ridden for two years at least, even though my mother used to sit my brothers and me out in the sun to wash our hair in paraffin, the best way to get rid of this scourge that the women in the neighbourhood had heard of. It was all a waste of time, though, and we always had to wait until the lice left of their own accord.

The train drew into a stopping station, prompting the roof passengers to jump down and scatter from the railway police who were looking for fare dodgers. I did the same. It required skills I had not acquired before, so I watched the others and copied what they did. The old man hurriedly lowered himself between two carriages with a skill that belied his age. He dangled himself into the narrow space between the coaches and squeezed himself through a window. I managed to do the same, and found myself in amongst a crush of men, women, and children. Beyond the crush I could detect the stink of bleach coming from the foul passenger toilets. I had to put up with that as best I could, until the carriages shunted together to a halt, allowing everyone to escape into the clean air at last.

I got out onto a station platform that looked much like every other one I'd seen. A century old, built when the British colonialists first came, dotted with little huts with pointed, corrugated roofs. The old man had been right next to me, but hadn't followed me off. I was so hungry, but had no money left to get anything. There were men, women, and children selling fuul and ta'miya sandwiches, fried eggs, tea, and even juice despite the cold weather, though most sold hot water. The aroma of barbecuing meat came from a stall behind which a man sat throwing chunks of meat into a pan of hot oil. He was surrounded by the better-off passengers, drawn by the alluring smell hanging in the cold air. I had to make do with just the smell. The renewed bellow of the engine had me rushing to clamber back up again onto the carriage roof. I had lost sight of my aged companion for good, and never saw him again. I looked up and down the train for him, but the people were so huddled up together it was hard to make out any one individual, however hard I tried. I had no idea where he had gone, so I decided to forget all about him, but then remembered he had left a little knapsack with me. I still had it there in my hand, but how could I give it back to him, if I couldn't find him? I would have to wait until we got to the next station. He was bound to look for me, like I him, so we would surely run into one another.

I thought about walking up and down the train carriage roofs looking for him, but the harrowing wind made it all too difficult. It was also too crowded up there, and I might fall if the train picked up speed beyond the lazy pace it had pulled out of the station at. Looking around, I saw some of my fellow rooftop passengers squatting asleep. I wondered how they could do such a thing. The carriage was easily narrow enough for them to fall from and die. I'd heard many stories of people falling off trains like that in the past. It was up to me to stay alert, then, until the journey – wherever it was taking me – came to an end.

I had decided to run away from home that unhappy evening when my father had come home early for a change, and began handing out his daily lesson. He hit my mother so hard she stumbled and fell to the ground and when my brothers and I tried to help her back up he turned on us. My father's belt repeatedly lashed our backs – all of us: mine, my five brothers' and nine sisters'. I was thirteen and my five brothers and three of my sisters were younger than me. My baby sister was not even one year old, and yet she had already had her share of beatings. Mother was always bearing children. No sooner did she give birth to one than she'd be carrying the next. Father wouldn't give her a break. He would beat her in the evenings until he'd stand over her, wherever it was, not caring less about his children's feelings. He was so far gone in drink he didn't know what he was doing. And Mother could do nothing to stand up to his punishment. However drunk he was, he could always find enough physical strength to fight anyone in his path. It was so shameful for us to have a father like that. In the street, in school, down any local alleyway, everywhere, everyone knew we were the madman's kids. You could tell our house from any other in the neighbourhood by the sobbing and bawling coming from it all through the night, and by the screaming and shouting at any other time of the day, for that matter.

The lord and master of the house's behaviour rubbed off on the rest of us, in the fighting, the screaming matches, and the blind rage sparked by the slightest pretext. Having a knife on you was normal in our house. One or other of the boys would often be seen chasing one or other of his younger brothers or sisters with a knife. It was

Photo by Samuel Shimon

NEXT ISSUE

TAYEB SALIH

CHAPTERS FROM THE MEMOIR

MANSI: A RARE MAN IN HIS OWN WAY

TRANSLATED BY ADIL BABIKIR

a daily event. It often ended up with one of us carted off to the hospital, probably bleeding profusely. Normal. Once my eldest brother stabbed one of his sisters in the backside. I was traumatised. I can see it now as if it were happening again right here before me, seeing again the dark blood pouring out of her.

I was pretty much the only exception to this culture of knife-waving, rowdy backwardness, as the neighbours used to say themselves to my face. The neighbours knew everything about our miserable household and its evil doings. Nothing was hidden from them. They were amazed I could emerge from this bizarre home a polite and respectable boy. I had no idea how I had done that either. I assumed it was simply that God had chosen for me to turn out like that. It was God who made me run away from my family hell and seek a life in another place too. That day I ran away, I left behind all my hopes and dreams I had once had for my family and for life in the village I'd spent the whole of my life till then in. The one thing it had given me, miraculously, was a great talent for learning, and I was always top of the class. For me to stand out with my intelligence this way, coming from the madly dysfunctional family I did, was indeed a miracle, as the teachers themselves would say to my face.

Nothing was hidden in that house. My father followed a regimented pattern. He'd leave early in the morning. Although he went to bed late, he was always an early riser, even if it meant him having only two hours' sleep. He had amazing powers, but he applied them to low pursuits, that's if he wasn't threatening to kill my mother and the rest of us. The first thing he'd do every day was warm up the municipal car – an old Land Rover with a dust-coloured cabin on the back. Before setting off, he would feed a tube into the petrol tank, suck one end, spit a little out, and then watch the fuel seep slowly into his plastic jerry can. He used to sell half the vehicle's fuel that way. Some man would come every morning dead on ten in the morning – never late – and take the petrol away in exchange for the few guinay he would give to my mother. She, of course, was not allowed to spend any of it, and had to turn it over to Father exactly as it was. If she'd spent even one guinay of it, she knew what her fate would be, but then, she was never spared a nightly beating anyway.

Father's job was driver to the village mayor – the man with the two-storey house lit up with electric light day and night that I mentioned before. Father appeared loyal to him, kowtowing to him all the time. The mayor liked him in return, and gave my father the money he wasted on his own entertainment. He never once threatened him with the sack or a pay cut. I very often saw Dad bowing and scraping to the mayor in his office, or to the mayor's wife in their home, while getting the vegetables, meat and bread ready for them in the morning. She was really shocked when she heard about father's reputation in the village. She once asked me: "Is it true that he beats your mother?" I realized straight away that the question was an improper one, so I looked at her without answering, and she realized I wasn't happy with her enquiry. Whatever happened in our house, it was our house, and our business, and that was my mother and my father she was talking about.

The day I ran away, my father had already decided to evict us all from the house anyway. He would often announce this when he came home drunk. We'd spend half the night in the street, or with a neighbour who had taken pity on us, and then go back home afterwards to life as normal. This time, though, he seemed serious. We'd spent more than half the night outside without hearing anything back. Mother didn't come to take us in. Father didn't call us from the darkness to come back in either. My mind started wandering into strange territory. I hated being in that place, in that house in particular. I told myself that I wasn't going to stay any longer. I had to go and seek a new life elsewhere. I didn't know where. I had no clear plan to speak of, but the main thing was to follow where my imagination led me.

A train was coming into the village station, less than half a mile away from us. That meant I could catch it. I was so full of joy when it set off, me sitting next to my friend, the old man, on the roof. The clanking together of the carriages gradually eased as the speed picked up. The only thing on my mind was to forget the past and head south for the capital. I'd find openings there that others had told me about before. I would be bound to find a job that would set me up. The main thing, though, was to get away from the pain of my daily life up to that point, and all the hatred and bile that went with it. I had to forget about school. What good was that to me now? Sooner or later, I would have left school anyway, for one reason or another. My brothers had been the same. If I had stayed, I would have reached the point where I couldn't stand it any more.

My elder brother was very much a case in point to me. He had done well in school like me. He'd earned himself an education, but one day lost patience with my father's endless harassment and lost his way. He started pulling blades on people like the rest of us, turned into a drunk like his father, and did nothing afterwards but chase after the girls in the neighbourhood. I wasn't going to go down that road. I promised myself that, and rode off on the roof of that train.

The idea of running away was not new to me. I had thought about it from time to time before. That house always felt alien to me. Whatever my father did was bad, and my mother did nothing about it. I knew she was constantly pained by it all, but there was nothing she could do but keep it to herself, as they say. She tried to live with the torment and keep her home together, though I don't know what kind of a home it was to her. When she talked about home, I always thought she must mean somewhere else, not our house.

The train drew near a major station after quite a journey. Hundreds of miles. It's all there deep in my memory to this day. It was a journey of destiny, one with as yet unknown consequences for a boy dreaming of a place far away from the hell he had lived in. The train had passed through dozens of stations, and along the way I learned how vast the country we live in is. It was the first time out of our village for me, and I discovered such diverse landscapes: desert stretching everywhere to the horizon, a river running alongside the rails, flowing against the train's direction, disappearing at times, only to reappear later. Farms full of greenery; others parched and barren. Bedouins leading camels through areas of grassy abundance; little pyramids scattered around, their peaks crushed in as if they had fallen from some planet or other; little cars stuck in the sand, and men heaving on ropes trying to pull them out. This was my country, though I had seen only a part of it, not even a quarter of it, as I knew from my geography lessons. We were a million-square-mile nation of paupers. I'd heard there were even forests in the far south, and wondered if I would ever see them. My mind wandered in all directions, not knowing what my fate would be, what was going to happen to me.

We entered the capital – the big city. I could tell it was huge from the high-rises looming up at me from every direction, from the streets crammed with cars and people, and from the noise and the smoke rising up from everywhere. I realized straight away that life there was going to be totally different from my village in the north. The only grand building we had back there was the mayor's. We had no paved streets. The air was cleaner there and you didn't feel so suffocated. Everyone knew everyone else, and everyone's business. The big city was quite different. The people seemed like they were living through the Day of Judgement. They talked to themselves, and rushed everywhere: why I couldn't work out. I watched it all from up on the train roof, comparing it all to the place of my birth. The biting wind dropped as we pulled into the station. It prompted me to quickly dive inside the carriage, fearing the police who had already started chasing after the stowaways on the roof. Some had jumped off and been arrested. I'd seen this happen so many times at previous stations, I made sure I escaped it.

The old man whom I had shadowed had rescued me at previous stations many times, but where was he now? I'd lost sight of him at the station before last, and wouldn't have known we were coming into the big city if it hadn't have been for the joyful chattering of the other passengers at the prospect. They were all jabbering away on the roof about what they were going to do, gathering their belongings and memories of the big city, preparing themselves for whatever lay ahead. How many of them, like me, had no idea what lay ahead? Looking around quickly, I couldn't see anyone around my age. They were all much older. The youngest of them seemed to be at least ten. I reminded myself that the quicker I got off the carriage roof, the better the chances of escape. This was something I learned from the old man.

The minute I rested my left foot on the rubber covering the carriage coupling – dangling down amid the crush of all the other

NEXT ISSUE
BUSHRA FADIL

A SHORT STORY
HAHINA AND HAWAHI

TRANSLATED BY JULIA IHNATOWICZ

stowaways keen to get off and away – I felt a firm hand from below grab hold of me and drag me off like a stone on the end of a rope. I felt my body spin at least three times in the air before I hit the ground. Another man, not the one who had pulled me off the roof, planted the sole of a giant boot on my back to hold me down. I couldn't see up any more as my face was crushed into the icy paving of the platform. Then, twisting my head with extreme difficulty, I could see out of the corner of my right eye the shape of the railway policeman who had mercilessly stomped on my back. It felt like I couldn't breathe and I was in quite a state, thinking I was going to die.

It was an unhappy welcome to the city. I was pulled up and led to a little office, behind which was a heap of buckled steel. It was a poky little room, but I soon realized I was not on my own. There were dozens of others who had been arrested like me. That was re-assuring, actually. At least I wouldn't feel alone. What mattered to me was whether they were good-hearted, polite types like my old friend on the roof, even if they were fare dodgers. The other thing was, I felt so hungry that my stomach hurt. There was little hope of fixing that before the police interrogation was over, and there was a whole row of people in front of me. And then what would happen to me? God alone knew.

I was the only young boy among the fare dodgers. All the others were men. No women. It felt proud to think I'd become a man by committing my first ever crime. I heard one of my fellow offenders swearing and cursing, not caring about the two constables nearby, along with a first lieutenant, as you could tell from the badge on his shoulder. The man yelled: "Any son of Adam should be proud to be an outlaw in this country!"

The others were all silent, except for two who muttered their agreement with the man, though not in the hearing of the officer guarding those arrested. He had a whip in his hand and he started flaying those trying to stir up trouble. Things calmed down after the whippings were handed out. I hadn't escaped a beating either. It took me instantly back to times my father would beat my mother, with each lash of the policeman's whip on my shivering body. The policeman even looked indistinguishable from my father to me, as though they had been cast from the same mould. The same heavy brow, the same trimmed beard, the same flaccid paunch, bloated

and undulating like the plains the train had passed through, a ciga-
rette burning away in one hand, while the other hand delighted in
administering the whip.

When I eventually came before the desk officer, he said to me:

"We'll let you go if you pay for the ticket, and that's me being
kind because you're so young."

I replied: "But I don't have any money on me."

He looked at the old man's knapsack, which I still had with me.
I don't know how I'd managed to hang onto it through all this pan-
demonium, but I had. He pointed at it: "What have you got there
in your hand?"

"I don't know."

My reply surprised him, as I could tell from the rumpled expres-
sion on his broad face. He spun round off his chair, ripped the knap-
sack out of my hand, and emptied it out onto the table. There was
an old Qur'an and some prayer beads made locally from the seeds
of the lalob tree. It was a small string, though, not one of the long
ones the dervishes wear for their night-time zhikr circles, when
they work up their rapturous adoration for the chosen one.

Then a pile of banknotes fell out – a little surprise I wasn't ex-
pecting. It looked like a lot, maybe one thousand guinay, given each
note was worth ten, and there must have been a hundred of them.
The officer slammed the palms of both hands down on the table,
stunned to see such a huge amount of cash, though not as stunned
as I was. That old man had been carrying all that money yet hadn't
coughed up for the price of a cup of tea, let alone food, for himself
or for me, who he had watched shiver from cold and hunger all that
time. I couldn't believe he hadn't realized how hungry I was. Any-
way, the police officer soon interrupted my thoughts: "Is all this

NEXT ISSUE
TWO SHORT STORIES BY
SARA HAMZA ALJACK

money yours?"

"No, sir, it isn't mine."

"Ah, so you stole it, then? Seems like we've got ourselves a thief here."

He didn't give me a chance to respond, but let loose a relentless volley of accusations and insults at me instead. This was nothing new to me. Our house back in the village lay near the police station, and I was quite used to seeing scuffles going on outside it between police and criminals there. It sometimes made me feel that both sides – the cops and the robbers – acted like criminals. This time, it was me in the criminal's shoes, and not much in the way of a defence to offer, either. What could I do?

I tried to explain, to tell him the whole story about the old man on the roof of the train. No, no, really, there had been an old man, and I'd followed him, and then he'd given me this bag, and then I'd lost sight of him and he must have forgotten all about me. It didn't wash with the policeman, though. He had me down for a thief trying to cover my tracks. I was barely allowed to speak in order to explain myself, anyway. I was still a young lad, not street-smart enough to stand on my own feet in the world of adults. I shut up in the end when it became obvious the officer wasn't going to listen. He only had eyes for the money, anyway. I wasn't so young as to not recognize that. "People will die for money, however they can get hold of it. All that matters to them is to get it," as I heard my mother often say.

He took me out into another office through a small door in the narrow hallway I hadn't noticed before. There was a higher-ranking officer there sitting behind a table with his head buried in a newspaper. He put it to one side when he heard what the officer had to say about me, the little train robber they had caught. He gazed at me a little while. He seemed well-mannered, unlike his colleague, but asked: "Where did you learn how to steal? Seems like you've come from a long way off."

"I'm not a thief, sir. I swear to God I didn't steal it. What happened was . . ."

Translated from the novel *Shawarma*,
published by Moment, London, 2014

RANIA MAMOUN

PASSING

A SHORT STORY

TRANSLATED BY WILLIAM M HUTCHINS

He visited me repeatedly and always asked me the same question in the same mournful way: "Why haven't you become a doctor? You promised!"

I would reply remorsefully: "Sadly enough, I haven't."

He would say: "I pinned my dreams on you. I thought you would fulfil them."

Then I would remain silent – either because I had nothing to say or because I was struck dumb by his disappointment.

* * *

Your scent was absorbed by the wall's cracks and mixed with motes of dust there. Then it wafted back to me, filling the room. When I turned to seek its source, it overwhelmed me, surrounding me. I extended my hand to seize it in my palm and thus to seize you, to feel your tender palm, your face, and your hand. I sensed your presence beside me, very near me, inside me even. I felt that if I held out my hand, it would bump into you.

Your scent opened memory's lanes and assailed me suddenly like armies of stinging ants, wreaking havoc on my eye, skin, pores, blood, and ear, which received the sympathetic vibrations of your voice. Memories flooded over me, and I felt the warmth of your embrace and of the bed when I slept beside you – instead of Mother – when I was a child.

When you came home from your office, I stuck to you like glue. Mother tried to pull me away, but I ignored her.

She told me: "He's traveling tomorrow."

I retorted: "But he'll return."

Now that I have grown up and you've passed away – after I have accepted your loss, which is hard to bear – I can no longer offer

the same response or be so sure.

Your scent fills all the interstices of the empty air and releases me from memory's whirlwind only to cast me into another one that is more extensive and deeper and that magnifies in me the sense of your presence near me. You are drinking tea from your mug, which we still have. How you loved your tea! After tea, you listened to the radio, lying on your back, with one leg propped on the other. Then you rifled through your briefcase and asked me to read one paper or another. Occasionally your specter appears in my imagination, where I see you perform your ablutions for prayer. I recall now your delight when we moved to this dwelling near the mosque from which the resounding call to prayer penetrated our hearts, shaking our bodies. You said: "What delights me most about the house is being near the mosque. Could we have a better neighbor?"

* * *

Today is Eid, and everyone is fluttering with joy. The muezzin is calling out from the mosque that God is great and proclaiming

God's uniqueness. The children repeat after him: "Allahu Akbar! God is most great! There is no god but God! God is most great! Praise God!"

My siblings' children run in and out merrily, wearing their new Eid clothes. Eid candy keeps finding its way to their mouths. They come to me and make a fuss.

Eyyad asks: "Where is the Eid present? You said you'd give us an Eid present." Then he adds innocently: "Quick! Give us the Eid present! We want to go to the swings."

Ziyad demands: "How much are you giving us? Give us lots of money – please?"

Back then I was adding the final touches to the house's decorations. I adjusted the drapes and pulled the new covers tighter on the cushions. I added embers to the censer so the sticks of sandalwood would complete the joyous atmosphere of Eid with their scent. I heard my sister call Mother: "Mama, Mama, come see what's wrong with Papa. He seems really weak."

My mother rushed to check on him. She touched him and spoke to him, but he didn't respond. She asked my sister to call my brother to fetch our neighbor, a doctor. That morning my sister had bathed him, dressed him in his new jilbab, sprinkled cologne on him, and told him it was Eid. He didn't seem to understand what she said or to realize that it was Eid.

He wasn't capable of understanding. You questioned him, but he didn't answer or give any indication he had heard you. He looked at you, but you imagined he didn't see you and was looking through you. His glances wandered around the room. You poured him the tea he loved and adjusted his position in bed, covering him carefully.

You asked: "Did he drink some tea?"

"Yes, he did."

* * *

I was his favorite child, and he loved me a lot. When he found me sitting quietly by myself, not chatting with other members of the family, he would ask: "What's wrong? Why are you sitting alone?"

"Nothing's the matter. I'm just sitting by myself."

"Go and talk to the other kids. I don't like to see you alone like this."

He gave me extra quantities of everything he brought us: sweets, money, sugar cane, beans, and games. He favored me with his affection, his company, and everything. If my siblings grumbled, he retorted that I was his youngest child. When I returned from school and asked my mother for lunch, he would tell me: "Go to the kitchen and fix some food. This is your home. Why are you so shy here?"

He frequently announced his great hopes for me: "I want this daughter to become a physician." He would always call me "Doctor", and I would be thrilled. Despite all that affection, I failed to fulfil his wish!

* * *

While we waited for the doctor, my father lay stretched out on his bed, and I sat by his head. Noticing beads of sweat on his brow and his bald head, I wiped the moisture away repeatedly with my hand – not a handkerchief. When his brow became moist again, I wiped away the perspiration once more. The sweat kept flowing, and I continued to wipe it off with my bare hand. When the doctor arrived, he found us surrounding my father. My mother was massaging his feet, my sister was holding his hand on the other side of the bed, my brother was standing not far away, and I was still wiping his forehead. The physician examined him meticulously, but my mother was staring at my father's eyes. She may have realized what was happening, because she began to recite the creed's two phrases. The doctor did not ask her to keep quiet. Instead, he continued monitoring my father's blood pressure, eyes, and pulse.

I saw my father's lips move. He recited the Muslim creed, following my mother's lead, in a low, scarcely audible voice. Then the sound faded, and the motion of his lips slowed.

In that parting moment, his forehead perspired profusely. His lips ceased moving, and the physician glanced up with a mournful look on his face. I was too naïve to realize till then that his spirit had departed as I was wiping the sweat from his brow. Perhaps it passed by me. Perhaps it collided with me as it passed. Perhaps it said farewell and waved or smiled. Even though I was right there, I did not see it.

TAREK ELTAYEB

Helmy Abu Regileh*

A SHORT STORY
TRANSLATED BY SALLY GOMAA

W
e all headed to Helmy's house covered in sweat and dust. We could not stop talking about our epic soccer game, which we had just brilliantly lost. We were walking slowly the way we usually did to let Helmy to keep up. He never ever asked us to wait for him but there was something about him that compelled us to slow down. It was not just out of respect for his feelings, we were moved by a mysterious, unnamable force. Even when we ran to catch the school bus, he was always ahead of us. We admired the way he limped forward with his body tilted at a sharp angle and jumped onto the bus, holding on to the door. More often than not, one of us would fall off and be seriously hurt, but not him. Perhaps this was one of Abu Regileh's miracles. "Abu Regileh" was the nickname we later gave him: the Miraculous Helmy or the Miraculous Helmy Abu Regileh.

We were a group of five from pre to middle school. And in the last two years, we were joined by Mahmoud el-Minyawi. He was a year older despite his small size. He had missed one school year due to the war raging along the Suez Canal. His family had had to emigrate from the city of Suez. As a "refugee" he was treated with contempt by his peers in both elementary and middle school. At that time, all the refugees who had had to relocate from the Canal to other parts of Egypt were stigmatized. For many years, they were viewed as outsiders through no fault of their own.

Helmy was our favorite. We loved descending on his house in small groups. His mother warmly welcomed us as if we were her own children. She always led us straight to his room even if he was asleep. He liked the ruckus we made to wake him up and he was immedi-

Photo by Hans Lobler, Vienna

ately out of bed, limping with his curious gait. His mom was from the countryside and she kept her beautiful original accent despite living in Cairo for many years. She understood that we were always hungry. So the moment we sat down, she walked in with her famous tray full of her distinctive delicious food. She made the best fried eggs with butter and she had the best feteer, stuffed with cheese and honey. Those treats, which we rarely enjoyed at our own homes, were always abundantly available at Helmy's. We used to wolf down her food as she watched us with a kindly smile. The feast usually ended with her excellent mint tea.

* * *

The strong bond that united the six of us was envied by many. Hardly a day went by without seeing each other after school. This was at the beginning of the 1970s. We had no way of communicating other than going to each other's house. Mahmoud el-Minyawi was the easiest to reach because he lived on the ground floor. All we had to do was tap lightly on his window to let him know we were waiting outside ready for our next adventure.

I lived on the second floor. At hearing a distinctive whistle followed by my name stretched in an exaggerated way, "Taaaaarek, Taaaaarek," I would stick my head out or wave my hand. In no time, I was downstairs. Fateen was the toughest to reach. We had to be as sly as foxes, carefully approaching his house and using his alias, "Pilot", to draw his attention. A red towel on the clotheslines was our sign to stay away. If we persisted in calling him, his mom would come out. She would yell loudly at us and accuse us of ruining her youngest son's future by being good for nothing losers.

As for Paulus, he was always available because he rarely stayed in the house. He usually sat outside on a round stone that looked like the one used to make falafel – a cylindrical stone, which was placed firmly at the corner of the house to protect it from passing traffic. This was where we always found him and where we held our meetings. Sometimes his invalid father came out to ask us to keep our voices down. Paulus's informal way of addressing his father always sounded peculiar to us. "Take it easy, Boss" or "Chill out," he would tell him.

* * *

Helmy was our best friend, the one with the kindest heart, the first to pay a sick friend a visit and to stick around until he felt better. Perhaps others' sickness moved him because of his gentle nature; perhaps he sympathized deeply because of his own handicap. I sensed the profound sadness he tried to hide, even from himself. He allowed no one to see his tears. Instead, he always came up with the funniest jokes and the wittiest remarks. His humor was treasured by all of us while his sarcasm was feared by people outside our group. He unleashed his sharp tongue against anyone who dared to offend one of us. He would invent a name that could stick to the offender for the rest of his school days and perhaps even for the rest of his life. He had his own unique vocabulary, along with his unique walk.

For Helmy's birthday, instead of a gift, we decided to give him cash. We convinced him to use it to see a well-known orthopedist. The orthopedist recommended another specialist who recommended another specialist and so on until he was advised to see a therapist. Each one of those consultations cost him a lot of money.

We saw Helmy walking out of the therapist's office with the usual sarcastic smile on his face. The therapist himself followed looking extremely angry. I was the only one who noticed the sadness in Helmy's eyes. This was why he avoided making eye contact with me. We were all there when the therapist told him clearly that his condition would never improve unless he admitted that he had a "condition" in the first place. Helmy told us later that the therapist saw his "problem" as a psychological one, which required intensive therapy going back to his early childhood. He joked that it would be cheaper and more effective to seek the help of a sheikh . A few prayers and religious chants would chase out the demons that seemed to have possessed him, he joked. Joking was his way to express his gratitude for what he considered a unique experience and a thoughtful birthday gift. From that day on, our way of handling any problem was to invoke Helmy's precious impression of the therapist's words: "After only ten sessions of intensive therapy, you will feel as good as new, son."

* * *

Once I went to see Nasser at his house. Since he was not home, his mom invited me to have some tea while I waited. I always dreaded one-on-one sessions with my friends' moms. Their brilliant interrogation methods always succeeded in unveiling secrets we had vowed never to share with our parents regardless of their pressure.

It was winter and the weather was unpredictable. As I neared Nasser's house, it started to rain heavily. I ran to take shelter at his house. As it would have been a long journey back home, I accepted his mom's invitation to have tea. But I prepared myself for her imminent attack with as much cunning as I could ever muster.

We sat in the living room on a colorful rug-covered couch. I tried to anticipate her questions and to prepare my own useless answers. I made up stories with fake names and characters in my head to distract her, on the one hand, and to waste time, on the other. I wanted to avoid being trapped into revealing one of her first-born's secrets. She always added the word "first-born" before his name as if it was a title like Dr or as if "first-born" was a unique blessing bestowed upon him by God.

Umm Nasser was a force to be reckoned with. She had already tricked two of us into admitting some of the follies committed by her "first-born". With unparalleled skill, she once extracted classified information from Fateen. The calmer she appeared, the more he babbled on until, before he even knew it, the fool had said too much. For a while afterwards, he and Nasser were not in good terms. From that day on, the six of us vowed to never ever share our secrets with anyone beyond our group.

* * *

Around that time, Nasser was suffering from bilharzia, which he was late in discovering, or, rather, which he was ashamed to admit. We were taking a leak once when I noticed the bright red color of his urine against the sand. First, he told me he had drunk lots of hibiscus tea at our Sudanese friend Abboud's house. But later he admitted that, in addition to a burning sensation, he had been seeing blood in his urine for a while. He was afraid to tell his family because he thought he had caught a sexually transmitted infection from rubbing against Mabsoutah's body while she was wearing nothing but a pair of panties. She had lifted her skirt up for him when she delivered milk to his house in place of her father. Nasser thought that counted as having sex. I understood then why he had had so many questions about pregnancy and marriage for Khalil, our sex expert.

Mabsoutah was only two years older than us but she had the body of a fully developed woman. She loved to flirt and to have boys rub against her and she took every opportunity to make obscene sexual jokes. We were fourteen years old, the age of sexual misinformation – all of which came from Khalil. Because he was a couple of years older than us he was our reference for everything to do with sex. He told us men ejaculated during sex and so did women. He said kissing caused pregnancy, which explained why some babies were born after only seven months. They were babies born from kissing whereas one needed to have sex several times to make a complete baby – each time made one part: one time for the head, another for the arms or the legs, and so on. He also told us that if a man was not on top during sex, he could get pregnant. We believed those myths and passed them on when it was our turn.

* * *

Nasser was treated for bilharzia by Dr Boutros el-Isnawi, who had volunteered to treat all the children of our neighborhood for free. Believing that he only treated school children, many parents sent their children to school not only for education, but also for the free medical treatment, which constituted a more pressing need. Thanks to Dr Boutros, not a single child had bilharzia. However, soon after Nasser was cured, he was bitten by a rabid dog and had to receive twenty-one injections at the local medical unit.

I went with him for his first appointment. He was trembling both before and after the injection. Within fifteen minutes of taking it, he started to vomit until nothing was left in his stomach. The same thing happened with the second injection. So, when it was time for the third one, we decided to spare him the torture and skip the appointment. We had to disappear for two or three hours. When he went home, Nasser had to act as if he had had the injection by showing the same side effects. We did this a total of four times. Each time, all four or five of us went with him.

However, his mom soon sensed that he was not acting the same way he did after the first two real injections. Among other things for example, she noticed that his appetite was no longer affected. Initially, she was delighted, but the remarkable speed of his recovery raised her doubts. At first, she played along but, like any mother in her place, she conspired to unravel the mystery.

She planned a meeting with Fateen on his own. Before he arrived, she prepared his favorite dessert, something called *bsissa*. As Fateen waited for Nasser, he could not help but smell the delicious freshly made *bsissa*. When a huge plate of *bsissa* appeared before him, the battle was already lost. Even before he swallowed his first bite, she started the inquisition.

"By the way, Fateen, since when did Nasser stop going to the medical unit?"

The bsissa stuck in Fateen's throat. To ease the pressure on him, she added with phony concern: "The poor thing told me how horrible the injections were and how he just couldn't keep taking them."

Her face maintained an exaggerated look of sympathy as she fixed her gaze on poor Fateen. When she said, "Eat up, my son," he thought she was saying, "Speak up, my son."

"Has Nasser really told you that," he said faintly.

"Yes, he did, after he made me promise not to tell his father. When exactly did he stop taking his injections?"

By this point, she made no effort to ease the pressure. And, like a complete fool, Fateen blurted out: "The third time, Tant ."

We used to call Umm Nasser "Interpol". Not only did Nasser approve of this name, I'm almost sure he was the one who invented it. It was how he referred to her sometimes. Recently, Umm Nasser said that she was concerned that we were skipping school. We had no idea how she had found out. But we were in fact skipping school about once every week. We used to leave after morning break to go to "the hill", as we called it, which was an open space about two kilometres from school. We went there to play soccer with a rudimentary ball made by our ingenious friend Mahmoud. He used to fill an old silk stocking with foam rubber, then wind it really tightly with rope until it was as perfectly round and smooth as a large navel orange. He would finally dip it in a special kind of liquid glue and leave it to dry for a few days. Thus, we were able to practise our favorite sport.

But we liked to play soccer on an open space behind Nasser's house more than on the "hill". The tough ground there was better than the sand that covered the hill. This change of place might have been the reason Umm Nasser's intelligence sources had identified us.

* * *

Umm Nasser did not offer me tea as I expected. Instead, she had made lentil soup with bone stock. Its overpowering smell alone was enough to bring the hardest criminal to his knees. When she placed a bowl of hot soup in front of me, I knew I was in trouble. As a pre-emptive strike, I said: "I just ate, Tant." However, what I said made no sense on account of my bulging eyes and slobbering mouth.

"But this is just a snack, sweetheart. Please have some soup, darling."

The smell of the fried onions on top of the soup conspired with the cold weather to destroy what was left of my resistance. I fell on the bowl, anticipating the first blow to hit at any moment. I knew that the lentil soup manoeuvre was the first move in the process of extracting information from me to be forever filed in her beautiful mind. By eating the soup, I was already co-opted into her plan. She brought me some sun-baked bread to complement the soup and continued with her kind words.

"Eat up, love. Take your time." This was followed by the usual formalities: "How's your mum? How's your dad? How's your sister, Hayat, and your aunt, Rouda?"

So far, so good, I thought. But things were moving fast. Where was Nasser, the fool? What was taking him so long?

To gain time, I asked: "Where's Nasser?" I hoped for a long answer.

"Oh, he and his brother went to Uncle Sanad's store to pick up a few things."

What the hell! Uncle Sanad's store was so far away! It was further away than our school and he didn't open till 3:00 pm. Despite these thoughts, I kept a stupid smile on my face.

Not before long, her next question crawled into the conversation like a snake: "How's school, love? Is it true your classmates are skipping school, as Mr Aref has told me?"

The way she kept calling me "love" signalled an impending disaster. May God help me! As for "classmates", I had no idea who exactly she was referring to.

"Well, some people do, but not everyone." That was the beginning of the end for me. I had spoken too fast and my answer was dumb. Sure enough, she followed by asking what "not everyone" meant.

I said, playing stupid: "Some boys skip school, but most of us don't."

"Come on, you've never done it?"

"Done what, Tant?"

"You've never, ever tried to skip school, you little devil? Not even once?"

I knew I was in no man's land. The soup had given me temporary strength, but it was all gone under the impact of the last blow. I remembered what happened with Fateen. That poor bunny. Here I was, trapped like a mouse.

"Never, Tant! Besides, where would we go? It's not like we could go to a cinema or a stadium."

"Not even if you were encouraged by what's his face, the kid who's driving his poor mother crazy, Helmy?"

"Helmy Abu Regileh? How would he be able to join us with his handicap?" I said with mock surprise. Then, in an attempt to turn round the conversation, I came up with my own question. "Is it true, Tant, that you gave birth to Nasser the same day Helmy was born?"

Umm Nasser laughed and the bracelets around her wrist made a little noise, like a soft song that transported her back to the past. Her story now appeared more important to her than anything I could have said. I sighed in relief. The ball was finally in my court. She started to tell the story as if it happened yesterday. I barely listened to her because all my attention was focused on the doorway through which I hoped someone would emerge and save me from my predicament. She said it was true that Nasser and Helmy were born on the same night. Umm Helmy had pneumonia at the beginning of her pregnancy. As her condition worsened, her doctor advised her to terminate the pregnancy. But her husband had just died and she wanted to keep the baby despite the risk.

"She gave birth to Helmy," Umm Nasser said, "a beautiful boy with a stunning face, the spitting image of his father. But too bad . . . no one is perfect."

Right at that moment, I heard a noise outside the door. My only wish was granted! There they were, Nasser and his brother walking in with many shopping bags. Nasser was happy to see me and gave me a hug, as usual. I thanked his mum for her hospitality and for her fabulous soup. In fact, everything she cooked was more than fabulous.

"Thanks, buddy. I just came from a 'private study group'," I told him.

His face showed fear because a 'private study group' in our vocabulary meant an interrogation by one of our parents. "Did you pass the quiz," he asked.

His mom thought we were discussing school and she prepared to leave the room with the empty soup bowl. "Would you like some more?" she asked me on her way out.

* * *

My visit to Nasser's house was part of an elaborate scheme. We had planned an important soccer match with another local team in the open space behind his house. The plan was to tell our parents we were going to study at Nasser's house while Nasser would tell his mom he was going to study at Mahmoud's. I had tucked two random delapidated books under my arm, as I always did, to give the impression I was going to study.

We were now late for the game. The other team had already arrived, along with a small group of their fans. Our team members were worried because we were late for such an important game.

Helmy was there. He attended every game, standing at the edge of the makeshift pitch. Only I noticed his sadness. Perhaps because of our deep friendship, I saw behind the constant smile on his face. I could tell from the way he eyed the ball intensely that he wanted to join in. But since no one offered, he always said he was there to support us. There were times when I saw him jumping behind the goal, which was marked by a couple of stones, as if he were the goalkeeper. I marvelled at his grace and his skill, catching the imaginary ball, but I admired him most for his ability to make something sublime out of his handicap.

At the time, I could not understand my feelings towards him. I did not possess an adequate vocabulary to capture such complex feelings. I did not even know what "sublime" meant. The only word I knew was love. I loved him in a way I did not need to intellectualize by thinking about why he was so strong, why he was so divine, or why we all loved him so much.

Fateen did not show up that day. Mahmoud laughed so hard as he told me that when they went to pick him up, his mother appeared from behind the clotheslines yelling that "The pilot has taken off!

Go find another loser so you can waste his time!" As he walked away feeling embarrassed, he noticed Fateen's head sticking out of a side window like a prisoner. Fateen's mum controlled the entire family. Not even his father was spared her sharp tongue. We dreaded her enough to stay out of her way or to change our route altogether to avoid running into her. The name we gave her, which Fateen knew, was "Dracula".

We could not start the game without our goalkeeper. So Nasser offered to do the job. "We can't afford to lose our best defense," I said.

For a while, I stood facing the crowds and the fans. Then, all of a sudden, I yelled at the captain of the opposite team as he was beginning to walk away: "We're ready to play, Captain."

Everyone watched in amazement as I walked towards Helmy. He was leaning on his good foot, waiting for the game to start. "You're going to be our goalkeeper today, Helmy," I told him. "Do a good job."

I spoke with authority. But my friends looked both annoyed and embarrassed. Sensing their unease, Helmy took a few steps back. I placed my hand firmly on his shoulder as I looked firmly into his eyes. He simply put his arms around me.

Mahmoud was the only one who came over to join us. "We'll win. This is our own pitch," he said as he tapped Helmy's shoulder.

Watching me and Mahmoud, our friends appeared baffled. The game started. We scored the first goal and for a short while we dominated the game. But we lost momentum once two goals were scored by the opposing team, one after the other. This was the result of Helmy being stressed. Our team was visibly shaken. The score now was 6/2.

During the short interval, we met in the middle of the pitch. I gave Helmy a telling-off and asked him to pay more attention to the ball. I told him he was an excellent goalkeeper but he needed to focus. I was yelling at him as if he did not have multiple sclerosis. Mahmoud reminded me to be careful not to hurt Helmy's feelings. But I told him pointing at Helmy: "Our goalkeeper is twenty times better than his opponent."

"It's OK," Paulus intervened. "You know he has a bad foot."

"But his good foot makes up for it," I yelled back.

This was awkward for everyone to hear except for Helmy. His

face glowed and he put on his unique beautiful smile. I knew that my words moved him and my mood switched from anger to joy. This was the real Helmy, the one who laughed in the face of tragedy, who had no time for self-pity, who put others' feelings before his.

In the second half of the game, he faced the ball like a lion. The crowds were stunned by his performance. "Helmy, Helmy, Helmy," they cheered. Their cheers inspired us and drew more people over to watch Helmy's amazing performance.

We wanted to win for Helmy's sake. From a distance, he looked so different to me, and, for a moment, I thought that there was nothing wrong with him and that his handicap was a guise he put on to deceive us.

* * *

We lost the game 7/3 that day. As soon as it was over, we ran towards Helmy. We hoisted him up in the air and hugged and kissed him as if we had won. We shouted his name over and over: "Helmy, Helmy, Helmy."

"Now, do you understand, silly, that you are the best goalkeeper we could ever have," I teased him.

I would never forget the gratitude in his eyes as I hugged him, and kissed him on his forehead. I looked away to wipe away the tears caused by so much dust in the air.

* * *

We all headed to Helmy's house covered in sweat and dust. We could not stop talking about our epic soccer game, which we had just brilliantly lost. We were walking slowly the way we usually did to allow Helmy to keep up. But this time he was several steps ahead of us, leaning confidently on his good leg.

Vienna, 2 January 2012

Note:
* Helmy's nickname Abu Regileh is after the famous Egyptian football player, Mahmoud Abu Regileh.

STELLA GAITANO

Is war the shortest route for saying No?

TESTIMONY OF A SUDANESE WRITER

My name is Stella Gaitano Jenishes. Stella is an Italian name that means the morning star. According to my father, I was born at dawn, but there was still a star glittering up there and my father said, "That's Stella". My father's name is Gaitano. I owe him an apology because many mispronounce his name. Even worse, his name is often misspelled; my first collection of short stories was not immune to this. Sometimes I would spontaneously make the necessary correction, but in many instances, I just let it go. As for my grandfather's name, it is the best proof that the Sudanese do not know how to pronounce or write their names properly. This Jenishes should have been James, but because those clerks who sat at the gate of the immigration office were too busy to hear the name properly from my father's mouth, they miswrote it as Jenishes and that was how it was permanently stamped onto

The South Sudanese writer Stella Gaitano was invited to Khartoum – where she was born and lived before partition – to speak at the Tayeb Salih Award activities about her life and writing. Her testimony is an invaluable contribution to understanding the complexities of place, family and language that make up Sudanese literary identity, "demolishing barriers and filling all spaces with love, tolerance and beauty". We are pleased to publish it here in full, in the first English translation.

our birth and educational certificates. It turned into a deliberate error that we consciously keep committing with great care, as any correction would cast doubt on our identity documents. Even when we went back to the South, we carried that error along as a souvenir from the mother country.

I was born in al-Mazad neighbourhood in Khartoum North, and grew up in al-Haj Yousef's al-Wihda sub-district (Souk 6). Al-Haj Yousef is a typical example of the worlds of the margin, those neighbourhoods encircling the capital. Neighbourhoods that play host to people displaced by wars, people who fall off the rocket of a stampeding city, and others who are attracted to city life and services not available elsewhere.

I am grateful for the chance that took me to the University of Khartoum. It was a turning point in my life. It was there I studied pharmacy and met my best friends – friends as faithful as the Earth, who never let you down. I also stumbled upon writers, poets, critics, and politicians, to whom I owe the birth of Stella the writer.

My social status? I am married, and the mother of two children – and of two books (with a third on the way, a children's book), and some articles replete with ravings and rants.

We the Sudanese, for some good reason or otherwise, tend to have an urge to know where a person hails from. I, for one, was a difficult case for many: short, with uncharacteristic features, and fluent, in Arabic. As a result, I was always introduced as "the southern writer who writes in Arabic". That description used to annoy me because it lent me a feeling of exclusion and I couldn't see why I should not be introduced simply as a Sudanese writer just like all the others. But I came to realize that most of the writers and critics used those regional distinctions merely for the purpose of introduction. As a result, I reconciled myself to the reality, as did many of the writers. After all, they all hailed from some tiny spots here or there but their presence extended across the million miles of the homeland, entering the sad households without the need for permission, demolishing barriers and filling all spaces with love, tolerance and beauty. Ironically, following the secession of the South, the "southern writer who writes in Arabic" description has become an inescapable reality.

Writing in Arabic gained me distinction because, at the time, no writer from South Sudan wrote in Arabic. Most wrote in English, and, in the absence of translation, their works did not find their way to the northern part of the country. That was why I decided to write in the language of the majority in northern Sudan so as to communicate with them more easily. While the fact that I was writing in Arabic took some northern writers and critics by surprise, it antagonized a southerner who wrote in English. At a special party we held in Juba in honour of a visiting delegation from the University of Iowa, many of them taught creative writing, I introduced myself, adding that I wrote in Arabic. That remark provoked the Southern writer. "What do you want from this language?" he snapped. "It's not your mother tongue!"

"I want the same thing you are looking for," I said. "You are writing in English, which is not your mother tongue, either."

I think we writers shouldn't think this way. We shouldn't blame the language for the sins of its speakers. Unfortunately, it seems that politics has poisoned invariably everyone, including some intellectuals. During the dinner, Professor Taban Lo Liyong, the famous novelist and poet, came to me and cast the following words in my ear: "Be the only Southern writer who writes in Arabic. That's an advantage. Never lose it. A good writer should write in the language he masters."

To me, language is the soul of the text. It lends life to our texts. Texts are like humans. We meet people that we love or hate at first sight. We meet people who impress us and win our respect or tempt us to befriend them, and others who do just the opposite. The same applies to texts. We use language to relate our own stories and those of people around us. I love Arabic. It's the vessel that communicates my own stories and my own culture — stories and culture that are quite different from Arab culture.

I had thought that I would never be able to write except in Arabic. However, after South Sudan became an independent state, English became the official language. I don't understand the logic behind imposing official languages. These languages do not express my identity but I am fine with using them as a means of communication, as a vehicle that takes me to other worlds and other nations that respect and celebrate beauty and diversity. As fellows in humanity, those nations have the right to read our creative work in the language they understand. I will be more than happy if "A Lake the Size of a Papaya" is translated into a thousand languages.

I had thought I would never be able to write except in Arabic, but my return to South Sudan has put me face to face with the challenge of reaching out to everyone, including English-language readers. Now I am trying to develop my language skills to be able to write in English as well. My Arabic published works have been translated to English and are now being published.

I wrote about wars and the agonies of displacement, and I documented the life of poverty, deprivation, and prisons. In *It's Boiling All Around* (a two-part story comprising *The Road to Death* or *Jail and The Road to Lunacy*), I was very close to the environment of those anecdotes. I may go even further and confess that I had a role in some of them. I know the kasha (police raids) and police cruelty. I know the blackmailing of mothers who prefer to lodge their hard-earned money in the hands of soldiers in order to avoid being taken to prison. It was a social and cultural confrontation between a state that is Arab and Islamic according to its constitution and a section of its citizens who have had nothing to do with the state's ideology. To those citizens, making liquor was their only source of livelihood, the only means to feed and dress their children and send a good number of them to some mediocre type of school. To the state, on the other hand, those citizens are nothing more than desecrators of the state religion, a religion that is not their own and of which they are almost entirely ignorant.

No wonder the State used its heavy hand to destroy that industry without offering those affected any alternative means of making a decent living — a halal means of living, according to the state's creed. But should a state have a creed? When the police launched their raids, spilled the white mareesa on the floor, and took the mothers to prison, the authorities had a clear conscience for having fought against vice. In the eyes of the local population, however, such acts meant nothing but the squandering of what meant food for adults and children and would lend them a feeling of fullness and pleasure after a full day. This is apart from the fact that such raids would culminate in the imprisonment of the family's sole bread-earner for several months. As a result, poverty and social grudges proliferated and those localities became a major breeding place for scores of homeless people, nutcases, and frustrated souls in desperate search of a way out.

Those cultural differences, though simple, had filled people with an urge to depart at the first opportunity. We did depart, eventually, but we still feel the bitter taste of those days. We had to live with irresponsible fathers who had been thrown into the abyss of unemployment and a vicious circle of drunkenness and violence against women and children and against their own selves. Our mothers entered prison dozens of times as punishment for their endeavours to secure a single meal a day for us and buy us a notebook and a pencil. Their best hope was that their daughters would not get pregnant during adolescence and that their sons would not get addicted to alcohol. In most cases, though, both fears materialized. That was a natural result of that environment, an environment of displacement and violence.

I, for one, consider myself lucky for having survived. From an early age, I chose the pen and the letter as the chisel with which to engrave all that colossal pain in my inner self. The scene, as I saw it, was of a state sending out soldiers armed with batons and guns to punish an "unruly mob" and teach them a lesson. As a result, society looked down on that section of the population with a mixture of accusations, fear, and disdain. The prevalent feeling was that those people were aliens who should go away. They did go in the end. It was a shocking and painful departure. Neither those who decided to go south nor those who opted to stay in the mother country managed to overcome their agonies. In the story *It's Boiling All Around*,

I featured a man who was bedridden and conscious of his helplessness. I reduced him to an eye that can monitor everything but can do nothing about it. The pain associated with that condition was too much of a torment to endure. He trickled out of his life.

I discovered how amusing it was to write about very private and local matters that engrossed readers' attention. I learned to write about myself, my mother, my people, and my far-away land. I felt the others had the right to discover other worlds beyond their imagination. In *A Pre-Rain Feast* the protagonist is called Olair, which means bewilderment. This is a common name in my tribe, the Latuka, which is one of the largest tribes of the Eastern Equatoria state. The Latuka express sadness by crying and dancing to the rhythm of drums, a crying of both the body and the soul. For that reason, I was not surprised at seeing Zorba dancing in pain with one leg in the film *Zorba the Greek*, based on Nikos Kazantzakis's great novel. So I discovered that such details are worth telling.

In selecting names for newborns, we tend to eternalise the tribal name, which our grandfathers and grandmothers consider as our original name. Each one of us has more than one name, including names ascribed to us by a grandfather or a grandmother or an uncle, which we have to accept gracefully. Naming is not restricted to the time of birth. You keep gaining new names throughout your life. These names are inspired by your physical features, such as tallness, shortness, black colour, strength, even physical defect. If your parents hail from different tribes, you will carry a heavy load of names. I am known as Stella but my tribal name is Ghari, which means the rejected. It is also derived from water and can sometimes mean the aqueous. Thank God my parents were from the same tribe. My mother's name is Lucia, after one of her grandmothers, but she has another name, Ikulang, which means the one born with a large belly button. My father Gaitano is also known as Ukood Araghi, a name he gave himself during early adulthood, which means a bird with curved wings ready to fly or attack. My sister Nagwa is called Edwa, meaning harvest. My brother Morris is Aghala, meaning "born with teeth". My aunt is called Emigok, the one with tiny ears. My son Omer is called Ogidi, the one born in the rainy season. There are also other names, such as Etari (born at night), Egudu (blind or bleary-eyed), and Imudu (pug-nosed).

We use names to document events, to celebrate beauty, and to reconcile us with our physical defects, without committing any violation of human rights. Olair is a baby born in bewilderment, Ofiri is one born in wartime, Emwara is one born in peacetime. A Pre-Rain Feast is pure fiction. In writing it, I recalled my collection of anecdotes and memories to enrich its images. I made references to rivers and lightning, and to charms, foretellers and superstitions, which are African beliefs deeply embedded in daily life. I decorated the story with references to the bush, to cassava and banana leaves, and I aromatized it with the smell of grandmothers on whose skirts lice leisurely strolled, grandmothers whose wishes could translate into curses on the heads of sons and grandsons. In this story, in an attempt to protect her grandson from the fate of his two friends who were hit by lightning when they were under the big tamarind tree, while he was safe asleep, grandma prayed that he would fall asleep whenever it started to rain. That spell of his grandma remained effective even after her death. With the first drizzle, Olair would fall asleep and instantly drift back into past memories at the age of six, specifically to the date of that incident. Towards the end of the story, Olair was helping his friends cross a raging river when it began to rain heavily. In the arms of nature, childhood memories came back fresh and vivid: trees in flames, mothers wailing, sounds of drums, grandma's tobacco-tainted saliva thick on his scalp, a big louse leisurely creeping and disappearing in the folds of grandma's skirt. In that story, I was trying to say that all beliefs – whether divine or earthly religions – are very difficult to get rid of. Belief can cause one to live full of hope or to die cursed and kicked out of the Lord's mercy.

About *A Lake the Size of a Papaya*, I love this story just as many of you do. It is closer to my heart because it was my bridge to having a voice of my own. I wrote it in just half an hour and did not do any further revisions or edits. It landed on my conscience like revelation or inspiration. I was shivering with fear and excitement, obsessed with fears that it might not fly well because of its strange setting. A woman who carries little resemblance to other women, a mixture of eternal motherhood and an inherent harshness typical of rural women who live in environments open to surprises, both pleasant and deadly. People who master fortune-telling and who understand the whisperings of trees, animals and colours, and who know how to communicate with nature. A mixture of faiths, superstitions and myth. How can I communicate all that at a time when one version of truth is prevailing over all other versions? It might invite ridicule.

I wrote it with great passion, and then I put it away in my handbag, as if trying to conceal a crime. Before writing it, I had spent time watching my real grandma, who had nothing to do with the fictional grandma. My real grandma was short and tiny, like me. She was a bit timid, like me. She feared illness, war, death, and barrenness. She had given birth to many children, who all died except my mother and another boy. For that reason, my mother gave birth to nine, of whom seven survived, all females except one. She used to say to us: "I have given birth to my own sisters and brothers. I wanted to compensate my mother for the death of her children." That was why grandma rejoiced at having grandchildren.

I rank in the middle among my sisters and that was why my parents didn't pay much attention to me until the day when they saw my picture on newspapers and TV channels. I was watching my grandma smashing to powder the clay bricks of our fence wall that had collapsed in the rain, and remoulding them to put the wall back in place. She was sitting on a low stool, singing a song she had composed in praise of my grandfather. It was the type of lyrics that all members of the tribe mastered, for everyone had to compose one or more songs as a way of documenting the events they came through. When my grandma rose and walked towards the courtyard, I could actually see the horizon through her huge ear hole that had been perforated with the help of a big thorn. That scene sparked an idea and it took me just half an hour to write it down. Instead of my real grandmother, however, I borrowed the image of another old woman I had seen before, who had been markedly tall and ugly. She had a strong smell and she didn't seem to be bothered by her unpleasant appearance. When the others made fun of her pug nose, she would say with indifference: "At least it's good enough to help me breathe."

The first person who read this story was the poet Atef Khairi. I was a senior high school pupil at the time, and had a part-time job at a copy centre in the University of Khartoum. After reading it, he threw the papers back to me and ran out. I was alarmed, but he came back after a short while and said: "This story will become your enemy one day if you don't keep up the same level." That remark sparked in me a feeling of fear from a demanding reader who always expected the same, if not better, quality.

My story *A Moon-Lit Night* was about fair struggle and renouncing vengeance and the need to hang on to hope.

Wilted Flowers, the eponymous story in my first collection, published in 2004 by Azza Publishing, is about selflessness, giving without wanting anything in return, and never quitting.

Maps of Unknown Worlds is a journey into the world of the homeless in big cities. The life of children trying to learn how to survive loathsome conditions. The handicapped and lepers displaying their physical defects and truncated limbs to win the sympathy of passersby. Examples of people who appear and disappear without anyone taking notice. Their death, like their life, goes unaccounted for.

One of the most common features of my stories is that I kill my heroes; perhaps I want to eternalize them, to save them from a life that was like death and give them a death as worthwhile as real life. Or, perhaps I chose such a passive end out of frustration, after getting too exhausted by selfish heroes gripping my pen and trying to dictate an end that suits them. It is essential that heroes die so that we feel the painful vacuum that their departure creates and thus strive to bring them back to life in different ways. I often endow gloomy stories with a glimmer of hope: a light, a smile, or a small green branch in a charred tree.

* * *

On the question of homecoming, let me quote the late Egyptian poet Amal Dunqul, "My bags are stacked on the shelves of memory". Perhaps we need to redefine that geographical area that accommodates several communities who have many things in common. Can that be called home? My home is now several patches of ground inhabited by different population groups that have many things in common though many of them deny the existence of such commonalities. To me, home is a void in memory, filled with war and displacement, killing and destruction, ceaseless aerial bombing and blood, dogs and vultures feeding on dead bodies, terror and hunger, collective graves and refugee camps. My home is a carcass that attracts humanitarian international organisations. A land trodden by strange soldiers wearing red, blue, and green caps, speaking strange languages. My home is a scene of perpetual fighting between brothers, in the name of religion, or identity, or tribe – different names for one thing: war. How can one feel at home when one's bags are packed, ready to go? Since secession, I have been living in my bags, shuttling back and forth between two airports, between two homes that I still consider as one; between a home that I yearn for and another whose alienation barriers that stand between us I am trying to break down. Home, in my opinion, is one-sided love. It is an inaccessible dream, an ever bleeding wound. I wish I had that positive energy that propelled my people to stand in queues for long hours to vote for Independence. They were armed with strong aspirations to build their dream homeland.

But is war the shortest route for saying No? After enormous losses, we finally yielded to regional and international pressure and came together around the negotiation table. Sitting on the skulls of victims, we distributed senior positions and military ranks amongst our numbers. My people have liberated themselves from the north, but many of them are still unable to liberate themselves from their own inherent defects that had long been blamed on the north. Yesterday's heroes will probably transform overnight into less than ordinary people, stealing public funds, indulging in corruption and leading lavish lifestyles. For the sake of protecting these privileges, they would not hesitate to ignite new wars that will claim the lives of thousands. Meanwhile, the majority of those in whose names all the wars have been waged are still experiencing the throes of hunger, disease, and ignorance, while the world's most luxurious cars sweep through Juba's ruined streets. A thundering collision between dream and reality. They always find thousands of justifications for waging war but they cannot find a single justification for waging peace for the sake of the downtrodden.

After Independence, I had to relocate to the South. There I found a yawning gap between the dreams of the public and that of the politicians. The public were so elated and proud they didn't bother to bring politicians to account for their blunders – small or big. I was happy for them, seeing that lofty feeling of pride in their tall figures. They were overwhelmed with a feeling that their long-cherished dream was coming true. They were transparent and pure, and they wanted to depend on themselves to build their new homeland. They answered the homeland's call and poured in from all corners of the world, braving brutal conditions: insecurity, lack of clean water and power, and politicians' narrow-mindedness.

But this latest war has shocked them and awakened them to the fact that things are not always what they seem. I felt sorry for them, and for myself, but in times of war we have no alternative but to believe slogans and lies so that soldiers can fight and so that the public can endure war's devastating impact.

As a writer, I had hoped I would not write about war and displacement any more. However, in my second collection of short stories, *Homecoming*, I found myself writing about a different kind of pain: about the southerners' suffering in the hands of their own compatriots, about their living in fear of each other, and their helplessness at seeing their dreams and expectations being crushed, one after the other.

I'm Scared, Mum is a story that captures scenes from the city today, where armed gangs roam the city at night terrifying people, looting and killing. It's a story of a widow who collects the compensation due to her husband who was killed at war, but before she can do anything with it, the gangsters break in at night and take away her children's fortune, her husband's sweat and blood, and her dreams.

I Kill Myself and Vanish documents the brother against brother war, and the dogs and vultures' feasting on human bodies dumped on the streets.

I have always been intrigued by the causes behind all this long-lived conflict between the north and the south, between the Sudanese living in the south and those living in the north. I came to realize that these causes were not strong enough. They were rather very tiny differences that could be found in every household and every society, but due to prolonged lack of response, they inflated into Africa's longest war, which acquired different colours and names before culminating in secession. On that day, I was wondering if we really needed to resort to that painful and shocking solution that split us into two states, one choked and the other paralyzed, both vying for the top rankings of the world's most failed states! Before 2011, the one-million-square-mile country was a failed state, but now the Sudanese in both the South and the North are a million times worse. Even worse, wars are still in full swing, under the same or different names. This is a grand farce, which the entire world should rise to address.

We have seen that people who had to flee the war zones in the Nuba Mountains, the Blue Nile, and Darfur, automatically took

refuge in South Sudan, and that most of the people who fled the re-
cent civil war in the South went north to Sudan. That makes me
wonder where the antagonism has come from. Now scores of
Northern Sudanese are in the South, working in all domains: doc-
tors, merchants, engineers, etc. Hundreds of Muslims throng Juba
mosques. They perform their religious rituals freely, without any
fear. Even Eid prayers and al-Mawlid – the prophet's birthday cel-
ebrations – are held in the open in grand squares. The adhan call to
prayer is one of the first signs of dawn in Juba, followed after a good
while by church bells. No one feels threatened. But who would have
joined the fighting if the slogan of enmity to Islam and Arabs had
not been flagged? Who would have voted for separation if the 'sec-
ond-class citizen' charges had not been circulated? We have come
to discover that there are still class differences created by corrup-
tion, that there is still exclusion consolidated by mismanagement,
and that ignorance, disease and war are still there. But we are run-
ning in a vicious circle because we shy away from the painful diag-
nosis and blame external factors for our own mistakes instead of
facing them. Admitting our mistakes is the first step. It can be a bit-
ter dose but we have to take it if we want to recover.

After that experience, I wrote *Fragrant Professions*, which I dedi-
cated to the soul of Dr John Garang. I wanted to emphasize that
professions do have fragrance: the tea seller, the *kisra* bread seller
(Hajja Amna, although she did not make it to Hajj), the *kaimout*
(peanut butter) seller, the mechanic, the porter, the intellectual,
the candy seller, and the dervish. I recalled the facial scars, the tall
figures, the ancient kings, and the alienated young generation. I
gathered them in one bus and gave them a death that befitted them:
drowning in the embrace of the great Nile. Aren't we in the throes
of an insane drowning?

TRANSLATED BY ADIL BABIKIR

MANSOUR EL SOUWAIM

A Rogue's Memory

AN EXCERPT FROM THE NOVEL *DHAKIRAT SHIRRIR*,
TRANSLATED BY WILLIAM M HUTCHINS

A Concrete Triangle

They brought me back to the massive building of solid stone and sturdy bricks. This grim structure has stood in the same place since the era of the English. It is a stately edifice that has challenged time's ravages and stood firm amid the city's surprising contractions and expansions. The party for me this time was exceptionally deferential and splendid, and they had reserved a private room to receive me. This luxurious chamber, which had an en-suite bathroom, contained two tall windows that received direct sunlight and bade the setting sun farewell. My quarters would have been fully appropriate for a dignitary. There was a large, comfortable aluminium bed at its centre. Its sides and legs were painted a lovely black that grew lighter and paler the higher you looked till it turned a fresh lavender at the bars between the legs. This cheerful colour had been created by detailed designs and beautiful, childish drawings. The mattress was cosy, tickly, and conducive to sleep. The moment you rested your head on the perfumed feather pillow you would doze off. My room also contained a lovely, medium-sized wardrobe made of gleaming, lustrous pitch pine. It would not hold many clothes but was adequate for an ascetic man – like me – with few needs. The small mirror in a gilt frame on the front of the wardrobe allowed me to see my face, cut my moustache, and trim my short beard. Two of the room's four chairs were the comfortable type with foam cushions. Though the other two were normal, straight chairs, their design was beautiful and elegant. More important than any of this were the large, colour TV and the digital media receiver they had placed in the room. These allowed me access to the entire world any time I wished. It took only a moment for me to press the button on the small remote control – as I am doing now, to lower the volume. This will let my ear heal and hear a different sound that I need even more. I will be able to travel and liberate myself through it and in it. I am Kusahi, a cripple. I listen now with my very being, with my pores, with my history, and with my memory of my past days. I listen to the train, to its whistle, to the rattling of its cars, and the wail and whine of the metal tracks.

I remember the rocking motion I felt when my magnificent mother, Karati Maryam, placed me on her lap, encircled me with one hand and with the other stuffed a scrap of cloth in her mouth to suck silicone adhesive from the fabric, which had been soaked in it. She rocked monotonously back and forth on the roof of the coach, moving slowly. I began to observe things, watching people's alienated faces and exhausted bodies. From the train's rolling roof I discovered creatures like donkeys and camels for the first time. I watched children run after the train to catch loaves of flat bread pitched from inside the coaches. Our fellow passengers on the swaying roof would give my mother pieces of bread and hardboiled eggs. Running their fingers over my soft hair, they would ask my name. "His name is Adam," my mother would reply. "Adamu." Then she would hug me to her chest and kiss me, letting me discover the taste of tyre glue on her lips, and sniff it delightedly. With innocent eyes, I examined the glum men who threatened to throw my magnificent mother off the train roof if she didn't pay. Then she would loosen a carefully knotted section of her thobe and give them the fare, while cursing them in her own special language, which I have forgotten. I remember those five days clearly – as if they were unfolding before me now – the long train twisting and winding while a distant banner fluttered at its rear. It climbed hills slowly and crossed high, scary bridges. Plumes of thick, black smoke poured from its front and then rose till they thinned, faded, and dissipated. The horrid soldiers drove men in front of them in a long line and gradually loaded them into carriages. I clearly remember the night's final watches when my mother was crushed by a soldier's massive frame, as he mashed and squeezed her near my feet. He was panting, and she was moaning; then they finished. She laughed and held me with one hand while she grasped the scrap of cloth with the other and began to sniff the glue. I started to doze off, plunging smoothly into sleep's orbits, as the train's carriage bounced and rocked me pleasantly, affectionately, and fondly.

I loved my mother, inevitably, and so now, inevitably, sense the bitter taste of loss at my eternal bereavement. My mother was magnificent with her fragrant aroma of silicone adhesive, her great affection, her little fantasies when she spoke to me in her language, which I have forgotten, and the way she stuffed me with leftover food, pieces of stolen candy, and the dregs of juice containers. Among those lusting after my beautiful mother were nasty soldiers, vagabonds, market layabouts, lepers, and the beggars at the grand mosque. My mother had soft, dirty hair, which straggled to her shoulders, and dreamy eyes, which roamed through the private worlds of her magnificence. My mother left me with young beggar women and went off to die in an insane jousting match with market roustabouts and hoboes, who were fortified by their stoned imaginations and drugged energy.

She left me with two girls, who started to move my tiny, wasted legs, because these young women refused to believe they really were dead and crippled. They tried to make me stand. Then I wept and called out to my distant mother, who could no longer hear. One of them carried me on her back and clasped my dead feet to her belly. She held out an old thoub and encircled my back and hers with it, fastening it carefully around both of us and making me one flesh with her. She grabbed my hands, pulled them beneath her armpits, and clasped them together in front of her chest. She began to shake her body with a slow rhythm to rock me. I laughed, and she looked at me out of the corner of her eye, smiling. She started walking with me on her back, beginning a daily circuit that would be repeated through the coming years, despite my magnificent mother's absence and tragic death. I clung to the girl's back as she turned onto the large avenue and slipped into the crowd of bodies in a perpetual motion that never waned or slackened – men, women, boys, girls – amid shouts and repeated screams, and singers' overlapping voices that were alternately soft and loud. Glittering, gleaming merchandise was exhibited on the ground: wristwatches, children's toys, sunglasses, shoes, textiles, handbags, and other items I could not identify. People surrounded us on all sides, rushing by hastily. She would lean to one side, straighten up, and then would begin to shake and rock me again. So I would close my eyes and allow all the rough fingers, soft fingers, sympathetic fingers, astonished fingers, and indifferent fingers – I would let all these hands rub my beautiful hair and then sympathetically drop small change into Wahiba's palm. During those first days, I was a fool-proof lure – a trap that spared no one when we strolled into restaurants and coffeehouses. She fed me while I was on her back. At bus stops, she would twirl me around and I would press my face against bus windows while she bounced and jiggled me. She jogged down empty streets along which crazy vehicles sped, and I felt tired and dozed off. I slept while collapsed on her back. I dreamt of my mother and the train's black smoke rising higher and higher. I saw my mother moan beneath the weight of the massive body, her eyes protruding as if she were dying. I started weeping while I slept and woke up. People were clamouring around me, and I found that the young beggar woman had clutched me to her chest. She was refusing to give me to an old woman who sat beside her with hands outstretched. That was the very same day my magnificent mother, Karati Maryam, died in a uniquely dramatic fashion.

My magnificent mother left me with some beggar girls – babysitters who used me as bait to solicit alms – while she went to look for her friends, who were homeless men and market layabouts. She found them in the familiar place, gathered beneath the high wall, as if they had agreed to meet her there, even though she had been gone a long time. They celebrated her arrival in their special way, making a hubbub, singing, dancing, and taking turns hugging, pinching, and kissing her. With extraordinary generosity they gave her an entire bottle of silicone adhesive, a tube, and a clean piece of cloth. Then they asked her to perform an Indian song for them, and she sang as she had never sung before. They stole a variety of fruits for her and competed with one another in offering her food. They proved – beyond the shadow of a doubt – their exceptional generosity as well as their love and admiration for her. They snuck her into a cinema that night. My magnificent mother, Karati Maryam, attended the cinema the evening she died and saw a Bollywood film filled with rose petals, song-and-dance routines, and blood. After the show, they found a smashed wooden crate at the cinema entrance and pulled the long slats from it to use as staves. They decided to recreate some scenes from the film and divided the parts among themselves. My mother became the heroine, who fought alongside the hero, but unlike him did not die. My magnificent mother, Karati Maryam, however, did die when the villain beat her with his stick. An inch-long nail sank into her head and penetrated her skull, grazing her brain or spirit. So life ebbed from her, and the heroine fell dead next to the hero.

Can a child forget quickly when he struggles to overcome loss and deprivation and cope with life? Did the child, Adam, forget the one creature he knew, the one person who had always been beside him throughout his first years? Magnificent Maryam slipped from his memory and was dispersed among various different fragrances, numerous eyes, and sudden bursts of laughter. She became a distant memory pertaining to a long-gone, chaotic period. Adam, this lovely child with an angelic face, gave himself to the beggar girl Wahiba. His stubborn, childish passion for her caused her to bond with him. So, with tears, teeth, and filthy fingernails, she fought to keep him. Weeping, she told them that his dear, departed mother had entrusted him to her. She kept hugging him, teary-eyed, as she rocked her body, rocking him too. She wanted him to fall asleep again and be spared the clamour and grumbling of the grand mosque's beggars as they quarrelled over him. Some suggested getting rid of him: handing him over to the police or dumping him in the street in hopes that some well-meaning person would pick him up. One suggested keeping him in memory of his deceased mother – their former companion – that pretty, half-crazed young woman who had been desired by all their men. Usha, an old lady, decided the matter when she patted his little head and declared: "We'll keep him and raise him like our own son."

And so, only hours after the tragic passing of my mother, I won the complete trust of a group of the grand mosque's beggars. I became one of them and a member of their troupe, which was the oldest and most venerable in the city. It controlled extensive squares downtown and in high traffic areas like the Arab Market, the Foreign Market, the street where ministries and large firms were located, the ancient Jewish and Coptic quarters, the boulevard with embassies, and the avenue with the most glitteringly beautiful restaurants and boutiques in the city. Our headquarters were at the heart of the city.

My crippled feet proved no handicap for me, and I ignored their weakness, because my late mother had trained me to fend for myself on the ground when she left me alone for hours on end and went off to attend to personal matters. I could crawl and scoot around on the ground in an astonishing and bewildering fashion. So I did not exhaust my new mother, Wahiba, by asking her to carry me all the time. I would slip off her and land on the ground when we approached stores with gleaming windows. I would drag my legs behind me and pretend that my waving feet were hampering me. Resting my weight on my rough little hands on the cold pavement, I would steal into elegant stores and scan their contents with my innocent eyes, which were haunted by misery and despair. Then I would look up at the merchandise displayed in glass cases or meticulously and harmoniously arranged on shelves. I would look around before fixing my pleading eyes first on the customers and then on the shop owners, who grumbled with disgust at the sight of me and my filthy palms, which were outstretched so humbly and sadly.

Umm Salama, who was Wahiba's older sister, and mine too, taught me the craft of begging with the techniques most capable of extracting money from people and melting their hearts with sympathy and compassion. She taught me to shed tears that would cascade down my face while I sobbed ardently on and off in a way that would disarm the most obdurate and hard-hearted folks. I quickly perfected this skill, amazing Umm Salama, because I had tears held in reserve since the passing of my magnificent mother. They were more than sufficient to keep me weeping, even for the coming century. In the street or when confronting hurried customers, I would execute Umm Salama's lessons, astonishing her. I would stretch out next to Wahiba and lie there for hours like a corpse, without moving any part of my body. I would crawl after Umm Salama, from place to place, scouting for ways for her to snag a client. I would cling with both hands and tightly grasp women's thoubs and girls' dresses. After only a brief time, I perfected all the tricks and happy games and could gratify the hearts of those who were fond of me and loved me when I watched and searched for them in rare, amiable moments. Umm Salama, where are you?

Kusahi, do you remember that period in the grand mosque, which was God's house and yours? Its outer wall extended for quite a distance that took you forever to crawl along. The solid concrete corners had light green paint at the base and bright white at their tops. The yellow colour of projecting stones of the building's wall gradually became dark brown toward the bottom. The stones were elegantly cut and set. You beggars soiled the lower tiers with your oils, fats, greases, and other filthy wastes. Kusahi, the grand mosque welcomes worshipers, loiterers, and people in need of shelter for the night by leaving its doors on the east, west, south, and north sides open night and day. The mosque's courtyard is always fragrant with musk and aloe. The prayer carpets are soft and resilient. On the wall, the large clock's pendulum sways left and right and right and left. You sway with it as you crawl between the worshipers – your palms outstretched and a tentative smile traced across your face. That time has vanished forever. You can no longer move through the mosque's courtyards, urinate in its toilets, or bathe in its cramped, humid baths. That brief period ended once the army came to power and focused their suspicions on all areas of the mosque. My God! How you enjoyed daybreak long ago, those cold winter mornings, dawn's pale light, the morning star in the distance glittering in the sky, the sweet sound of the call to prayer waking you, calling you to separate your flesh from Wahiba's warm body.

You creep quietly from beneath the blanket you share with her and watch her roll over as she mumbles incomprehensible words before she returns to her sound sleep. The cold morning air stings your face and chases away the remnants of sleep still clinging to your lids. You turn your neck and inspect the bodies scattered along the wall, huddled together and conjoined in memorable clumps. You watch as a body splits off, separating from another who can now stretch out and draw the meagre, threadbare cover around his body. Grandmother Usha is performing her prayers silently behind you as the sweet call to prayer continues to echo through the courtyard. You crawl away, timing your advance to greet the first worshiper who arrives – a burly man with a long jilbab and a thick wool shawl that hides the features of his face. You meet him at the threshold of the east portal after you have crawled fifty metres. The huge man stops, gazes at you for a few moments, and then leans down to run his fingers over your hair. He whispers, "Glory to God . . . Glory to God!" He takes your little palm and thrusts a small coin into it. Your appreciative looks follow him as he strolls into the mosque. You hold the coin between your palms. Glancing around, you ascertain that you have been the first to score this morning.

One month Grandmother Usha took us to a mud-brick house in a distant shantytown. When she prepared to travel there, her movements were disconcertingly tense as she collected her supplies of sugar, tea, and coffee. She counted her coins covertly. Then she placed two light-weight, dirty containers, together with her other things, inside a large bundle that she fastened carefully. She made the rounds of her mendicant friends – Hajj Ibrahim, the amputee, Halima who is extremely old and never leaves her spot, and the rest of her beggar comrades, bidding them farewell as she prepared to depart. Umm Salama and Wahiba estimated our time of departure by tracking the old lady's activities and gestures and began their own preparations with awe-inspiring and hyperbolic celebration of the trip. They took me to the ablutions cistern in the mosque and turned on the faucets till they splashed water over my shrivelled, naked body, which they scrubbed with a sponge and soap. They worked hard, exhausting themselves to wash my thick hair and to remove the layers of dirt caked on my chest and neck. I surrendered to them, realizing it was impossible to resist once powerful Umm Salama grabbed my wrist and turned me every which way until water streamed over my entire body. They devoted a lot of time to making me presentable, wanting me to emerge gleaming and beautiful so they could show me off to people on the street, the bus passengers, their friends in the distant shantytown called "Revolution", and finally Hajj Muhammadu, the only person who still called me Adamu, now that my magnificent mother had passed.

In the bus I clung to Umm Salama's neck and sat on her lap. Like her, as we departed, I started to watch for glimpses of the buildings of the enchanting city's eastern neighbourhoods. Wahiba stood beside Hajja Usha and gripped the edge of the seat with both hands. She also craned her neck to see the dazzling sights the bus passed. Umm Salama's fingers pressed against my arms when the elegant villas with their splendid architecture came into view. I fastened my eyes on the colours, which changed in an astonishingly harmonious way from deep green to a vegetable green on the roofs of eastern-style structures that I thought were little mosques but that were reserved for different, private individuals. The colours of the scattered, European-style villas ranged from a haughty white, to refined pink, and even to an arrogant sky-blue. Hajja Usha's mind wasn't on the beautiful scenery or the gardens surrounding the buildings and beautiful villas. Grasping the headrest of the seat in front of her, her lips pursed, she had withdrawn into herself and radiated a profound, Sufi silence. We quickly passed huge grocery stores with numerous goods displayed inside and out. We regarded everything with the enormous curiosity of children who ride bikes full speed over green grass pursuing a young runner, friendly birds, or colourful balls. Umm Salama hugged me and shifted my position on her. As we left all that beauty behind us and trees and wide open spaces replaced it, her lips tickled my ear as she said, "Tashdir: loot." This was jargon she had shared with me early on – Umm Salama's secret – and the start of her escapades and mendicancy, which were sped along by the wheels of our despicable age.

My God! The dilapidated, mud-brick hovel – who can conjure up for me today the fragrance of the magical, mood-enhancing incense embedded in its walls? Who can provide me today with the savoury taste of that slow-cooked chicken broth? In this crumbling house I learned to read and write two full years before kids my age and was washed with water fortified with verses of the Qur'an and blessed by the sincerity of my magnificent teacher Hajju Muhammadu. I followed him through his countless devotions, prayed nightly and daily prayers at his behest, wrote out with my own hand his talis-mans and amulets on paper or wooden reading tablets, and filled dozens of bottles with pure, curative, protective Qur'an water that never goes bad.

There was a single room, made of rammed earth, at the centre of the mud-brick house. Occupied by Hajju Muhammadu, it was crammed full of wooden tablets, yellowing books, glass bottles, and white slips of paper. When we arrived, Hajju Muhammadu and Hajja Usha secluded themselves beneath the venerable palm tree where lessons were taught. They conversed for a long time in their private, difficult language – in fact into the wee hours of the night. I never grasped the essence of the bond that united them but saw that they loved and understood each other – as if they were two lovebirds who had vowed eternal loyalty. Wahiba and Umm Salama passed the night of our arrival anxiously and impatiently waiting for morning to come; then they would meet their male and female friends, who had been students of Hajju Muhammadu, and tell them, in great detail, stories and tales of events that definitely had not occurred. I too was waiting, but for the children's class, when I would be able to hear their reedy voices, which leapfrogged over each other, recite chapters of the Qur'an. I didn't know then that I would join their recitation sessions the next day and continue with them for many months.

On the afternoon of the second day Hajja Usha took Wahiba and Umm Salama away with her, returning to the city. They left me in the care of the smiling old man. I sat among the youngsters on the frond mats by the venerable palm and began to recite with them short chapters from the Qur'an. Although at first they taught me cautiously, they were soon astonished by my ability to pull myself across the ground and to memorize quickly and accurately. In a few days I caught up with them. Then I even surpassed their accomplishments. My beautiful calligraphy also was superior to theirs, and I wrote inscriptions on the tablets, on my drawings, and on the decorations I had made in the margins of my tablet . I only rarely went out to the street with them, but they loved me and were wild about the athletic feats I performed to entertain them – spinning round on the ground or standing on my small hands and waving my dead legs in the air. I told them some of Umm Salama's invented stories about the fabulous city that lay beyond the grove of trees surrounding their community. They would crowd around me when the lesson ended and listen to my white lies. They wouldn't budge till Hajju Muhammadu scolded them and ordered them to go home.

Good-hearted Hajju Muhammadu treated me with great love and affection. He would have me sit beside him when his few women visitors came to ask him to reveal to them – on the authority of his yellow book – surprises they could expect in the coming days and to provide them with the raw material for happy and blissful dreams. He would write charms on lucky sticks of incense, prepare amulets and protective talismans for them, and fill glass jars with holy, prophylactic water. All this time I sat beside him assisting him by handing him little slips of paper, pencils, the inkwell, and the holy water preserved inside large, blackened calabashes. When men with powerful bodies and rippling muscles came and bared their backs and chests, which were inflamed with excess blood, he would ask me to light the fire of the small brazier and stay near him as his nurse's aide. I handed him the instruments for his therapy: special glass cups of various sizes, gauze, razor blades, and sharp lancets. I watched with astonishment as he pressed the cups to a man's body to collect the bad blood. Then he would swiftly drain blood into them with a sharp razor and gentle, expert taps. The spurts of blood released would turn black. He did not charge exorbitant fees. The most he asked for a complicated operation that required the intervention of higher powers would be an aged, white rooster. My most unforgettable memory of Hajju Muhammadu is of him preparing to stew an aged cock. He would grind its bones and then pound its flesh – before cooking it slowly over a low fire till it was done. I would wait till late that night to savour the tastiest broth in the world. Hajju Muhammadu was carefully planning the course of my life. He loved me like his son and had me drink litres of prophylactic holy water. He also washed my legs and feet with it, hoping to cure

them so I could race around him like the other children. He hung
a small amulet around my neck and told me, "This will protect you
for ever and ever." When he secluded himself for private devotions,
I suffered from separation's agony for the first time. Hajja Usha's
visits were intermittent and not predictable. I felt heartbroken and
could have wept for Wahiba, my mother, my beloved, my feet, and
my tongue. I missed the street and its people as my months of con-
finement within the dilapidated walls grew longer and longer. I re-
cited and memorized verses of the Qur'an and prayers and
devoured the legs of venerable roosters. During that period of tem-
porary separation from Wahiba's body by the wall of the grand
mosque I would wake at dawn to find Hajju Muhammadu smiling
at me as his prayers beads passed through his fingers. I would begin
the day with ablutions and prayers – the prayers I never performed
when I was at the grand mosque. I will never perform them again,
even though I write charms and amulets and cure people with tal-
ismans and sacred incantations. Regular, ritual prayers and his spe-
cial prayers exhausted me as I prostrated myself beside him. I
covered my forehead with dirt and waited for him to complete his
amulets, recitations from the Qur'an, and unintelligible hymns. I
slept with my forehead pressed to the ground and dreamt of the
long-lost Karati Maryam. I saw her dance among red roses as a
streak of red blood stained her forehead and spilled down her face.
I dreamt of the spacious streets and the long crawl that extended
to my spirit and splintered it into strange, unifying harmonies of
self, enveloping its days with a cellophane of pain and moans.

One morning my eyes opened without me seeing Hajju Muham-
madu's smiling gaze. Instead he lay in bed inside his cramped, low-
ceilinged room amid his tablets, flasks, and yellowed books. He
coughed quietly as he looked at me, smiling. Hajja Usha arrived with
some men I did not know. They crowded into his room and spent
the entire day with him. When they left, they announced that he
had died and departed to eternity.

I returned to the wide-open road, to the wall of the grand
mosque, to the market crowded with people, to loud voices. I re-
sumed crawling between people's feet, performing somersaults on
the pavement, and waving my dead feet in the air. I had lost my
good-hearted teacher Hajju Muhammadu, whom I would never see
again except in dreams that shimmered like faraway rainbow mi-

rages. I returned to find that the status quo had changed. I was sep-
arated from Wahiba, and Umm Salama took charge of me. I accom-
panied her on her distant daily trips, scouting beyond the precincts
of the grand mosque and the grand market. Wahiba, who was now
charged with accompanying Hajja Usha, looked upset when she saw
me clinging to Umma Salama's back as we prepared to explore a
new area. The old lady, Grandmother Usha, offered one last, terse
bit of advice to anxious Umm Salama. Running her dry fingers over
my hair, she said, "Stay close to him and keep a keen eye on him."
Then this elderly grandmother turned sadly to Wahiba, who was
very quiet, and told her: "Come on! Let's get a move on." We sep-
arated, and Wahiba grasped the stick to drag Hajja Usha behind her.
Then they disappeared in the crowd. Umm Salama jiggled me more
than once to make sure I was seated firmly on her back. She locked
her hands beneath my butt, chafing my face with her coarse hair,
and laughed and laughed. So we set off. We went in the opposite
direction to Wahiba and Grandmother. The farther we went, the
fewer commercial establishments and people there were. The street
grew wider, and the traffic increased. Apprehensive, Umma Salama
crossed cautiously and carefully in front of the vehicles. Her heart-
beats pounded beneath my hands. I was more sad than frightened
about being separated from Wahiba a second time – from her inno-
cent laughter, her little games, the rancid smell of her hair, and the
vigour with which she defended me against attacks by vagrants,
market layabouts, and beggars, who were more vicious that mean
policemen. I pressed my face against Umm Salama's back and mois-
tened my forehead with her sweat, which was flowing profusely. I
sniffed with delight the powerful odour that emanated from her
armpits as she navigated that long, wide road. Vehicles sped past us,
beneath huge mahogany and teak trees; they flashed by, disappearing
in a wink of my eye. The few pedestrians scattered in all directions
– like bubbles. What a long errand this was! We did not pause a sin-
gle moment till Umm Salama lifted me off her back and deposited
me beneath her. With the sleeve of her dress, she started to wipe
away the flood of perspiration that drenched her face. I turned
around to inspect our surroundings – an intersection of several
streets with traffic lights, which turned from red to yellow to green,
and a traffic cop – in a white uniform – who directed traffic with
his hands and blew his whistle loudly. Before us was a slab of bur-

nished concrete that shone like a mirror. Umm Salama carried me across one of the streets to the concrete triangle, which was a traffic island between three roads. She dropped me on the white and black squares of the triangle and – in a soft whisper – filled me in on my new occupation. "Wait till the vehicles stop and then crawl toward them. Approach the car's door, knock on it, hold out your hand, and wait." She stroked my hair the way people did, and tried to arrange it before she walked off and disappeared.

Alone on the concrete triangle, seated on its black and white squares, I watched the traffic signals change: green to red to yellow. The vehicles came to a full stop but then quickly sped away as their engines roared and their horns created a pandemonium. I cringed there. When the policeman's whistle repeated its shrill call, I cowered even more. I clung to my spot but experimented with different ways of sitting that would spare me some of the heat of the concrete beneath me. Raucous bus passengers turned to stare at me indifferently before their buses shot off. I could not see the features of passengers in private sedans because of the tinted glass. Their vehicles jerked nervously before they took off, leaving me in my same position – huddled on the concrete, not having budged.

I wasted so much time that first day! I was standing on my hands when Umm Salama returned. She leaned over and whispered: "Adam, you poor dear!" She sat beside me and shaded me from the sun's midday heat. Then she pushed me gently to encourage me to crawl out and greet my first automobile, which was red. I had not noticed the quiet purr of its engine when it came to a stop at the light, but Umm Salama directed my attention to it by poking me with her elbow and saying: "Riches." I hesitated but then sped off. I traversed the short distance from the traffic island to the car in two leaps that were so skillful that even I was surprised. The first day I begged from that concrete triangle, no one responded when I knocked on the gleaming red door. When I turned, Umm Salama gestured with her head. So I knocked on the door again. Then the engine purred gently, and I looked up to find that the lights had changed: red, yellow, green. The red car started and drove off. I never saw anyone inside it.

During that steamy day with its fiery heat, Umm Salama gave me time to adjust to my new assignment and waited till I had scored my first donations from drivers – their alms, their gifts. A convertible stopped behind us; then a voice called out: "Turn around." I found that a slender young man was poking his head out and dangling paper currency from his fingers. I grasped it quickly while horns around him tooted to demand that he move along. I held the valuable paper money in my teeth and returned with a leap to Umm Salama, who was waiting eagerly and triumphantly. She seized the money, folded it carefully, and then tucked it into the small pocket of my short trousers.

Luminous and sparkling, stinging and fiery, recapturing many memories, the vehicles' dazzling headlights reflected on the bodies of other vehicles, and lit up the red, green, and yellow traffic signals. These lights collided with the body of the traffic policeman and reflected the phosphorescent green of his short uniform. The lights of the vehicles, of all those vehicles, fell on and scattered over that cold concrete triangle, illuminating the small, rigid body that lay in a heap among the black and white squares. His dead legs were drawn beneath him, and his face was hidden by his hands in a sea of darkness. His ears picked up the engines' whine and their soft purring, which resembled music and allowed him to swim dreamily in his own dark sea. Rocking the darkness, the roar of speeding machines scratched his eyelids with successive white spots, like shadows. The drone vanished, and an engine rocked the area with a harsh, convulsive roar, shaking his house of concrete and adding to its air pollution. The burning taste penetrated the roof of his throat and scratched inside his nose. The small body shook with a brief spasm of coughing. Then it was stiff again, isolated from the tumult. It was still and motionless as it waited for nocturnal donors, for their magical appearance, their light footsteps, their visionary presence as they tossed small coins into his metal container, where they rang loudly enough to dominate all the other sounds.

In the evening you would find us tired and exhausted – like two tormented ghosts – our bodies clinging together, as we moved deftly and warily from street to street, avoiding dark places and ruined buildings. The two of us were startled at the slightest sound from gloomy areas and dead alleys. We would quicken our steps in the still night of the city. We encountered some vagrants, who were staring at the ground or gesturing toward the sky, and detoured to avoid them. We kept our distance from the shadows of the massive trees and proceeded along the smooth, asphalt pavement in the dim

light, avoiding the path of speeding vehicles that raced insanely to-
ward their destinations. When we reached the entry to the cinema,
Umm Salama said: "They've left." She clasped her hands firmly be-
neath my butt and added, "Hold on tight!" Then she started running
at full speed while I cringed, closed my eyes, and cleaved to her
solid back as I clutched her chest, which was sprouting and ripening.
The vagabonds and market layabouts saw us run by – terrified of
meeting them. They clapped their hands and stomped the ground
with their feet. They created a resounding noise by blowing long,
twisting whistles. They roared with laughter when they saw me sway
rhythmically on Umm Salama's back and almost fall off. The beg-
gars' fires were visible as we approached. They looked like flashing
traffic signals, lighting up only to vanish behind the bodies clustered
around them. Before reaching them we walked beside the wall,
where we met a group of lepers, who were gathered around their
quiet fire. Some were feeding and others were conversing in whis-
pers. Their inflamed eyes stared hatefully at us. They fell silent when
we approached and passed them quickly. Then they let out a morose
burst of laughter at our backs. We slackened our pace; before us
was the circle of beggar girls and half the homeless women. They
were giggling as they listened to the tales of a young vagrant, who
usually camped near the mosque. Umm Salama paused near these
women and let me down. I supported myself on my hands and
found myself heading toward the young homeless man, who started
to examine my face and body. Something like a cunning smile
formed on his face. Umm Salama suddenly turned on him and
bopped him on the head. She said, "Martuq, you liar, why are you
looking at him like this?" This young hobo, Martuq, who was to be-
come a valued friend in later years and who was the first person to
call me by a name I will always treasure, vanished into the crevices
of his reluctant memory before retrieving a name from scenes of
variety films, as he fabricated a meaning with his incendiary imag-
ination. Rubbing my dead feet with his little hands, he exclaimed:
"He's Kusahi!"

He then leapt to his feet, bowed dramatically, and added: "Kusahi
the King."

The young beggar women and vagrant girls laughed and seized
hold of me to seat me in their midst. I laughed too when I heard
them repeat this new name in order to memorize it – so they

wouldn't ever forget it: Kusahi the King. On that long-ago evening Umm Salama and I found Wahiba waiting anxiously for us with our supper of asida – a rye flour and butter porridge – with a hot sauce on a plastic tray. We ate as if famished. While I laughed, Umm Salama recounted, more than once – as she did every day – all the events of our day in detail. I giggled contentedly when Wahiba hugged me and called me by my new name: Kusahi the King.

How many years have passed while you crouched on the concrete triangle's squares, regarding with sad eyes the children's beautiful faces when they glanced down at you from behind car windows? You saw them throw banana and orange peels at you and toss out wrappers from chocolates and biscuits. The latter flew up into the air and soared high above you before landing on the concrete beside you. Kusahi, you loved seeing the children and would turn flips and spin about to amuse them after you caught the pieces of candy they threw you. How long has it been since you rested on Umm Salama's back and lovingly supervised the development of her small breasts, adding more of your body's weight to hers each day as you grew quickly? When, Kusahi, in which year, did the velvety faces of women begin to attract your attention as they stared through their car windows, oblivious to your existence, when you leapt like a quail across the roads? Remember! Squeeze your forehead and jog your defective memory!

One day Umm Salama came back early, and Martuq was with her. They both reeked of that odour that you relished and missed. This was the fragrance of your dead and forgotten mother. Umm Salama asked you to show Martuq your extraordinary skill in spinning around and doing flips. As she begged you, she leaned over, and her moist breath, which smelled of that fondly remembered odour, re-turned you to the lap of your magnificent mother, Karati Maryam. You turned a somersault and demonstrated your astonishing abili-ties. You stood on one hand and then on two. You twirled your body around while standing on your head. You spun on your butt and made your hands into speeding propeller blades. Your ally, Martuq, joined in your games and turned somersaults near you. He picked you up and leapt around with you, leaping over the cracks, moving like a sparrow from square to square. Then, suddenly, they left you alone, and penniless. Martuq had pounced on the "wealth" of the day. Umm Salama colluded with him, and that upset you. All the same, you said nothing and silently watched her protestations of in-nocence as she departed.

Umm Salama rebelled and broke Grandmother Usha's sacred laws. She ran off with her defiant breasts, which resembled horns that she used to ram the elderly granny's staff with. At night she slipped into the gathering of female beggars and homeless girls. She left quietly and slid in among them, and they moved to make room for her, hiding her with their lean bodies. She also grabbed young Martuq when he crept in and hid among the female bodies. Then other young men – lean and tall – infiltrated the gathering later in the night, squeezing themselves into the huddle of girls. Umm Salama upset Grandmother's system, which had been precisely cal-culated. She began to take me to hang out with the homeless girls around the stores and restaurants of the foreign market, where they would scrounge stuff and occasionally shoplift – while quarrelling all the time with the tall, adult homeless men who operated in that market. Umm Salama began to resemble the magnificent Maryam. She would carry me in one hand and stuff a piece of cloth soaked in silicone adhesive in her mouth with the other one. I started to roam

Mansour El Souwaim's novel *Dhakirat Shirrir* was translated into French by France Meyer and published by Editions Phébus, Paris, in 2012. Here, we introduce to readers a short excerpt from a review by Catherine Simon published in *Le Monde* newspaper.

Memories of a street child

Though they tell the life of a child, these memories do not belong, strictly speaking, to a coming-of-age novel. From the off, the circle is already closed: bad boy from birth, little Adam Kusahi, nicknamed Kusahi the broken one, will remain so. Since he left the belly of his mother – the powerful solvent-perfumed Karati Maryam – with poverty, drugs, vio-lence of down-an-outs more vicious than the police, he learns everything very quickly. Born a paraplegic, his legs inert and atrophied, Kusahi plays his disability to soften the hearts of onlookers.

Mansour El Souwaim knows how to tell a story like he is there himself:

around with the homeless girls. Beneath the cool, shady awnings, they would sneak a look in the shop windows and their displays of impossibly expensive clothes and then gaze at the breasts of impassive mannequins. I would also run my fingers over the glass and stare with great curiosity at the gold chains and jewellery displayed behind the windows until horrible voices scolded us and chased us away. The girls would stand for long periods outside fine restaurants gazing at young men courting young women who were happily devouring huge burger sandwiches. My friends would – when their normal methods of securing the price of tubes of silicone adhesive failed – place me on the ground and ask me to earn the money to rescue them from the quandary by crawling between people's feet with my hand outstretched. I, Kusahi, never disappointed the hopes of those extraordinary lost girls, who doled out pleasure, pain, and death.

Dhakirat Shirrir was first published in 2005 by the Abdel Karim Mirghani Cultural Center, Omdurman, Sudan, and won the Center's Tayeb Salih Award for the Novel the same year

long hours passed on the concrete traffic island, a triangle at the junction of three roads where the apprentice beggar tries to glean coins from drivers. Or, later, the unending wait of a whole tribe of streetkids fleeing police raids, hiding in the sewers . . . Fraternity, solidarity, and compassion are not absent from these oppressed lives, but it is a fraternity of young monsters, products of a rotten society, where only the strongest rule.

If the reality is dark, however, Mansour El Suwaim's powerful lyrical prose is, itself, full of light . . . He has succeeded in producing a formidable story, homage to the streetchildren of Sudan and elsewhere.

EMAD BLAKE

The New Novel in Sudan

The art of novel writing in Sudan blossomed with the foundation of its modern civil state, at the hands of the British, in the first half of the twentieth century. Cultural contact with Egypt had its role too – an influence apparent in what is, according to many scholars, the first Sudanese novel *Inahum Bashar* (They Are Humans) by Khalil Abdullah al-Hajj. Published at the end of the 1950s, al-Hajj's work showed itself to be remarkably influenced by Egyptian writer Naguib Mahfouz, a feature similarly noticed in the novels of his contemporary, Abu Bakr Khalid, such as *Bidayat el-Rabi'a* (The Beginning of Spring) and *Al-Nabi'a al-Mur* (The Bitter Spring).

General opinion, however, tends to agree that the author of the first Sudanese novel was, in fact, Malkat El-Dar Mohammad. Her book, *Al-Faragh al-Areedh* (The Wide Hollowness), was written in the late forties, though not actually published until 1969. Prior to this, efforts at narrative literature in Sudan did not really live up to the art of novel writing as we understand it today. There was, for example, Othman Mohammad Hashim's *Tajuj: Ma's-sat el-Hub wal Jamal* (Tajuj: Tragedy of Love and Beauty) (1948), a literary adaptation of a romantic folktale from Eastern Sudan. Similarly, there was the joint literary project of Mohammad Ahmed Mahjoub and Abdel

Cover of The Wide Hollowness

Halim Mohammad, *Mawt Dunya* (Death of a World), which took the form of a series of letters that sought to reflect social life and an image of the Sudanese intellectual.

The growth of the middle class in Sudan may also, to some extent, have encouraged the flourishing of novel writing. Education became more widespread, and a new culture, and new systems and modes of production in society began to emerge. In Khalil Abdullah al-Hajj's previously mentioned (They Are Humans), for example, the author focuses on the hardship of working-class

Abu Bakr Khalid

life in 1940s Omdurman. Soon after, groups such as the petty bourgeoisie were addressed, and such issues of social marginalisation are still evident in Sudanese novels today.

Like poetry and short stories, the novel in Sudan continually oscillated between reflecting foreign influence and trying to produce a local school, inspired by the local cultural heritage. Various schools of political thought and intellectual and ideological currents within the country also played their part in novel writing: from socialist realism and the French existentialist school of the 1960s, to the magical realism of the 1980s and 1990s, to a more modern style of literature with the dawn of the new millennium.

Yet in the minds of those well versed in Arabic literature, whether Arab or not, the Sudanese novel cannot fail to be associated with Tayeb Salih and his celebrated *Season of Migration to the North*. Published in the mid-1960s, this novel claimed a school of its own, disengaged from the Sudanese and Arab novel, and drawing on the author's experience as a young émigré in London in his early twenties. In *Season of Migration to the North*, Salih confronted the crucial issues of his time, such as the clash of Eastern and Western civilizations, as well as boldly employing sex and a style of writing we might term the 'impossible easy'. As a parallel example from within the country, we have the novelist Ibrahim Ishaq, exploring the cultural environment of Western Sudan. Unlike Salih's balance of dialect and more neutral language, Ishaq exclusively used the local tongue in his dialogue. In fact, most critics would agree that it was these two writers who were the true driving force behind the transformation of the form and content of the Sudanese novel.

cover of Season of Migration to the North

In spite of this, it was poetry, and, to a lesser extent, the short story, which remained at the forefront of the cultural scene in Sudan between the early 1970s and the late 1990s. Whilst this period saw the publishing of many diverse novels, an unfortunate pattern, of writing one or two books before falling into oblivion, seemed to prevail for most novelists. Penning works of fiction could hardly sustain a steady income and, as a result, amounted to little more than a hobby, pursued in one's spare time. All this stood in the way of novel writing spreading and taking root in Sudanese society. Even the acclaimed Tayeb Salih stopped after five novels and turned to journalism,

Ibrahim Ishaq

writing articles for newspapers and magazines. Moreover, issues within publishing itself were preventing newly written literary works from reaching Sudanese readers. Manuscripts were locked up for years, only to be met with criticism and mockery when they were eventually published, as being completely out of touch with

their modern audience.

With the turn of the millennium, however, the Sudanese novel flourished in a spirit of openness and true revolution. Pushing poetry and short stories to the margins, it was now time for the novel to take centre stage amongst the new wave of young writers. Most wrote from abroad, where they could read and immerse themselves in the culture of the "Other" – with fewer concerns over problems of publishing. This explosion in novel writing was fuelled also by the increasing maturity of Sudanese society itself – culturally and more generally. Life in all its forms had reached a complexity, no less alleviated by tough political and economic circumstances. The country witnessed class inequality and several civil wars, leading to the division of the country into North Sudan and South Sudan in 2011. Thus, the image of social maturity, crystallised in the novels of this period, can hardly be isolated from this turbulent context.

The themes addressed by these novels were numerous and everchanging. Some reflected on social reality, with its political and social issues: marginalisation, and the crisis of the ongoing war in the south for half a century, followed by the Darfur War in Western Sudan. In others Sudan's cultural heritage and local tradition were illuminated through delving into the country's history and cultural and ethnic diversity, which is a model of intermingling between Arab and African culture, religion and patterns of global awareness. Importantly, successful efforts of new authors to disengage themselves from foreign schools of thought contributed to a distinct Sudanese literary current, still taking form today, and which is wide-ranging in its richness, experience, treatment and concerns.

This is by no means to overlook Sudanese literature composed in English, whether during the current or previous century. We may

draw attention, for example, to Francis Deng, who wrote his fa-
mous novel *Cry of the Owl* before South Sudan's independence.
Translated into Arabic and published in 1989, the novel reflected a
new direction in the South Sudanese novel, in its social and cultural
image and its concerns, but which was little discussed in the north
as a result of political isolation. Likewise in English are the works
of the UK-based writer Leila Aboulela, and Jamal Mahjoub, who in
recent years has turned to writing crime fiction under the pseudo-
nym Parker Bilal.

One concern does, however, constantly loom over the Sudanese
literary scene: that of surpassing the legacy of Tayeb Salih. A national
icon in the Sudanese consciousness, his books – previously banned
from circulation with the advent of Islamist rule in 1989 – can be
found in virtually every household. However, a different wave of
opinion is beginning to speak out, highlighting how greatly life in
Sudan has changed, and noting that modern literature is featuring
themes and styles that are more modern compared to Salih's liter-
ature, which paints the early phases of the Sudanese state, before
life became so complex and modern cities began to emerge. Khar-
toum today, for example, is a complex, intermingled world, with
ten million inhabitants from a multitude of cultural backgrounds,
barely resembling the Khartoum of Tayeb Salih's books.

We are met today with a vast array of prominent Sudanese au-
thors, such as the prolific Amir Tag Elsir, who writes about topics
relating to the Sudan of the present and past. His best-known novel
Mahr el-Sayyiah (The Dowry of Cries), 2007, revolves around the
history of the Sultanate of Darfur in Western Sudan. Similarly we
see the works of another prolific novelist, Abdelaziz Baraka Sakin,
in particular *Al-Jungo Masamir al-Ardh* (The Jungo: Stakes of the
Earth (2010), which explores the society of seasonal agricultural
labourers in Eastern Sudan and issues of cultural, economic and
ethnic marginalisation; as well as his *Messiah of Darfur* [Ed. see page
153 below for a review], which deals with the conflict in Western
Sudan. The works of Emad Blake, on the other hand, move between
his local environment and issues affecting the entire Arab region,
for example in his novel *Aalam Uday* (The World of Uday). He is,
however, best known for *Shawarma* (2014) [Ed. excerpted in this
feature on page 74], which spans across three political eras in
Sudan's modern history up to the present day, told from the per-

Jamal Mahjoub   Amir Tag Elsir   Leila Aboulela

spective of a youth who flees his broken home to Khartoum. Vi-
enna-based Tarek Eltayeb, though with fewer titles to his name, is
well known for his novel *Cities without Palms*, [Ed. a runner-up in the
2010 Saif Ghobash Banipal Prize for Arabic Literary Translation],
which discusses migration to Europe in the last quarter of the twen-
tieth century. Likewise well known are the works of Hammour
Ziada, whose novel *Shawq al-Darwish* (The Longing of the Dervish)
won the Naguib Mahfouz Medal for Literature in 2014 and was
shortlisted for the 2015 International Prize for Arabic Fiction. Set
during the Mahdi Revolution against the Turks in the late nineteenth
century, the novel provocatively discusses the potential of religion
to turn into violence. And there is the prolific Ahmad Al Malik,
whose works are characterised by the undeniable flavour of magical
realism, and has been consistently published since his first novel in
the late 1980s, *Assafir Akher Ayam el-Khareef* (The Last of the Autumn
Sparrows).

In fact, the sheer number of Sudanese novelists today makes com-
piling an exhaustive list somewhat difficult. However, in terms of
popularity amongst the younger generation, leading names include
Mansour El-Suwaim, whose novel, *Akher al-Salateen* (The Last Sul-
tan) (2014), is based on the life of Ali Dinar, former Sultan of Dar-
fur; Hisham Adam, whose subject matter varies from the Spanish
Civil War to issues within Sudan, as seen in his novel *Kajoumi*
(2015)[Ed. see page 30 above]; and Mu'tassim al-Shair, author of
Edfununi fi tel Abeeb (Bury Me in Tel Aviv) 2013. Looking at works
by women authors, we see, amongst many others, Sara Hamza Al-

Issa al-Hilu

Jack's novel *Khiyanata'eth* (That Betrayal), 2013; *Ibn al-Shams* (Son of the Sun), 2013, by Rania Mamoun, and the prolific Buthaina Khidhir Makki, whose novels are particularly vocal about women's issues in Sudanese society today.

Amidst the vast literary output of the new generation, the work of the early pioneers has all but come to a close, except, that is, in the case of Issa al-Hilu, regarded today as the 'spiritual father' of Sudanese literature. One of the most active voices in the cultural sphere for around half a century, particularly as a journalist, al-Hilu is best known for his short stories, although he has published a number of novels, too, the most recent being *Al-Ward wa Kawabees el-Layl* (Roses and Nightmares) 2013.

In spite of all these works, the Sudanese novel continues, to some extent, to face challenges to its development, particularly in the actual publishing – most of which takes place overseas, in Cairo or Beirut. The issue of local censorship – and sometimes even seizure – has prevented a number of works from reaching readers. The 2015 Khartoum International Book Fair, for example, saw the ban-

Ihab Adlan

Hammour Ziada   *Sara Hamza Aljack*   *Muhsin Khalid*

ning of Ihab Adlan's first novel, *Asfal Qaa' al-Madina* (Down the Bottom of the City), for allegedly violating public decency. Aside from this, other problems relating to the social environment persist today. Whilst globally open, Sudanese society continues to be the prisoner of tradition and conservative values, especially given the effect of a quarter of a century under Islamist military rule. This is not to mention the evident marginalisation of cultural activism and closure of venues through which creative writing and art can thrive. Recent years have witnessed the closure of a number of centres for thought and enlightenment, and the banning of several literary works. In the case of novelist Muhsin Khalid, a censorship report wrote of one of his novels: "It moves the senses and intoxicates like wine, and that is why it is religiously forbidden." Worth mentioning, too, is that literary criticism is not really keeping pace with the fictional output. Indeed, serious attempts at criticism of the new novel are few and far between, while newspaper articles are more complimentary comments and press reports than literary criticism.

But none of the above is able to obscure a bright picture that continues to evolve: of young people in the second or third decade of their lives, experimenting with their writing and yet unable to reach out to the reading population. Some have even resorted to using the internet and social media. It is clear that a new body of literature is being written in Sudan, one that is too broad to accommodate or reflect in this limited space.

TRANSLATED BY ROSIE MAXTON

HEAD OF AZZA PUBLISHING
NUR AL-HUDA MOHAMMAD NUR AL-HUDA

"My main goal is to bring Sudanese creativity to the rest of the Arab world"

INTERVIEWED IN CAIRO BY AZZA RASHAD

TRANSLATED BY BECKI MADDOCK

Nur al-Huda Mohammad Nur al-Huda, Head of Azza Publishing House and one of the major and daring publishers in Sudan, was born in 1946 in Khartoum, where he received his elementary education. In 1967 he obtained a higher diploma in Library Studies. Khartoum University then sent him to the United Kingdom in 1983-1984. Following his return he worked at Khartoum University Publishing House until 1991, when he was dismissed for no legitimate reason. That year he founded Azza Publishing and to date has published over 500 titles, comprising important works in the fields of philosophy, literature and the sciences. He is the publisher of Abdelaziz Baraka Sakin and Stella Gaitano, among others.

The novel has become the most read genre, and literary prizes have played a significant role in this.

Nur al-Huda M. Nur al-Huda, at his stand at the Cairo Book Fair, January 2016. Photo by Azza Rashad

Let's begin with the two years you spent in the UK. What did that mean for you?

Those two years in the first fortress of democracy, from Oxford University to Cambridge, via its world-famous museums, exhibitions and libraries, established within me a singular faith in democracy, even in the field of publishing. The democracy of knowledge. From there, just a brief glance at our titles shows that we publish all political and intellectual trends and movements, that the quality of a work is the sole criterion we take into account, irrespective of whether the author is a Marxist or a Liberal or a supporter of the Muslim Brotherhood.

What made you establish Azza Publishing?

From the beginning I chose the subject of Library Studies because I loved reading and culture, and I discovered in it the way to bring this culture to everyone. I worked for a long time at Khartoum University Press, and after being dismissed unfairly, I founded Azza Publishing so that I could continue to practise the profession I had learnt and excelled at, which I love, and which is proven by the fact I have handed it on to my children.

What type of books do you publish? Is there a focus on a particular genre, for example?

We publish 30% literature, including novels, poetry and short stories; 20% political books; 10% history. The remaining 40% are educational books and research – religion, science, thought, philosophy, economics, etc. The main focus is on quality.

In your opinion, what type of books attracts the Sudanese reader?

The Sudanese usually incline towards reading political books. The bestsellers are those that discuss the conflict in Darfur and the Blue Nile, and books with titles such as *Sudan, War of Resources and Identity*, *Identity and the Breakup of the Sudanese State*, *The Characteristics of Sudanese Society*, and others. After politics comes history, followed by novels and poetry. However, recently some changes have occurred in the Sudanese reader's temperament, and the novel has jumped to first place and become the most read genre.

How did that happen?

Literary prizes have played a significant role in this respect. Monetary prizes entice both writers and publishers, as does the extensive media coverage of these prizes and the establishment of their presence and importance. All this has propelled novels to first place on the reading scene.

In terms of literature, who are the writers that you publish?

The publishing house is open to all creative talent. For example, we have published the novelist Abdelaziz Baraka Sakin, who was obliged to leave Sudan for Vienna because of the confiscation of most of his books.

> The quality of a work is the sole criterion we take into account, irrespective of whether the author is a Marxist or a Liberal or a supporter of the Muslim Brotherhood.

How does the cooperation between publisher and author work?

It depends on the situation of the author. If possible he contributes to the publishing costs in exchange for a percentage of the profits; if that is not possible, the publishing house carries the total cost and gives him a fixed share of the profits. Things happen flexibly, they are not fixed. However, the real stumbling block comes from the Ministry of Culture's Department of Literary Works, which places obstacles in the author's contract with authors, stipulating legal requirements that are more than the costs, and makes it difficult to agree any contract with an author who is outside Sudan. This means that publishers are forced to smuggle abroad information of what they want to print.

How many copies of a book do you usually print?

A thousand copies is the minimum run for any book. I content myself with that and am happy to publish that number.

What is the situation of book distribution in Sudan?

Difficult. We are accustomed to difficulties and we think up ways to deal with them.

Do your books reach the bookshops in all Sudanese cities?

Yes, I have a distribution agreement with a bookshop in each Sudanese city in return for a maximum of 30% discount on sales.

In the whole of Sudan? Including the South?

Yes, we even have distributers in South Sudan, which I consider a part of the body of Sudan that has been removed (and this is a big mistake). But the connections to the Sudanese there continue and personally I hope that the body of Sudan will be joined together again.

Are there particular obstacles that impede the spread of books published in Sudan?

There are no libraries or lessons about using libraries in schools; and at all the various educational stages, there is nothing to promote the importance of reading and knowledge, so we find that most graduates from the University Libraries Department do not find work. The problem of methods of learning that rely on dictation and abridged works rather than on scientific research can also be considered among the great obstacles, in addition to other factors that Sudan shares with the rest of the Arab world, such as worsening illiteracy and poverty.

Tell us about the costs of book production, the selling price and the taxes imposed on you by the state.

The problem with books in Sudan is the high cost of printing and its poor quality, which is due to lack of modernisation in the print-ing industry and the absence of modern machinery; also the exor-bitant fees imposed on us by the Ministry of Culture for us to obtain the requisite ISBN number for any book. As for imported books, they are very expensive, due to the taxes, customs and fees – at ports, airports, for instance, and then also the administrative costs.

In addition to taxes you pay zakat[1] on books. Do you pay it on each book separately?

In fact zakat is levied on each title that we print, as it is considered a commercial unit, but it does not take into account that the printed book might not to be distributed for a year or two, or perhaps more. Nevertheless, we pay zakat on it each year, as it is deemed a commercial unit. This is baffling, but the most surprising thing is that there is zakat on books at all!

> Counterfeiting of books has become an insupportable problem . . . Egypt is the Arab country where this counterfeiting or print piracy occurs most, without any legal obstacles.

What is the sum that you pay as zakat?

The amount varies and depends on their mood, but all told it is a burden.

If I were in your place, I would have left this profession long ago.

I cannot be anywhere else. This is what I studied. This is the profession I have practised my entire life, which I will continue to follow until I die, and which I will leave to my children after me. Books are my life.

Can you explain to us the interaction between the publisher and the censor on works that you want to publish?

We have had 24 books banned, and for this reason we started printing 70% of our books outside Sudan.

And how do these books re-enter the country?

We slip them in, here and there. It is unavoidable. We are forced into doing that.

If we take the book *The Sudanese View and the Production of Failure* by Amru Mohammad Abbas as an example, why did the security authorities ban it when it reached al-Obaidiya customs post in North Sudan after it had been approved by the Ministry of Culture's Department of Literary Works?

There are no standards or rules governing this approval. Suddenly, they said, "It must be banned". But in the field of literature the ban is usually because of a claim that it offends public morality because of some words that incite rancour from some quarters. The book is judged on a moral rather than artistic basis.

Is there any organisation in Sudan that defends books from bans or confiscation?

The Council of Journalists and Printers says that it is responsible for newspapers and magazines, but not for books.

> I must say to you, with greater bitterness, that imprisoning people in Sudan does not require laws.

What about the Sudanese Writers' Union? Does it not object?

The authorities dissolved the Sudanese Writers' Union some time ago.

And if I were to say to you, with great bitterness, that banning or confiscating a book is, in the end, a lesser evil than imprisoning an author for years because of his/her book, using Hisbah[2] law as a blasphemy law, as in Egypt for example. What do you think?

I must say to you, with greater bitterness, that imprisoning people in Sudan does not require laws.

In a country in deep crisis like Sudan, it surprises me that all these difficulties are placed in the way of book production, in the way of knowledge, without which there is no way out of a crisis. I want to ask you: Do you think this stems from the ignorance or stupidity of officials or is it intentional?

In my opinion it is intentional. There is no real will to develop people through knowledge acquisition. They want people to be ignorant. How ridiculous this is today, when knowledge is available to anyone anywhere, thanks to the technological revolution, and when what has been banned on Sudanese soil reaches the people through the internet.

In general, what are the difficulties facing the Sudanese publisher?

Perhaps the cost of printing, taxes, customs and fees, which are taxes by another name, are difficulties that the publisher can endure, and the possibilities of a ban or confiscation are difficulties to which he becomes accustomed. However, the counterfeiting of books has today become an insupportable problem. The counterfeit book is sold for half, or even one third, of the price of the original book, which causes both the publisher and the writer to go bankrupt.

In which Arab country is this phenomenon of book counterfeiting most prevalent?

Egypt is the Arab country where this counterfeiting or print piracy occurs most, without any legal obstacles. However, Sudan is the greatest consumer of counterfeit books. As a consequence of severe poverty, the reader is interested in the low price of a book, even if it is counterfeit.

Are there any particular proposals to overcome these difficulties?

There are some local Arab authorities introducing laws to penalise the counterfeiters, and the introduction by UNICEF of measures supporting intellectual property rights and the allocation of courts to investigate counterfeiting. But I also count on the effectiveness of condemnation by society to eliminate this phenomenon.

Are there book fairs in Sudan?

Yes, there is the Khartoum Book Fair.

What is your assessment of the Khartoum Book Fair?

Unfortunately, most years of the fair have lacked the organisation necessary for success. The bureaucratic mentality that runs the fair each year does not respect the Sudanese reader (who spends from his living expenses in order to buy books), and is not interested in inviting the big international publishing houses. Last year, although there was a fair increase in the number of exhibitors, it was an increase in quantity, not quality, since heritage books and religious book still constitute 70% of all those exhibited, while 20% are educational books and only 10% published in Sudan itself. But the worst thing was that counterfeit books represented 50% of those displayed at the fair. And, in addition to this, there was an absence of any cultural activities accompanying the fair, which is what the Sudanese citizen needs.

How would you suggest it could be better organised?

I would suggest combining all cultural activities – the fair, the two Tayeb Salih literary prizes and the Nile Festival – into one cultural month. But it is still fundamental that the world of books will not develop except in a climate of freedom.

Which Arab book fairs have you attended, and how useful are they?

I go to many book fairs – Cairo in January, Muscat in February, Riyadh in March, Abu Dhabi in April, Sharjah in November and

Qatar in December. Not to mention my participation of many years standing at the Frankfurt and London fairs. Of course, the fairs are useful for me as I present Azza Publishing with my titles, so it provides an opportunity to get to know us. I also find it useful meeting other Arab publishers and exchanging experiences. My main goal is to bring Sudanese creativity to the rest of the Arab world, on the one hand, and to the Sudanese expatriates in the various Arab countries, on the other, and the latter welcome every occasion.

Do you have a children's books department?

No, unfortunately this would require huge financial resources.

So, what is the situation for children's book publishing in Sudan?

Children's books are published in low-cost, local, popular editions for Sudanese consumption only and are not exhibited outside Sudan at the Arab book fairs.

In this difficult profession of yours, how do you view the future of the book?

Without a climate that guarantees freedom of expression and freedom of creativity, without real democracy it is hard to imagine any future, not only for the book but also for the citizen himself. The main thing I count on now is the Sudanese author, whose creative talent arises from the cross-pollination of several cultures: Black African, Arab, Berber and Nubian, which gives him a special cultural quality, which assists him in confronting the forces of oppression and tyranny, and supports him in reaching the level of our writers now, whether in the International Prize for Arabic Fiction, the Katara Prize, or others. I count to the same extent on the Sudan-based reader who has the desire for knowledge, who actively participates in fairs, both at home (despite poverty) and abroad, where the jilbab and turban can be seen at the London and Frankfurt book fairs. This is the reader that I count on for a better future.

Notes:
1 Zakat is a mandatory annual religious tax, on certain kinds of property and used for charitable and religious purposes, fundamental to Islamic law and one of the five pillars of Islam. It is enshrined in Sudanese law.
2 Hisbah in Islamic doctrine means accountability in accordance with Sharia law. This law is commonly referred to in English as the blasphemy law.

Volker Kaminski Reviews

Der Messias von Darfur
(The Messiah of Darfur)
by **Abdelaziz Baraka Sakin**
translated into the German by Günther Orth

Liberation strategy

In his fifth novel *The Messiah of Darfur*, Sakin — one of Sudan's best-known contemporary authors — tells the extraordinary story of a charismatic 'prophet' who gathers his disciples together in war-ravaged Darfur in western Sudan. His aim is to make them question their lives so that they can be 'free'. Astonishingly, the prophet is called 'Issa' (Jesus), and 'Son of Man', marking him out as unusual in a society characterised by the Muslim faith.

However, although his message is filled with love and humanity, his own situation is in stark contrast to this: 666 soldiers have been sent to eliminate him and his small band of followers. The reader fears the worst, but is not immediately 'delivered'. Instead, we are taken on a journey into the country's recent past, where we hear about war, destruction, and misery on an epic scale, affecting countless numbers of people. We share in the fate of a people killed en masse in a civil war between government troops and rebels, a people with scarcely a chance of survival.

There are, however, a few strong individuals who fight back bravely, taking drastic action — like Abdarrahman. A war orphan, Abdarrahman evolves from victim to rebel: she marries a soldier, who himself was forcibly recruited, and demands that he kill least ten Janjaweed. However, she then takes matters into her own hands, gets hold of weapons and exacts her own revenge. The prophet, who actually preaches peace, would be entirely on her side in this because his personal motto, which is also the motto of the book, is: 'It

Cover of the Arabic edition

is easier for a camel to go through the eye of a needle than for a Janjaweed to enter into the kingdom of God.' The terrible Janjaweed (literally: 'devils on horseback') are an actual ethnic group – nomadic tribes deployed by the government as militias during the war and characterised by their unusual cruelty and unscrupulousness.

Abdelazizi Baraka Sakin

And how does the story of the prophet on the mountain conclude? It's a fairy tale ending: the prophet and his troops, together with all the soldiers and their captain, fly up to Heaven, carrying their crosses on their backs like wings. This may seem escapist, but perhaps it's the only way to leave the misery of the present behind and find some degree of comfort. So it can also be regarded as a liberation strategy in which, with such a serious and depressing theme, the author repeatedly makes use of irony and satire, thereby distancing himself from his subject matter.

An impressive book by a clever author, in a congenial German translation by Günther Orth, as yet unpublished. It is to be hoped that this translation will soon find a good one.

NEXT ISSUE

DARWISH
BY *ABDELAZIZ BARAKA SAKIN*

A CHAPTER FROM A NEW NOVEL
TRANSLATED BY SPENCER SCOVILLE

Olivia Snaije reviews

Nouvelles du Soudan (Short Stories from Sudan)
by Ahmad Al Malik, Stella Gaitano, Hisham Adam, Abdulaziz
Baraka Sakin, Abdel Ghani Karamallah and Rania Mamoun.
Translated by Xavier Luffin
Magellan & CIE, Paris, 2009. Part of the "Miniatures – Nouvelles du
monde" series, in collaboration with *Courrier International* magazine.
ISBN 978-2-35074-160-4, pbk, 95 pp. €12.

Literary reflections
of a diverse reality

As the Arabic to French literary translator Xavier Luffin recently said: "It is interesting to get past one's colonial history and see what's being translated into other languages."
Indeed, in *Nouvelles du Soudan*, a collection of short stories from Sudan translated from Arabic to French, the English-language reader will discover writing from a wide range of authors not necessarily available in English. In his informative preface, Luffin writes that Sudan has been a most fertile literary terrain since the 1940s, but that unfortunately much of the literature remains unknown in the Arab world and in the West, apart from the writings and poetry of Tayeb Salih and Mohammed Al-Faytouri. For the past twenty years Sudan's cultural, ethnic and religious diversity has been reflected in its literature, remarks Luffin. Although they all write in Arabic, these authors are also Nubian, Darfouri or from South Sudan. "They evoke grave events that are reflections of Sudanese reality today. But the skill and elegance of the authors, the humour and dreamlike style of some that recalls Latin American magic realism, transforms [these writings] into small treasures, bearing witness to both a harsh reality but also of a literature that begs to be discovered."

The collection begins with a short story by Ahmad Al Malik called *Le Char D'Assaut* (The Army Tank). Subtle, ironic and very funny, it describes how one man's life changes after he invests in an army tank. Invoking inflation, military rule and society's necessary hypocrisy in order to get by, Al Malik uses absurdity and deftness to describe a debilitating economic situation.

Stella Gaetano's *Des Mondes inconnus sur la Carte* (Worlds Unknown to a Map) is a harrowing account of a brother and his handicapped sister living on the street with no outlook for a better life.

In Hisham Adam's *Lanji, la vendeuse de merissa* (Lanja, the Marissa-Seller) a young girl from a small village in South Sudan dreams of visiting the capital. When she is chased from her village during the civil war, she makes her way with difficulty to Khartoum and discovers it is far from what she had dreamed of.

Une Femme du camp Kadis (A Woman from Kadis Camp) by Abdulaziz Baraka Sakin takes place in a multicultural market where a woman is arrested for selling alcohol. Sakin shows the all-too-common contradictions about the reality of alcohol in Muslim cultures.

Abdel Ghani Karamallah's *L'Âne du Prédicateur* (The Preacher's Donkey), is an example of the author's penchant for using animals or objects as narrators. Here, a donkey is the storyteller. He is a philosopher and a historian who, despite his enslavement, has strength of character and a thirst for freedom. Illustrating the relativity of a hard life, Karamallah's donkey describes humans who are for the most part brutal and ignorant, with a few rare moments of

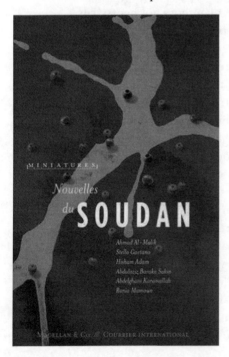

kindness and generosity coming from women and children.

Journalist and writer Rania Mamoun's contribution is a devastating story of hope versus desperation in a man trying valiantly to overcome poverty in *Histoire de portes* (Story of Doors). From his home, to the bus he rides towards a job interview, to the door to the office where he is hoping to work – doors open and close to him, cruelly symbolizing the narrator's utter lack of control over his destiny.

In a mere 95 pages, the selection of short stories in this collection reflect powerful and engaging story-telling recounted in an astonishing variety of styles.

Clare Roberts reviews
two novels
by **Amir Tag Elsir**

Ebola '76
translated by
Chris Bredin and Emily Danby
Darf Publishers, UK, 2015.
ISBN: 978-1-85077-274-3, 134pp,
pbk, £8.99.

French Perfume
translated by William M Hutchins
ANTIBOOKCLUB, USA, June 2015.
ISBN 978-0983868385, 160pp, pbk, $15.

Comedic calculation

The novel *Ebola '76* is an unexpectedly comical take on a tragic epidemic, the publication of its English translation timely in light of the recent resurgence of the disease in West Africa. The anthropomorphised Ebola disease itself becomes the novel's central character as it leaps from victim to victim and leaves a path of destruction in its wake, but not before judging the virtues and vices of each individual. In this way, Ebola becomes not only the most terrifying of villains, but also, the ultimate judge of society.

What is remarkable about Amir Tag Elsir's novel is that not one of the characters is portrayed in a particularly favourable light. All have their secrets, jealousies, self-importance and adulterous desires, and Elsir does not encourage his readers to feel an ounce of sympathy as the deadly disease picks off its victims one by one. Even the main protagonist, Lewis, a textile factory worker recently named the town's Man of the Year, is far from likeable, not least because he carries the disease across the Congolese border on a visit to his deceased lover. Rape, harassment and poverty are rife in the

Amir Tag Elsir

town of Nzara, even before Ebola strikes. Even the weather is sluggish.

Equally striking is the humour inherent throughout the novel, the subject matter of which is clearly far from comical: from a description of a tragic sequence of events culminating in a pigeon flying into a hospital window, to the disappointment felt by Lewis's wife when he miraculously recovers from the disease – 'he had ruined all the plans she'd formulated for her newfound widowhood' – Elsir pokes fun at everyone and everything, leaving, like the deadly disease itself, no-one unscathed. A renowned magician becomes enraged when he is unable to impress his fellow travellers with his magic tricks as they flee the disease, terrified, while the town's wealthy expats, airlifted away to escape their near-miss with death, congratulate themselves as 'intrepid explorers' on 'their little run-in with a Third World epidemic'. Meanwhile, Ebola is flattered to hear the death it causes described to be 'the most excruciating known to man'.

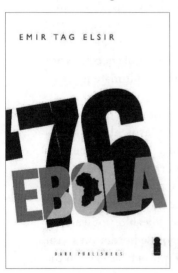

Despite the absurdity that pervades the novel, tragedy is never far from the surface. Caravans of refugees, closed borders, hysteria of the masses and terror – 'a law unto itself' – reigning free, are depicted vividly. Bodies both dead and alive pile up in the town's central meeting place (renamed as 'Ebola Square'), as the town's few doctors struggle with insufficient resources. In such conditions, the inherent lack of empathy for any of the characters is a surprising response to such subject matter. At times 'cackling with glee', at others 'squirming with anxiety', the 'wicked sorcerer' that is the disease calculates its every move.

Ebola's most crucial role in this novel, however, is to bring to the
fore the flaws already possessed by each of the characters, before
plunging them into the darkness of death.

The dark reality
of the unreal

The novel *French Perfume* is a disturbing tale of one man's
growing obsession with a figment of his own imagination.
Reality blurs with insanity as the lonely protagonist Ali Jar-
jar, a well-known member of the poverty-stricken Gha'ib commu-
nity, lets his imagination get the better of him, to devastating effect.
Entrusted with the task of welcoming a foreign female guest to the
neighbourhood, he and his community get swept up in the excite-
ment of her imminent arrival, but, to their increasing frustration,
their visitor continually delays her arrival in town.

Meanwhile, the ever-fanciful Ali Jarjar gets carried away by his
preparations. Not only does he take the liberty of embellishing the
very limited information he already has about the Frenchwoman,
but, with the help of a computer-savvy acquaintance, he uses the
internet to find out as much as possible about her in order to pre-
pare for their time together. Everything he does is in preparation
for a woman about whom he knows next to nothing. His over-active
imagination, fuelled by the details he has found on her online, leads
him to 'salt and pepper' reality to the extent that he holds an imag-
inary wedding with a heavily edited photo of his bride and embarks
upon a relationship (both emotional and physical) with a woman he
has yet to meet. He soon loses touch with reality, drowning in his
own fantasy. The reader follows his downward spiral, first with
amusement, then astonishment, and, finally, alarm as his obsession
grows. Eventually, he becomes unable to discern between the jeal-
ously he imagines his community to feel and the pity they actually
feel towards him. By the end of the novel, the community's sense
of discomfort is acute, and Jarjar reacts with disproportionate bru-
tality.

The prime accomplice to the protagonist's obsession is technol-

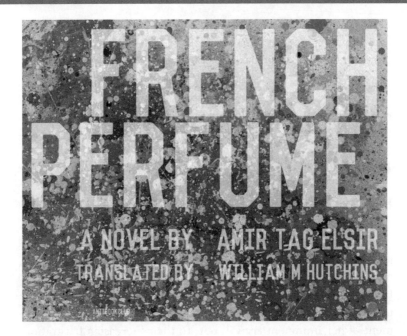

ogy. Raised in a community with little if any access to the outside world, he is introduced to the internet in a local coffeehouse. His first tenuous attempts to research the visitor online help him to narrow down the possible persona of the Frenchwoman. From this quick search, he can gather enough detail to build up an idea of her appearance, likes, dislikes and habits. With the help of his vivid imagination, he can fill in the blanks himself.

As a writer Elsir is entertaining and unpredictable, shocking and dark at every turn. His characters are well-respected members of the community, but misfits — lonely outsiders who dwell more in their own minds than in reality. An exaggerated emphasis on the importance of the virtual is clearly a point of intrigue to Elsir, although it is taken to a new level in *French Perfume* [Ed. recently longlisted for the 2016 BTBA Best Translated Book Award of Three Percent, University of Rochester, NY]. Although few of us can imagine our own minds distorting reality to such an alarming extent, a warning can be taken from this novel, in a world in which the lines between the imagined and the real have never been more confused.

الجائزة العالمية للرواية العربية
INTERNATIONAL PRIZE FOR ARABIC FICTION

EXCERPTS FROM
THE 2016 SHORTLIST OF THE
INTERNATIONAL PRIZE FOR ARABIC FICTION

Numedia by
Tareq Bakari

Destinies: Concerto of the
Holocaust and the Nakba
by Rabai al-Madhoun

Mercury
by Mohamed Rabie

Praise for the Women of
the Family
by Mahmoud Shukair

A Sky Close to Our House
by Shahla Ujayli

Guard of the Dead
by George Yaraq

TAREQ BAKARI

Numedia

EXCERPT FROM THE NOVEL

TRANSLATED BY WILLIAM M HUTCHINS

❝Why this village in particular?" (She asks me why? Oh! You should instead ask the woman who dropped me here when I was an infant the way someone drops a banana peel or anything else they think worthless. Or, if you want, ask this village. They might provide you with a bit of information about the nights I wept silently whilst helplessly confronting thorny questions.)

I replied: "Because on the one hand this village is beautiful – as you will see – and because this hotel belongs to me now."

Her mouth fell open, and she shouted incredulously: "Really, Darling? When did you become an investor?"

We shared an insane round of laughter, and in this paroxysm of fleeting delight vowed eternal love for each other. I was secretly laughing at the emotional hypocrisy from which I could not liberate myself, even though it cost me dearly. We frequently embrace projects far beyond our capabilities, even when we doubt we will ever attain the stature necessary to keep these vows. All the same, we plunge into this quagmire, if only to lend the moment we make such a vow a special excitement. Lovers' vows, though, exactly like lovers' roses, quickly wither.

I was watching her expression while she rocked to and fro as if laughing to herself and regretting that I was roiling her pleasure. When she finished breakfast, I took her by the hand and we left quickly. At the moment that Ighram's morning surprised me, I sensed I was traversing an abyss on a thread finer than a hair, or treading on a sword's lethal blade.

The village spread out like a cluster of grapes falling freely down the mountain slope. In official documents the community is referred to as Kasr Anned, but all those who love it know it simply as Ighram. Its yellow houses are beautiful! They stand hugging each other as they flow down the mountain and hug the foot in a chaos that only residents perceive as orderly.

We walked past fields of maize that stood proudly, like my pain, and watched hardworking farm workers lift mattocks high enough to touch the sky and bring them down to split open the belly of the earth – as if seeking revenge for some wrong beyond my ken and, I assumed, beyond theirs as well. I felt upset that when they leaned on their mattocks and stared curiously at us, they never recognized me and saw nothing in my features comparable to theirs. In the crowded parade of days they had lost track of me. One day an outsider had left them, and one day an outsider had returned. When Julia grasped my arm, I became aware of her presence and thus she rescued me – if only temporarily – from a pain that had suddenly begun to throb.

"Murad, please tell me quickly the special secret of this place. You certainly didn't choose it by chance?"

I sensed she was trying to run toward a whirlpool that I would only escape by having my heart broken. Julia did not realize she was grasping, through his pains and sorrows, a man formed from ink and pain. At the height of my bewilderment and fascination with a place covered by almost three decades of dust, my psychiatrist had suggested: "Try to mingle with other people, even if just occasionally. They're not an inferno – contrary to what you think. Explain to them as much as you can about your ordeal. If you can't, invent some other person, call him whatever you want, and talk about him instead. You need to liberate yourself from your own persona and image."

Julia squeezed my arm to remind me she was waiting for an answer. I had not organized my thoughts adequately and panicked. Yes, I panicked and told her: "Because I was born and raised here."

She stopped me, and her face registered her astonishment, which made her even more beautiful. The blue of her eyes penetrated me. "So you're from here. That's gorgeous, splendid!"

As we followed the road back to the village, she asked me many questions. Actually, most follies commence with a slip of the tongue or some other fleeting misstep. Beginning with what I had blurted out, I constructed a life unlike my own. Perhaps it was the life I should have lived. It was a total fabrication, which gave me parents, a home, a herding dog, and many other such things. At the entrance to the village, some curse – I don't know which one – made me say to Julia: "Later I'll tell you about a stranger who left here as a child. People had found him, a baby wrapped in a white cloth after a woman abandoned him here. They named him Udad, and that's a Berber word meaning 'mountain goat'. We grew up together and sat at the same table in school – that's Udad."

* * *

"You're not our son, and that's all there is to the matter."

When Emhannad said this he was holding me in his burnous, which reeked of the tobacco he stayed up late nights processing. I was weeping profusely. Yes, I remember quite clearly how I wept. This may be the first memory I can recall in some detail. Then women's trills sealed our chilly embrace. I didn't grasp the secret reason for those jubilant trills or of the subsequent ones but later deduced that they announced my rebirth. Emhannad, with the members of his family gathered around, continued as if attempting to withdraw the sword he had plunged into me: "Udad, one gloomy morning, the fates drew me to a side road that had never been my preferred route. I found you there, only a few months old, wrapped in a white cloth. You weren't crying then; you were gazing at the sky. I looked in all four directions thinking I might catch a glimpse of the hand that had delivered you to such a destiny – but to no avail. I brought you home. You're one of us – remember that very well – but not of our blood."

This truth was more than the heart of a child who was not yet six could bear; it did, however, let me see the future more clearly and explained many matters that had seemed difficult to understand back then. I had not, for example, understood why I had such a strange name: Udad, or "mountain goat" in the Berber language. I didn't know why children laughed loudly when they stared at me and whispered to one another too softly for me to hear. I had never understood why some people cast me rancorous looks while others gazed at me with enormous compassion. I did grasp, though, that my heart had shattered like a vase that can never be repaired and that it was permanently deformed. Since the moment Emhannad's dry visage confronted me with the truth, I have felt very much alone and defenceless, in a war not of my choosing. I sensed later that the heavens had forced me into this war, not to repay me for my long nights of weeping but, instead, for my mocking guffaws.

Udad – me as a child – matured like a grain of wheat that eventually bursts through the earth's crust, and his questions matured along with him. This was especially true when he saw Emhannad's biological children fly into their mother's embrace after school or enveloped in their father's expansive burnous on cold days when Udad's only solace was provided by tramping through Ighram's fields and watching its wild goats scale the mountain with extreme agility while avoiding the lure of the abyss with extraordinary dexterity.

Pinocchio, who was created by a lonely carpenter to alleviate his solitude, wasn't a normal wooden foundling. Instead, he faced the agonizing question of how to become a real boy. This other more human foundling, Udad, communicated in a language composed of apprehensions and echoes in order to, like the others, alleviate his solitude. Like the others, he loved and wept. Like the others, he ate normal food and walked through the markets. But he lacked a biological sibling. Nature had singled him out and deprived him of many things. Over the decades, these deprivations matured with him and revealed themselves, just as his existence emerged defective from non-existence, when he was asked to offer his pathetic life as the price for this error.

The days that followed the secret's revelation proved an unbearable inferno, thanks especially to my grandmother Umm Emhannad. Ill-health had begun to mangle her, transforming her into a crazy bitch. This ghost-like woman was knocking on the doors of forgetfulness, struggling with its blanking out. I still remember her face, which was almost brown, with its topology of pronounced ridges and deep wrinkles, and her hair that henna had transformed into something resembling the tassel of a maize plant. She hated me, actually despised me. Whenever she had an opportunity, she reminded me I was a bastard and therefore a person with no kin or lineage. I used to wonder how such a shrivelled body, less than an inch from the grave, could hold and retain the amount of rancour and hatred she did.

On a very gloomy day when I shared this black epoch of my life with the psychiatrist Dr Ben-Hashim, while I struggled to restrain the angry tear in my eye, he asked me with all the intrusive malice of shrinks: "Isn't possible that you killed her?"

I remember I laughed, then, with phony bravado; perhaps that tear retreated when I replied: "Frankly – I wish I had, but the fates beat me to it."

I haven't forgotten the day the old woman forced me to contemplate ending the chaos of my life by killing myself. At the age of twelve, this young human goat decided to abandon the life that had abandoned him from the very beginning. One melancholy morning, when her daughter-in-law and all her grandchildren were present, that old woman cast curses on me merely to vent her sadism somewhat, and because I responded to her only with silence. Then she grabbed my long hair that fell in a fringe over my eyes and began to slap my face with her veined hand. I stood there like a peg planted in centre of the house, without resisting at all, because for the first time my heart had filled entirely with sorrow; and no additional worry could flow into it or occupy it; further concerns would necessarily skirt it.

What most devastated my heart that day wasn't what she did to me but the silence of the rest of the family and their collusion with this grandmother. Not one of them lifted a finger or intervened in any way to avert this tragedy. In keeping with their perverted logic, they did not seem to think that anything untoward was happening. They considered themselves neutral observers, even when confronted by a calamity. Perhaps they hated me for my academic success. So long as I live I will never forget the day she dragged me by my hair and her saliva wet my face. The instant I escaped from her grip I slipped quickly to the door, drying my tears and wiping her spit off my face and clothes. It was raining, and normally rain increases sorrow. The sky had finally turned its attention to me and was shedding tears. I wept for a long time as I climbed to the summit of the mountain, ignoring my heart, which was pounding the drums of danger.

The child of twelve stood on the mountain top and thought about ending his life by leaping into the bottomless abyss. At the time, the only name I knew for myself was Udad – which in the Berber language means "wild goat" – and for the first time I realized that the name suited me. I was facing the abyss like a wounded goat, and with only a step or two my body would become airborne. Then I would relieve Ighram of my dissonant presence that threatened the purity of its progeny, and in turn find relief myself.

My clothes, which were soaked from a thunderstorm of rain, squelched loudly, and the urgency of the downpour became more powerful than at any time in the past there, as the portals of Judgement Day opened wide for a child on that rainy day. If I had leaned forward a little, I would have lost my balance and fallen head first. Then my fate would have been quickly sealed. Similarly, a jump on my part would have landed me on my feet or on my back. In either case, my fate would have been decided, too – perhaps even before my body disintegrated like chalk dust down the valley's waterfalls. I don't know precisely how much time passed as I stood there dumbfounded on the balconies of death. In any case, that day my hesitation eroded my resolve to the point that I wished the mountain would swallow me whole, the way the corner of his castle had swallowed the Greek. Then I would be spared the curse of suicide. Later, I wept because my wish to die had weakened. I wept as I had never wept before, convinced that this time I had lost everything.

The fountainhead that had fed my tears ran dry, and my pain lessened a little. I gradually understood that the logic of my circumstances stipulated that I should think differently at exactly the moment I sensed I had suddenly become a man.

As we stood in the middle of one of the mountain gullies, which had swallowed Udad (me) after he (I) returned, vanquished, from the mountain top, I told Julia: "Udad – my childhood friend – tried to kill himself by leaping from the summit but chickened out, changing his mind. He returned, but life, which had treated him unfairly, decided to thread him through the eye of a needle. He was coming down from the mountain when the heavens released their downpour over his small body, and the gullies of Ighram became avenues of sorrow and menace. In order to retrace his steps he was obliged to cross each gully, one by one, till he reached this particular one." I kicked the dry dirt of this gully – not to show it was responsible but to protest the grievous affliction it had subjected me to. Then I flicked the ash from my cigarette and continued, while I watched Julia, who was waiting for my words with obvious interest.

"When the skies of this village trill with woe, all the curses of the heavens and the earth meet in these gullies where water collects gradually. Each small gully empties into the next till all the water ends up in the great valley, where it swallows Ighram's fields and nearby dwellings. As I said, Udad crossed all these small gullies, but when he reached this one here and started to ford it, the water came coursing down, and its swift current swept him off his feet. In just a few moments it had tossed and turned him the way the sea's waves toss and turn a small boat, and dragging him along as if he were a plank of wood. The farther along into the valley he was swept, the stronger and more violent the current became."

Published by Dar al-Adab, Beirut, Lebanon, 2015

RABAI AL-MADHOUN

In Yad Vashem

EXCERPT FROM THE NOVEL

DESTINIES: CONCERTO OF THE HOLOCAUST AND THE NAKBA

TRANSLATED BY PAUL STARKEY

There were four of them, hovering in hope of finding a passenger who'd finished his visit to the museum. They were chattering in Arabic. As I approached them I became their prey, their hoped for passenger, despite the fact that I'd come from the opposite direction —¬ the direction of people making their way to the museum. Two of them got up from their plastic chairs and greeted me with a single question, preceded by two smiles designed to ensnare me:

Wanting a taxi, Hajj?"

I ignored the question, and asked them: "Excuse me ... where is Deir Yassin?"

My question disappointed them. One of them whispered in a disinterested tone, which I heard: 'this guy looks like he's just run away from Deir Yassin and yet he's come to ask about it!'

The same man replied to me: "My friend, you can't see anything from here. The fact is, there's nothing left of it except for a few stones. If you like, I can take you to Gafat Shaul B, just by the Hospital for Psychiatric Disorders – the loony bin, that is, if you'll pardon the expression – which is very near to it." Then he fell silent.

When he received no reply or comment from me, he continued like someone retracting his offer: "Anyway, Deir Yassin is behind the building ... [pointing to the south wing of the museum] in that direction. Go past the building. Stand and look to your right, though you won't see anything. The village is more than three kilometres away."

"OK," I said to myself, "if it's like that, I'll postpone the sightseeing I came for and dreamed about, and wander around for a bit inside the Yad Vashem Museum. That was part of my trip, anyway."

Once again, I wondered about the value of a visit like this. Was I being truthful and convincing when I told Salman, who'd asked me whether I would really be visiting Yad Vashem, that I wanted to explore how the victims I'd be visiting in order to remember them, stood in relation to the victims on the other side? How could one keep the memory of the Nazi destruction alive, for example, by bombing Gaza? And what was the difference between being burned in gas ovens and being burned by Apache rockets? Then again, what had I gained when I gave up counting the number of souvenirs and unusual presents, the smells of herbs and spices, and the smiles of Palestinian peasants decorated with mint and thyme, and came here to count the names of victims whom others had garnered from other worlds, on whom the most hideous crimes had been committed? At the entrance, my speculations fell away from me and I paid them no more attention. I passed a small glass office, where a young man in civilian clothes was sitting, reading a newspaper. He didn't ask me anything and hardly registered my presence as I walked past him. I entered the museum through a long covered corridor, broken up by a sharp corner, to a point where the museum's contents are divided between halls designed in the most beautiful and artistic way. I passed through most of the halls, both big and small, and stopped in front of several tables providing information, either in the form of pamphlets placed on the tables, or else on computers. The Hall of Names made me pause and captured my feelings. I studied the names and examined the features of the victims, who continued to scrutinise me as I looked at their faces and tried to gauge their feelings at the moment the pictures had been taken. Moments that would no longer be there for people who had been reduced to skeletons or whose corpses had disappeared. I lifted my head to follow the features and names upwards until my gaze reached the hall's circular extremity, open to the sky, At that moment, the faces of thousands of Palestinians, some of whom I knew but most of whom I did not, gazed down on me. They were pushing and shoving, as if they wanted to come down into the halls of the museum, spread through them, and take their places as victims. I felt sorrow for those who were ours and those who were theirs, and I cried for those who were crowded together in the sky, looking for a place to assemble their names. I woke from my reverie in the sky, and whispered to myself, as if someone was chiding or punishing me: "In this museum that you are visiting, Walid, in the name of every name in it, a name among you is killed, and sometimes several names. And so that the Nazi holocaust of the Jews should not be repeated, the Israelis, in the name of the holocaust victims, light in our country many fires, which may in the end themselves become a holocaust."

I was silent.

I finally left the main building, preoccupied and dejected. I turned to the right and walked on in the direction the Palestinian driver had shown me. The semi-circular path took me to the back of the building, where I found myself close to a tree-lined strip of ground, no more than a few metres wide, which ran parallel to the building and ended up in some slopes covered in woods, which stretched for a considerable distance, perhaps three kilometres, as the driver had surmised. The whole length of the tree-lined strip had been planted with small signboards. I went up to one of them and started to run my eye over the names of Jews who had been among the victims of the Nazi slaughters. Underneath each name had been written the date of death, though some had no date. There were boards that bore the names of Jewish families that had been exterminated in their entirety. On the opposite side, parallel to the walls of the building at the rear, the victims' names were displayed in a different way. There was a small hut made of stones, with a twisted, roughly circular ceiling, which ended in a circular opening like a large hole. I stood for some minutes inside the hut, contemplating a work of art that aroused in me a mixture of emotions – admiration for the idea, and the suffering that had inspired it. On the walls of the hut, which had no definite shape, identity cards and documents had been scattered. There were also scraps of paper of varying shapes and sizes, with phrases written on them like instructions, and the names of victims, some in handwriting, which grew closer to each other and more tightly packed, the nearer they came to the ceiling. I found myself continuing to read them one by one with a strange curiosity, until finally I was gazing at a distant blue sky whose shape and size were defined by the opening in the ceiling. Artistically, the message had reached me. And as a human being, I understood it. I had to remember these victims, and their last, smuggled words. I asked God to have mercy on them twice: once as victims of the Nazis, and a second time as victims of those who traded on their tragedy.

I turned a little to the right. The scene revealed groups of people waiting in two small queues in front of two iron gates that looked like entrance gates. I went up to a lady with an expression of worried anticipation on her face and asked her in Hebrew: "*Sliha, gvirti,* excuse me, madam, why are these people gathering here?"

She looked at me, astonishment now written all over her face, making me feel that I had come from another age. Despite that, she answered me with a cheerfulness that had neither surprise nor anticipation in it: "They want to visit the other museum, on the other side over there." And she pointed to an area in the distance situated on some mountain slopes whose features were difficult to distinguish. I didn't interrupt her as she explained to me what she meant: "Listen, sir, you're a stranger, in fact it looks as though you must be a complete stranger! These people are waiting their turn to visit the Zikhron ha-Filastinim museum, that's the museum of Palestinian memories. It was built recently following the historic peace agreement that was signed just two years ago between the two peoples of the country, and which ended the bloody struggle that had lasted more than a hundred years. There are brand new electric cable cars like buses – you'll see them when you get nearer, they call them 'tele-buses'." They are each large enough to hold twenty passengers. They carry visitors there along cables that stretch for three kilometres or more, and of course they work in both directions. Isn't that wonderful?"

Before I could reply, a ringtone could be heard from a small device that she was carrying. She apologised to me and looked at the device then started to mutter happily, as if she were addressing me and the device at the same time: "That's my granddaughter Abigail, she's apologising, she was going to come with me on my visit to the other museum but she's changed her mind, she's inside, wandering around with some friends of hers. Perhaps she didn't find the prospect of my company very attractive. She's right – my company is never very amusing for people like her, but it might appeal to you, mightn't it?"

"Appeal to me?" I asked.

"Why not? The electronic ticket's already reserved, anyway ..."

She interrupted herself to stretch out her hand to me with her mobile, saying: "As you can see, there are two sets of numbers, each containing five digits. As soon as you touch one of them, the entrance gate will open for you, and you board the tele-bus. Then the set of numbers disappears from the device and is wiped from its memory ..."

"Perhaps you'd like to accompany me, Mr ..." she continued.

"Walid Dahman," I said, quickly filling the gap, as I welcomed her invitation and thanked her for it. "Tala. Tala Rabinovitch," she responded, introducing herself to me.

We postponed any further conversation and headed for the assembly point, from where we arrived at one of the two doors, which was clearly indeed an entrance door. It was fitted with a small numerical screen. Tala looked at her phone, touched somewhere on the screen, and a green number appeared on the screen opposite. The entrance gate opened and she invited me to go through. I passed through the cross-shaped barrier, which closed behind me, and waited for Tala to pass through. She did the same thing she had done before, the door opened a second time, and she passed through.

So we found ourselves beside some doors that opened electronically just by approaching them. We went through one of them to find ourselves immediately in front of the tele-bus door. A large number of other visitors had already boarded before us. In less than two minutes, the vehicle, which was like a tourist téléférique, had moved off.

The view from above was stunning and took the breath away. As the area opposite slowly drew closer to us, allowing us to look at it closely, Tala explained to me: "Some years ago that" – and she pointed to the far-off spot that we were presumably aiming for – 'that was the Shaul Gafat B settlement. Now we call it 'Ir shel Slihanut, which means the City of Tolerance. No one uses the name of the settlement any more, it reminds us of the period of struggle, which no one wants to remember. Now there are Palestinian Arabs living in the city as well. By the way, Mr Walid, any citizen of the new state can reside anywhere in the country. He is classed as a resident of the city he lives in, though he remains registered on the electoral roll of the region where he was born, or where his name was registered after the general census that was carried out a few months after the two peoples of the country had been unified."

That was extremely interesting. I felt the value of my visit to Yad Vashem. The visitors to the Palestinian museum that we were heading for would doubtless also feel at peace after their visit to Yad Vashem — a peace that would prepare them for their visit to the other museum opposite. "Truly, the rights of the dead victims become equal when the rights of the living are equal," I said to myself.

Then I turned to Tala and said: "At last, this has become a homeland for everyone, hasn't it?"

"Exactly, sir! Albeit with a certain amount of acceptable and welcome differentiation with regard to national rights and the expression of identity with all its subtleties, including language. Arabic has become an official language of the country, and everyone here speaks two languages. We have become Swiss, with two languages, Arabic and Hebrew."

"But you haven't tried speaking Arabic with me!"

"Because I only speak it a little. I'm from a previous generation, from the generation of the struggle, as we're called by those who call themselves the generation of the historic peace agreement – or the "peacemakers", as the intellectuals among them like to call themselves. But if you spoke Arabic to any schoolboy, he would answer in proper Arabic."

The tele-bus approached the terminus then slid smoothly and gracefully onto the ground-level platform inside a clean room that had been built of white Palestinian stone.

We left the platform together and made for a large building containing several wings and offices. It took some time for us to get out. As I walked, I carried with me the question that I had put to the four drivers without receiving any clear answer: "Where is Deir Yassin?" I put the question to Tala, who pursed her lips – lips worn out by several things, not least her love of chatter. But this woman, who had just been speaking to me about a state for all and equal rights, didn't want to talk about the village of Deir Yassin, and gave the impression she had never heard of it. Was it because she belonged to a generation for whom the history of the country began with the proclamation of the establishment of the State of Israel on 15 May 1948, the anniversary of the Palestinian Nakba, and considered anything before that date to be a void, or a "black hole" that gobbled up everything in existence? I turned to Tala and said: "Madam, if you don't understand what happened at Deir Yassin, and remember its lesson well, the "others" won't understand what happened to those victims at Yad Vashem."

At that moment, a woman appeared from behind me, came up to me and asked me with a peasant's stutter: "Do you want Deir Yassin, Hajj?"

"Yes, madam. Do you know where it is?"

"I come from Deir Yassin myself, sir, from the Darwish family. My name is Widad. But my mother is from the Zahran family. Her entire family perished in the massacre. The Jews killed them and piled them up on top of one another, children on top of grown-ups, women on top of the men. There's no trace of Deir Yassin now, not because the Jews destroyed it all that time ago, but because the site has become the Memorial Museum that we're going to now. You'll see it in a minute. I'm excited, I work there!"

We left the "Jewish Station" building. I looked around for Tala. I hadn't heard her voice since the woman from Deir Yassin had appeared, and I couldn't find her. She had disappeared as if she'd passed by in a dream, from which I was woken by Widad's shouting: "Here's the memorial, sir! The museum's behind it. That's the side of it, you can see it from here."

I lifted my head, to be met with a sight that linked earth and sky as this world is linked to the next. I found myself facing a gigantic memorial, whose base covered almost sixteen square metres, and was about a metre and a half high. The memorial itself had been designed in the shape of a four-sided rocket, which grew narrower the higher it went, until it turned into a thin line that disappeared into the sky. Starting from the body of the rocket, a moving beam of light rose up, showing in succession, inside a rectangle of light, the name of a Palestinian martyr, which shone for a few seconds, then moved up, for its place to be taken by another name. And underneath each name appeared the date of birth and date of martyrdom.

I continued to follow the names as they shone and rose upwards. They had been arranged at random, reflecting the wish of the designers that everyone should be equal, with no distinction between those who had been martyred sixty years ago and those who had fallen victim to the latest Israeli raids on Gaza.

The names followed one another, lighting up in my eyes and awakening my memory before ascending: Fatima Jum'a Zahran, Safiyya Jum'a ... Suddenly, Widad shouted out: "These are all my relatives." And she proceeded to repeat the names and to weep: "Fathi Jum'a Zahran, Fathiyya Jum'a, Yusri, Fatima, Samiha, Nazmi ..." and she wept.

Published by Maktabat Kul Shee, Haifa, Israel, 2015

MOHAMED RABIE

Mercury

AN EXCERPT FROM THE NOVEL
TRANSLATED BY ROBIN MOGER

Chapter 4

One evening, I'd received a message informing us that a technician would be coming to produce a mask for each of us. He would be at the tower in no more than two hours. The message requested that we be clean-shaven for the cast to be taken.

At first I didn't understand what was being asked of us. True, we carried out our orders to the letter, as though we were still officers with the Interior Ministry, but what did masks have to do with the task at hand? The whole thing was absurd.

The technician asked me to lie down on the floor and placed two thin tubes in my nostrils. He covered my head, my hair, and my neck, then poured a cold, damp paste over my face, waited a few minutes for the paste to dry, and lifted the mould. Inspecting the inside of the mould, he told me that this wouldn't be the final one, that he would make another mould from which to cast the mask. I was on my way to the bathroom when he asked what design I'd like. "Hold on," I said, "Let me think about it."

We had treated the business with the masks as extra-curricular entertainment – something frivolous but fun. Our unusual situation meant we welcomed any distractions at all, but I was considering motivations greater and more profound than providing distractions to the troops; the leadership had some undeclared objective in all this. I held my counsel and told myself we would find all out soon enough.

When I went back in, the technician had finished making moulds for everybody. They had also chosen faces for their masks. All had gone for comic actors. One had picked Fuad al-Mohandes and had asked for the actor's famous black-framed spectacles to be added as well. As I thought about what I'd like, the face of Buddha floated before my eyes.

If it was a memory, it was a very obscure one. I couldn't recall having seen the face anywhere before. A picture of him in a magazine or newspaper, perhaps? Maybe I'd watched a documentary about him. In my mind, Buddha was associated with wisdom, but really I knew nothing about him. Was he a prophet? A god? Did he worship cows? I had no idea why I asked for a Buddha mask. Later, a few people would come to call me Buddha. For some in the resistance, it became my nom de guerre, but my personality would be more readily associated with mystery than wisdom. Others would assume that by making this choice I thought myself superior to everyone else – to those who chose celebrities for their masks. I later found out that all the snipers received masks made especially for them by professional sculptors, and learned, too, that this was a privilege granted only to the elite – to those who had killed, or were about to kill, large numbers of people.

When the same technician came back to see me, he took the mask from a wooden case and very carefully handed it over. And as I put it on, and felt the touch of cold metal, and discovered that it didn't fit exactly over my features, I asked him what the point had been of making the mould in the first place, and he said that the purpose of the mould hadn't been to capture every detail of my face, but to get a rough idea of my measurements. "This is a mask of solid metal," he said, "an alloy of aluminum and other lightweight compounds. It's inflexible but affords protection for the face against small fragments of shrapnel."

Mask in his hands, he said: "Don't worry, it will never fit your face exactly. It will never become your face." Well, he had been wrong about that.

For several days, I wore it just a few minutes at a time before taking it off, and then the period I spent masked grew. I would go days with it on, would wear it in place of my face, would forget I had a face of flesh and blood. I would gaze into the mirror, unconcerned by the sight of my gleaming, immutable metal reflection – knowing that it wouldn't age, that it was immune to changes in the weather and the aging effect of cigarettes. Taking it off every few days to shave, I would become afraid – so afraid to look at my own face while shaving that I had to ask a colleague to do it for me. I'd tremble when I came to bed. Against my will, I would lay it aside and would feel as though I were standing naked before millions. I would put out the light and, masked, walk over to my little bed, and I would not remove it until I was under the covers. And I would lay it beside my head in readiness for when daylight came. I would put it on the moment I woke. For months on end, I would do this. And then the madness reached its peak, and for a full six weeks I slept with it on.

With time, I came to realize that I wasn't substituting the mask for my face as I had first thought, but putting a barrier between myself and everyone around me, though they were my colleagues and friends, the people I believed in and trusted most of all. Like me, I saw them go into decline, hanging onto their masks, refusing to take them off for extended periods of time. Once his face had become familiar, I wouldn't smile to see Fuad al-Mohandis. I would develop the strangest ideas about the characters around me. Would completely forget all the conventional associations of those laughing, smiling, frowning masks and would forget, too, the original faces. I would create imaginary faces for their bodies, and whenever we received a group of snipers whose true faces I had never seen – just their masks – their actual personalities wouldn't come into it at all: nothing would stick in my mind but details of those borrowed identities. I would reach a point when featureless masks – with no noses, ears, lips, or eyeholes, just a grille of very fine wires that the wearer could see through while his own eyes remained completely ob-scured – would leave me in a state of complete bewilderment. We were breaking down without being aware of it, throwing up barri-ers around us and ensuring they were buttressed and maintained.

It went further. I lost the ability to aim unless I was masked. It happened when I was lining up a target standing by the Maspero building. The officer was waiting for a car to pick him up; it was as rare an opportunity as you could get. According to protocol, I shouldn't have waited or hesitated. We had standing orders to snipe soldiers and officers on sight. I took off the mask to get a clearer look through the scope's narrow, round eyepiece and as I got back into position and searched around for the target I found that he was looking straight at me. The target, at a distance of approximately a kilometre, was staring into my eyes with a defiance that my hands shook to see, and if it hadn't been for the last vestiges of common sense, I would have assumed he was actually looking at me and that he recognized me. I moved back from the eyepiece in a daze and put on my mask, then looked through the scope to find that the man had turned his face away and was looking at the Nile. Much reassured, I took aim again and fired. I didn't kill him because he was an officer of the occupation, but because I was convinced that he had seen me.

After taking out that target, I never again removed the mask while taking aim. The mask had become the secret to my precision, and maybe, without my realizing it, the secret behind the accuracy of the entire Tower Group.

For days and days, I studied East Cairo from behind my mask. I felt no need to hide behind the scope and heavy rifle. I did not give in to curiosity and inspect all the little details that the scope would let me see. Up here I was immune, protected by height, distance, and my mask. I was an ancient Egyptian god with a borrowed face, whose true features no man could ever know, do what he might. A Greek god, full of contempt for the world that he had created – killing whomever he chose, deserting whomever he chose, sleeping with whomever he chose, impregnating whomever he chose. And the day a drone came with a message, telling me that my colleagues and I were now free to select targets and snipe without checking back with the leadership, I felt that my divine status had been confirmed, and I told myself that what was to come would fulfill me utterly.

Now I had the green light, the five battleships became easy pickings: close range, immobile, and, should we so desire, quite sinkable. And that was why we ignored them. Long distance, arbitrary targets in East Cairo were now our main concern, and bulky drones brought us vast quantities of ammunition. We had abandoned our beloved Dragunovs and now relied exclusively on two models: the McMillan Tac-50 and the Barrett M107. We must have poured thousands of half-inch rounds into East Cairo.

I killed the Minister of Foreign Affairs. I received a message telling me his car would pass along the Corniche within the next quarter of an hour and that it would be stopping at some point between the Semiramis and Maspero. On tenterhooks, I tracked the black Mercedes and, as it sped toward the Maspero building and I realised that it was going to go on without pulling over, I had no choice but to fire five rounds into the vehicle. At last, it did stop, but only thanks to my bullets. Nobody got out. I killed the Minister of Information. I was watching the outside of the Maspero building through my scope when he stuck his head out of one of the windows, chattering away on his cell phone. A happy coincidence indeed. I don't think it was more than three seconds between my spotting him and opening fire. I killed what could have been a general from the Fourth Army of the Knights of Malta who drove past in his armored car and got out to inspect a checkpoint. His moustache and eyebrows were what got my attention — the mismatch between his salt and pepper hair and the lone lieutenant's star on his shoulder. I killed him, and I'm still not totally sure whether or not he was a general in disguise. I killed a former colleague, a major in the police, who was sitting on a balcony at the Semiramis. He was dressed in civilian clothes, slumped beneath an umbrella, drinking beer straight from the bottle and smoking. I recognized his face but couldn't remember his name, just that I had graduated a few classes ahead of him, and I supposed that if he was relaxing like that on a hotel balcony he must have done well for himself under the occupation. So I shot him.

One hot, listless day, I aimed my rifle in the general direction of Bulaq Abul-Ela and opened fire at random. Three hundred rounds buried themselves in the district's buildings, and I had no idea if I had killed or injured anybody. Then I turned the gun on Tahrir Square and fired through a gap between the twin wrecks of the Nile Hilton and the Arab League. I hit a large number of cars, and buses, and pedestrians until the square had cleared completely, and then I went on firing into the deserted space until my gun jammed.

I didn't stop to consider what I would say to the leaders of the resistance to justify my actions, or to think about the reprimand I would get. I didn't care about my fellow snipers, standing around unable to understand what I was up to. And when I was done and I turned to face them, I saw only the immobility of their masks, kept on to hide their quaking eyes.

Chapter 5

E verything here was old, and I don't just mean that the furniture and walls had seen twenty years come and go – they were so old and dusty I couldn't tell which era they belonged to. It wouldn't have made much difference if we had met in a tomb.

There were five of us, including the leader of the resistance, Major General Kamal al-Asyuti. I had met him once before, when I'd been an officer at the Interior Ministry and had later learned that he was our leader. He looked thinner than I remembered him. His cheekbones jutted, his front teeth stuck out, and his eyes bulged. White hairs outnumbered the black. Then there was his aide, Brigadier General Suleiman Madi. Him I knew well, and I knew his story. He had been a detective his whole career, had never transferred to another department – the very essence of an officer who dedicates his life to police work and cares for nothing else, not even the standard pastimes of hunting and marksmanship, not even research. Suleiman Madi was a one-dimensional man without dreams, ambitions, or expectations – nothing more or less than a work machine. I had been astonished to hear that he had not carried on as a cop following the occupation and had chosen to join the resistance, evincing a patriotic zeal quite at odds with his character. Then I had started to notice his methodical fingerprints all over the resistance's actions and the violence meted out to the recruits and officers of the Interior Ministry. The last two officers I didn't know, but the presence of the organization's two most powerful figures gave an indication of this meeting's importance.

We stood, since sitting on the filthy chairs was out of the question, and a lamp on the table illuminated the room and cast its light onto us. The meeting, it seemed, was going to be an ordeal for everyone.

Al-Asyuti spoke first. "So, the drone wasn't lost after all," he said, pointing at my shoulder. Suleiman Madi, the aide, looked over at me and nodded: "We dispatched it to inform you about the meeting but it never returned. We assumed it had been broken or stolen, and we weren't sure if the message had reached you or not. Don't ask me why, but it appears to have become quite attached to you."

Was Madi trying to make a fool of me?

"How can a drone disobey its orders and attach itself to someone?" I asked.

"It rarely happens and then we have to reprogram it to factory settings. It'll operate normally after that. Anyway, we have no choice. Drones are scarce these days."

Al-Asyuti looked around, studying our faces. With a sweep of his hand he said: "Everyone's here. Let's begin."

He appeared to be in a considerable hurry, and infirm as well, having trouble holding himself upright. Why I felt sorry for him I don't know. He stared absently at the floor as though searching for something he had misplaced. To us three, Madi said: "We're missing one officer, but his mission is a little different to yours, so we can start without him. In any case, we have absolute faith in you, just as we do in him."

He turned to me.

"Incidentally, he's in charge of the drones. In a few minutes, he'll be here and he'll take that one off your hands."

For a few moments he was silent, gazing at us each in turn, then: "The resistance has tried everything to drive out the occupier. You know what we've done. You have been our long arm in these operations and not one of those many assassinations would have been possible were it not for your skill and bravery. Civilian casualties were unavoidable, and we have never blamed you for them. If anything, perhaps there should have been more. At the end of the day, the occupation is still with us and civilians are going to have to make more sacrifices. Why shouldn't we become that land of five million martyrs?"

Smiles appeared on everyone's faces. Al-Asyuti remained completely silent, completely preoccupied – with us in body, but his mind elsewhere.

Madi went on: "You're the cream of the resistance snipers, and the mission to come will be the hardest any of you have undertaken. By hardest, I don't mean technically difficult; I'm talking about the ethical side of things. Each one of you will have to debate this with yourselves, but I hope you will stay pragmatic and levelheaded. This kind of opportunity doesn't come along that often. We're standing atop a volcano of public rage and we mustn't let the chance slip."

Public rage? Where? I hadn't noticed any in the last few hours. There wasn't any rage out there at all.

Published by Dar Tanweer, Beirut, Lebanon, 2014

MAHMOUD SHUKAIR

Praise for the Women of the Family

A CHAPTER FROM THE NOVEL

TRANSLATED BY JONATHAN WRIGHT

I had to call off the trip. Sana grumbled then lapsed into silence, as she usually did when anything took her by surprise. She started to busy herself inspecting the clothes she had packed in the suitcase. She took them out of the suitcase and put them back in the wardrobe. With a mixture of sadness and a sense of loss she looked at the swimming costume I had bought her a few days earlier.

When we had made a trip to the Dead Sea together, I had worn my swimming trunks and swam in the water. Sana had her own private ritual: she took off her shoes and held her dress up above her knees. The water washed over her legs and made the hem of her dress wet. When the women of the family gathered together one evening she told them what she had done, as evidence that she didn't observe the code of modesty. I sympathised with her and she sympathised with me because I had to carry the weight of the family on my shoulders, the burden that my father had entrusted to me. For some time Sana and I had been looking forward to taking a break from the family and its worries.

I am Muhammad bin Mannan al-Abdallat, known as Muhammad the Youngest, to distinguish me from two brothers to whom my father gave the same name in honour of his own father, Sheikh Muhammad, who was a man of considerable importance in the desert. The other brothers, known as Muhammad the Elder and Muhammad the Younger, went in opposite directions, and my father took an aggrieved attitude towards them. On numerous occasions he told his sons openly that he placed his confidence in me and held out hope that I would reunite the family, protect the women of the family from harm (what had happened to my sister Falha and the worry that caused my father had been quite enough), and perform glorious feats that would exalt the name of the Abdallat tribe, which had expanded and branched out and now had members scattered everywhere.

When I told him I was going to marry a divorced woman who was three years older than me, he looked at me and said: "You're joking of course." "Not at all," I said, "I'm not joking." He saw this decision of mine as a severe reversal. He almost lost confidence in me and put me in the same category as my brothers, Muhammad the Elder, Muhammad the Younger and Fuleihan, who had himself committed many grave offences. It was then 1962. He was still giving me one piece of advice after another and assuring me I could choose a beautiful virgin from among the girls of Ras al-Naba or from one of the villages around Jerusalem, but I wasn't persuaded.

Sana came to our house and behaved decorously and with poise and spoke unpretentiously. I had told my father that her ex-husband was her cousin and fifteen years older than her. They had lived together for three years but she couldn't put up with the way he only thought about his business. She took a dislike to him and they agreed to divorce. They went to court and stood in front of the judge, and I was taking the minutes for the session. Sana stole my heart from the first moment.

My mother said she was a woman worthy of praise. She and her parents spent the whole day in Ras al-Naba. After Sana left my, father told me: "It's with God's blessing."

That was twenty years ago. Now I'm 42. I've been through many troubles, most importantly family troubles but also Sana's problem. In a way the two are related. This trip we had planned was part of a ritual we had adopted to give Sana some relief from family pressures. There was nothing she could do about her problem but as a result of it she suffered in a way that flared up from time to time and then died down. Every now and then she would suggest we separate but I would never agree to a separation because I loved her and because my work in the sharia courts made me reluctant to go through with a divorce, since in most cases divorces were unfavourable to the wives.

I worked in the sharia court in Jerusalem. I got a job there in 1958. It wasn't a very important job but for some time my relatives believed I was an important official because they saw me in my dark blue suit with a blue tie and a white shirt, and carrying a black briefcase, in which I put papers and files, and I believed them. I thought I was a civil servant of significance, although in the civil service hierarchy I only counted as junior. My self-confidence increased and I thought I could please my father by fulfilling his wish that I bring the family together.

Muhammad the Younger was always competing with Muhammad the Elder for influence over me, to determine my course in life. They each tried to persuade me of their own intellectual convictions. I was cautious and not enthusiastic about tying my fate to convictions that might prevent me from considering all possible options or that might burden me with responsibilities that would be too onerous. Before I got the job Muhammad the Younger told my father he knew the director of the religious institute in Jerusalem and the director would be willing to accept me for training as an imam who would lead people in prayer on Temple Mount (Haram al-Sharif). I hadn't thought of becoming a sheikh in a turban, although I was religious by nature, and I wasn't enthusiastic about my brother's suggestion, and neither was my father.

My father wanted to arrange a job that would earn me some money, a part of which would go to him, because he was no longer confident he could depend on his flocks after investing his money in land he had bought here and there, and he didn't want to receive any money from my brother Fuleihan, because it was tainted money

* * *

I'm Fuleihan bin Mannan al-Abdallat. My father called me Fulei-
han in memory of my uncle Fuleihan, who was killed in one of
the wars of the Ottoman Empire. My brother Muhammad the
Youngest thought that I was the obstacle to the mission my father
had assigned him. I don't know whether he still insists on believing
this.

He told me he had cancelled the trip to Beirut. "I expected that,"
I said. I had had the radio glued to my ear since the morning. Lis-
tening to the radio at certain times of day has become one of my
few habitual pleasures. At night, I spend two or three hours watch-
ing television programmes, such as the news bulletins, light enter-
tainment and popular music with songs sung by beautiful women.

I love women singing. That might be the source of the disorder I
suffer from, and of the complications that made my brother Muham-
mad the Youngest see me as an obstacle. When the famous Lebanese
singer Samira Tawfiq appeared on the screen I was rapt. I looked at
the mole on her left cheek as she swayed back and forth, so com-
posed and so upright, singing, "You with the white kuffieh, what
can I say? My heart burns for you, and what does your heart make
of me?" Whenever I hear the song it takes me back to earlier years,
and I remember the time when I was at peak strength and in my
prime, and during the song I would get angry if Rasmiya made any
noise in the kitchen. I would shout, "I don't want to hear a sound."
Samira Tawfiq's singing would bring me raptures of delight. I re-
member how I used to listen to her voice coming to me from the
radio and how I enjoyed imagining I was meeting her to tell her how
much I admired her. I used to see pictures of her in Achabaka mag-
azine, where I followed celebrity singers and musicians.

All that was in the past, before I ended up in this state, though it
still recurs whenever I see Samira Tawfiq on television. I remember
how much I wanted to meet her, and I go back to daydreaming about
her and enjoying everything about her. Then I wake up to the real
world around me and find that my only consolation is Rasmiya, who
complies with my desires. Rasmiya is no longer young, but although
she's in her fifties she still has enough feminity to please me when-
ever I look at her body and hug her. She sleeps by my side as if she
were still in her twenties, and although I'm no longer capable of

performing, I can give her pleasure and I can tell that she has enjoyed it. In the meantime we go over all the moments of companionship and all the things we have discovered together. I fell in love with Rasmiya when she was engaged to her cousin. She wasn't in love with him but she agreed to the engagement to please her parents. I'll never forget the ordeal I endured because of my love for her.

Now I sit in my wheelchair in the yard and see al-Awda camp nestled on the plain under the June sun. I'm following news of the war on Lebanon, the war that disrupted the trip that my brother Mohammad the Youngest and his wife Sana planned to make.

Rasmiya is standing close to me after finishing sweeping the yard with a broom and sprinkling the courtyard with a little water to keep down the dust and for relief from the summer heat. She leans her arm on my shoulder. I love it when she stands so close to me. She listens to the radio and seems anxious as she lifts the hem of her dress on both sides and tucks it into the waistband of her underwear. The whiteness of her legs shows beneath her dress because she no longer wears those long drawers. But she doesn't stay near me for long, so I'm always reluctant to let her go and I'm impatient for her return. She's energetic, flitting from place to place like a butterfly. She disappears inside for a while, then comes back carrying morning coffee for the two of us, with a deep sadness in her eyes. She says to me: "Tell me anything new, Fuleihan," and I say, "There's nothing new but the constant bombing and the bloodshed, Rasmiya." We drink the coffee, anxious in a way we have often started to feel.

When I stole her from her fiancé I didn't realise how outrageously I had acted. I was carried away in a moment of folly and curiosity. It got out of hand because Rasmiya took a liking to me. I didn't intend to offend her relatives, who had been forced to leave their homes in the village of al-Wasmiya. They came to this place close to Jerusalem. For weeks they slept under the trees until some tents arrived. It never occurred to me that I would see Rasmiya or that I would be attracted to her. I came with my first wife and my family and my clan from the desert. I was on good terms with my wife, and it never occurred to me that I would marry a second wife. My mother Mathila had suffered from second wives because of my father's polygamous inclinations. But Rasmiya upset my calculations and took me in a direction I had never imagined.

Although I had enough education to qualify to work as a clerk in a road-building operation or with some other company I never lost my desire to herd sheep and goats. With livestock I could see nature at work, producing the pasturage that I awaited impatiently every year. From the flock I obtained my livelihood and the animals gave my life some meaning, although I later found several other ways of making a living. I accumulated greater wealth than any of my brothers or other members of the al-Abdallat clan. It was herding livestock that brought me to Rasmiya or maybe it was what made her appear in my life. But now I can't get up from this wheelchair, and the reason for that is that Sarhan, Rasmiya's cousin, tried to kill me years after what happened. Sarhan said nothing until the right moment came but when he joined the resistance he remembered the offence I had caused him. He shot me but didn't kill me. My legs were incapacitated after the bullet lodged in my pelvis, and something of mine more important than my legs was also incapacitated.

Rasmiya first caught my attention when she used to come to the foot of the hill. I discovered she had been displaced from her home and from the place where she was born and where she had lived till she came of age. She had also been taken out of the school where she was having lessons and had been forced to leave the village and the trees and water that were there, and the fields and plains and hills around it, to come here under duress to live in a camp with tents that were so disconcertingly close together that there was no privacy and a safe, decent life wasn't possible. I would watch her from a distance and feel sorry for her and I could see how cruel fate had been to her and her family. I started to sympathise with her and then I began to see her as a soulmate.

At first I didn't distinguish her from other women. I saw many girls that looked like a flock of goats, wearing faded clothes and shabby old shoes on their feet. They lifted up the hems of their dresses on both sides and tucked them into the cloth belts they wore round their waists. Then you could see the long drawers they wore underneath – drawers of a kind that our women in Ras al-Naba no longer wore and wouldn't dream of wearing. When I saw those drawers for the first time on the girls in the camp, I took a dislike to them. Why did they need to wear such things?

I saw them at the foot of the hill that skirted our land in the springtime when they were picking mallow and thyme and other herbs that were good to cook in times of hunger. I saw them in summer at the foot of the hill when they were gathering firewood, and I wondered what was behind the disaster that had forced the people to leave their houses and fields and orange groves.

She would come to the foot of the hill and I could see the lower part of her drawers, which were made of cheap cloth. I no longer felt any aversion to her when she was wearing drawers, unlike earlier. Her drawers acted on me like a challenge: they were so determined to stop me seeing her legs that I felt an even stronger urge to take them off and discover the good things they were hiding.

I approached her one morning and didn't expect her to avoid me. But she did and I realised that she wasn't thinking about me and was paying me no attention. She was busy picking mallow at the foot of the hill and she seemed to be avoiding me, although her pert breasts under her dress posed an unexpected dilemma for me. I saw her long drawers and had an overwhelming desire to find out what they were covering. I felt a fever course through my body. I called her and said, "Hey, you girl, what's your name?"

"Why do you ask?"

"Do you trust what I say?"

She hesitated a moment before answering my question. "What do you mean by that?" she said.

"I'm sitting on a rock and you're sitting on a rock."

I don't know why I brought up this Bedouin ritual. In the desert, it was the custom for a prospective husband to propose in this simple way in the open air but we abandoned that practice after we began to rely on written marriage contracts. She thought about what I meant and didn't seem to understand my intent. When she saw the desire in my eyes, she moved away saying, "No, I don't want to."

I let her walk away but I could no longer forget her. Whenever I saw her my blood seethed with passion for her. I used all possible methods of getting close to her. I would stand not far from her, take my reed flute out from under my belt and proceed to play it. I played dance tunes and sad tunes. I played the tune of the song "Ala dalouna, ala dalouna, our loved ones have gone and didn't say farewell", and all the while I couldn't take my eyes off her as she continued to pick mallow and other herbs. She was listening to the tunes I played although she pretended that she wasn't.

Published by Hachette Antoine, Beirut, Lebanon, 2015

SHAHLA UJAYLI

A Sky Close to our House

A CHAPTER FROM THE NOVEL

TRANSLATED BY NANCY ROBERTS

I sat down in the transit lounge to wait my turn to go to my gate for boarding. I began watching the airport employees and travelers on the other side of the glass as they came and went nonstop. I love watching people in airports. It's as if, being beyond the gravitational pull of their usual surroundings, they're more spontaneous and natural than they would be otherwise – in a temporary state of liberation. An airport is a place where most people are getting ready for a new story of sorts, although we Syrians have our own kind of story to tell in this connection. The minute we get through the passport clearance section, we feel as though we've been given a new lease on life, a birth certificate announcing that we aren't wanted by any national or international security apparatus. If you're a Syrian who's done any traveling, it's an experience you can relate to even if you've never said a word about politics in your entire life, since you're always sure you'll end up having a run-in with the authorities for some reason or another, even if just because they confused your name with somebody else's!

An official at the gate announced that boarding had begun, so I got up and went to stand with four others in the line designated for first-class passengers. As the line inched forward, I found myself moving to the quiet rhythm of the steps of the man in front of me. After our passports had been checked, I noticed a look of exhaustion and resignation on his face. With a fair complexion and light hair, he looked to be around fifty. He was of medium to slender build, and had an unaffected elegance about him. He was wearing blue jeans, a black shirt, and black running shoes without laces.

By the time I got to my seat, he was already sitting in the one next to me.

I wasn't in the mood to socialize. I was too full of memories of the sweet times I'd spent in Tunisia, where I'd managed to see all the people in the world whose company I most enjoy. We'd been to attend the Conference on Arab Youth and Cultural Development in the coastal city of Gabès, where we had spent evenings filled with laughter that I'd been sorely in need of after months of misery that had felt like years. It was the first conference I had attended since fleeing the unrest in Syria and the war brewing there.

My traveling companion received me with what seemed like the quiet enthusiasm of someone who knew me already and had something to tell me. A few minutes went by as we got ourselves settled and ready for take-off, each of us on his or her own island. Then came time for lift-off, the moment of anxiety that we all experience no matter how seasoned a globetrotter we have become. It was the moment that brings people closer. He turned to me and, after scrutinizing my features two or three times, blurted out: "My mother died today, and I'm going to bury her."

Not knowing what else to do, I squeezed his hand, and kept hold of it for almost the entire flight. I wanted the lifeblood of tender sympathy to make its way from my hand to his, from my heart to his. I wished I could hold him in my arms, but we can't necessarily do everything we'd like to!

After I'd let go of his hand, he introduced himself, saying: "My name is Nasser Amiri. I'm an international consultant on climate and drought."

Hmmm …, I thought, and what do I know about things like that? All I know about geography could be summed up in something Edward Said wrote to the effect that geography was our first enemy.

What helped me ease into his world at that moment was the fact that several months earlier, I had attended a conference at the Jordanian Society for Scientific Research that had addressed a variety of topics, including health sciences, the economy, education, and others.

Life coaches sometimes encourage us to do as many random things as possible. We should attend conferences nobody else would attend, read books nobody else would read, talk to people nobody else talks to, and trust in the possibilities of chance. That's why I'd decided to attend the sessions on climate change while everybody else was attending the ones on the economy and education. The first lecture was given by an Indian professor by the name of Mannava Sivakumar. After hearing him speak, I decided to attend all the other presentations as well, which went from ten in the morning till four in the afternoon. I was especially impressed by Dr Sivakumar's paper on the little offenses we commit every day against the environment without realising it until, over time, their cumulative effects end in natural disasters. We sat together at lunch and talked, and he expressed surprise that I was attending sessions so far from my field of specialization.

The following afternoon I passed by his hotel and took him on a tour of Old Amman, including the city centre and the Roman Amphitheatre. I treated him to knafah from Habibah, a famous local confectionery, and we had coffee on the balcony of Café Jafra surrounded by quaint old shops. Sivakumar talked to me about how solutions to the problems of climate change start not with his specialization, but with mine – which is to say: they start with culture, not with geography or meteorology. They start by changing people's ways of thinking about how to relate to the world and its resources, not by sending coded messages to the clouds, the winds, and the waves.

So, then, the enlightening days I had spent at the Jordanian Society for Scientific Research talking to a world-renowned climate expert had been a training course from Destiny that would help me decipher Dr Nasser Amiri's personal map!

* * *

The airplane that had brought us together touched down at the Queen Alia International Airport. During the flight from Istanbul to Amman, our conversations had ranged from the general to the personal. I learned that Nasser had studied at the University of California at Santa Barbara, that he had been married to an American woman, from whom he was now divorced, and had three children – two boys in college, and a daughter who had been living with her grandmother in Amman. He told me his mother had been Syrian, describing her with the word "Shamiyah" after the manner of Jordanians and Palestinians, who refer to Syrians as "Shawamm". She belonged to the Haffar family, well known in the city of Aleppo. He went on to tell me he was working at the Center for Arid Land De-velopment in Dubai. As he related these details, my mind wandered to his daughter. What would happen to her now that her grand-mother was gone? My heart went out to her.

I snapped out of my sympathetic reverie as I realized that Nasser was asking me a question.

"Are you divorced, too?"

Strange! I thought. Is that the impression I give? On the other hand, I reasoned, maybe it was just a wishful thought that had sur-faced in my traveling companion's mind. His question served as a map legend, if I might borrow a term from the field of geography. It was a small enough question in and of itself. However, it was the kind that reveals the true size of the space I had come to occupy in another person's mind.

I wanted to be as brief and straightforward as I could – to open the door between us to the extent that would be appropriate for mature adults with a proper estimation of themselves and others, and who strive for relationships that go deep enough to endure.

"My name is Juman Badran. I'm a Syrian living in Amman, I have a PhD in Cultural Anthropology, and I'm working with the Nether-lands-based Solidarity Foundation. I'm not divorced – actually, I've never been married. Five years ago I went through the kind of loss you've just experienced yourself, and it was excruciating! It's the kind of thing that seeps deep inside you and leaves a dark spot on your heart that nothing will ever be able to erase. It becomes a part of who you are from then on. It colors the way you look at things – even the way you walk! You might be able to hide it from other people, of course. But it stays there as a sign that you've lived, and that you know what it means to suffer."

At this point I shut myself up lest my friendly contribution turn into a sermon. As a matter of fact, people who've been through painful experiences are fond of comforting others. They talk about the things they've been through as a heartfelt humanitarian offering, and they do it with a healthy dose of pride tinged with amazement at their own maturity, at the riches they've gained through suffering and – even more – at the courage it took them to get through the ordeal. I have to confess, I was pleased with the last thing I'd said to him, since it made clear that my having held his hand for such a long time hadn't been random or meaningless, but an expression of genuine empathy.

Before we began making our separate ways through the crowd of fellow travelers, Nasser asked for my telephone number. Grief-stricken though he was, he was still engaged with his surroundings. He gave me a missed call right away, and on the screen there appeared the number that would become the one indispensible thing in my life in the days to come.

* * *

Ten days passed, in the course of which I worked like mad, trying to recover the sense of self that had been obliterated by the war in my country. I immersed myself in data, statistics, and stories of women who had been forced by the violence to flee their homes and homelands. I had been one of them myself just a few months earlier. My sisters Salma and Joud were still in Syria, and whenever thoughts of them intruded into my consciousness, I would get depressed all over again. I knew I wasn't where I was to offer anything to anybody else but, rather, to flee the war. In Aleppo where I had been working, they had begun targeting academics. Dr Muhammad, a history professor who had been my colleague and office mate in the Faculty of Humanities, had been hit by sniper fire on his way from the university to his house in the Bustan al-Qasr neighborhood.

Among a number of contradictions in my head was that alongside a sense of how lucky I was to have found a safe haven and rewarding work, I also felt defeated, and miserably guilty for having left Dad and my two sisters in a war zone. When Nasser's face hovered in my consciousness, peering at me with those deep, gentle eyes, a happy feeling would come over me and I would let myself break into a huge grin, hoping it would wash away the sorrow I was carrying around on the inside.

Nasser called, as I had expected him to, after the initial wave of grief had passed, leaving behind the sweetness of the solace I had managed to pass on to him during his first hours of loss. He had called looking for another type of solace, one I knew only too well. What he needed now was to talk.

We arranged to meet that evening at the Blue Fig in Abdoun. My relationship with places in Amman was still limited and awkward. In Aleppo, by contrast, I'd had a special haunt of my own, a place

where I would always be at certain times. I had a table that was re-
served specially for me, all the employees knew me by name, and
they used to give me and my guests special treatment. They knew
what I liked and what I didn't like. They even knew when I wanted
to write and when I wanted to spend time with friends.

Nothing – not even a restaurant in the Ritz, a coffee shop on the
Champs Élysées, or a pavement cafe in Prague – could have equalled
a session on the terrace of the Baron Hotel – a diminutive building
in the heart of Aleppo, located on the street to which it bequeathed
its name in 1946 in recognition of the nationalist role the hotel had
played during the period of French colonialism. Up until that time,
the street had borne the name of Henri Gouraud, the French com-
mander who had entered Damascus after the Battle of Maysalun
and, with a contemptuous kick of a certain Muslim warrior's tomb,
uttered his infamous words, "Wake up, Saladin. We're back!" When
the Baron Hotel was built in 1906, it consisted of 31 bedrooms and
two bathrooms, after which the Mazloumian Brothers added on a
third storey that featured a separate bathroom for each of its sev-
enteen rooms.

To the east of the hotel lies the renowned Aziziyeh neighbour-
hood, home to a large Christian bourgeoisie, whose sidewalks are
dotted with elegant cafes – Wanis, al-Shallal, and Cordoba. The
restaurants are fronted by lush hedges and flowers that were planted
in the bed of what was once the Queiq River, which was filled in
after a proliferation of flies threatened to cause an outbreak of leish-
maniasis disease. These restaurants were once gathering places for
artists, writers, businessmen, and statesmen who spent their
evenings listening to music performed by unnamed Armenian bands
which, obscure though they were, had a knack for creating nostalgia
for the 1940s and 1950s, when it was popular in Aleppo to dance
to the strains of tango and waltz music.

Next to the Baron Hotel looms the Bab al-Faraj Clock Tower,
which marks the site of one of the city's historic gates. It's so fa-
mous, it's said that unless you've seen Bab al-Faraj, you haven't seen
Aleppo – even though the city has six other surviving gates. The
clock tower is located near the National Library, a place of pilgrim-
age for lovers of reading, research, theatre and the arts. Between
the hotel and Bab al-Faraj Square run narrow parallel streets in the
area known as Bustan Kullab, or, as the locals say it, Bustan Kullayb,

which is full of shops that sell used car parts and agricultural equipment, as well as cheap hotels like the Suez Canal Hotel, the Unity Hotel, and the Syria and Lebanon Hotel, which have just one bathroom for every four or five rooms. You find restaurants there that serve Armenian kebab and kofta, and nightclubs like the Moulin Rouge and the Crazy Horse, whose pavements are populated by women wearing headscarves and face veils side by side with airline stewardesses, while inside the clubs you'll find many Russian and Ukrainian women employees along with a few local hookers.

If you sit on the hotel terrace and look across the street, you'll see the local branch of the Arab Writers' Union, whose aging building hosts lectures and literary evenings that used to rescue us from the tedium of academia and from the dead silence of long winter evenings spent with our noses in books. On the next street along is al-Kindi Cinema, its entrance plastered with salacious advertisements for old movies that were box-office flops. In front of the posters stand mesmerized teenagers devouring falafel sandwiches, their eyes fixed on the tantalizing pictures of naked women. Most likely, however, they'll continue on their way to the other old buildings that line the street, or head for al-Quwatli Street's clothing and shoe stores that are always having sales of locally made merchandise or low-priced, mediocre goods made in China.

Cinemas like al-Kindi suffer no lack of patrons no matter what kind of films they show. Their clientele consists mainly of couples – teens, pre-teens, and a few college students who have despaired of finding a place to be alone together. Once they're inside, the theatre attendant lights the way to the seats at the back with his little flashlight. Then he looks the other way while, safely ensconced in darkness, they proceed to ignore the film, which they've already seen a million times, for some amorous smooching and quick sex. Not one of them, of course, has ever given a thought to how al-Kindi Cinema and al-Quwatli Street got their names. And the phenomenon repeats itself in nearly every city in Syria!

Published by Difaf Publications, Beirut, Lebanon, 2015

GEORGE YARAQ

Guard of the Dead

EXCERPT FROM THE NOVEL

TRANSLATED BY RAPHAEL COHEN

I contemplated the corpses that nobody had claimed; they were starting to turn blue. I was used to the way they looked, their faces and clothing, the pose their stiffening bodies assumed. A vague bond grew between me and them.

I memorized the features of every corpse, despite the hourly changes they underwent. Features brimming with health and toned with life faded into a blue-stained yellow, a mixture that stood for death. I hated the colour blue, the first sign that the body had started to decay and decompose. On clear days, I often avoided looking at the sky to stop the blueness reminding me of the blueness of death.

I was sad about the corpses when I knew the story of their death.

Their memory roiled through me. The smell of bread, ink, or chalk, or of sweat from toiling in a factory or restaurant, clung to their souls and bodies. The cake seller, the oven hand, the lad on the school bus, the tramp, the wretched scavenger in the rubbish tip; the corpses of those, and those like them, pained my heart and shook my faith in God.

Wasn't the daily grind to find something to eat enough?

What had they done to deserve to die like that?

They were accidental victims, and we, who still enjoyed the breeze, the sunshine, and a few pleasures, were the accidentally alive.

Corpses that showed signs of an easy life did not evoke the same sympathy as the corpses of the poor and ordinary.

It was something involuntary.

I often derided a corpse whose person was dressed in a jacket and tie and still reeked of perfume. An elegantly dressed corpse seemed to put the others down, or at least I thought so. Other corpses I thought humble in comparison. I would lift the leg of the chewing-gum seller and place it on the chest of an elegant corpse, or do something else to redress the balance of justice.

I could not be impartial, even though it was against hospital rules.

I was biased towards the corpses of the wretched, those whom fate had oppressed and turned into humiliated beings living on the breadline. I was biased towards them because I was one of them. I felt we had many things in common, and I tried to make their corpses comfortable in this place where I was in charge.

Sometimes, I would delay the turn of a corpse whose time had come to be shrouded on the refrigerator slab, jumping the queue with a corpse that had come in later, because the second corpse was someone poor and oppressed while the first was someone well off. I did not have any guilt complex about it.

I did what I did with an easy conscience.

A good many of the corpses I did not handle the way the living should treat the dead, or in the way someone with my job was supposed to behave. Many times I spoke to a dead person and revealed my innermost thoughts.

It is not true that people die when their heart stops beating and the brain stops functioning.

I often felt I was not alone in the morgue, although there was no one there.

I felt the place was full, its cramped space almost bursting, especially when it was quiet.

The quiet freed the souls from their bodies and they hovered around them.

I listened to breathing fraught with strangled words in voices that wanted to say something but did not speak.

I was not imagining it.

To begin with, I convinced myself that what I heard was a total illusion, or just voices in my head.

I did not dare say anything about it.

I was afraid people would say I was a bit mad, or that I conjured up spirits and communicated with demons.

Now, I am certain that what I heard, and still hear, was not a figment of my imagination or a result of the films I had seen. I rarely watched the television here at the hospital, and what I watched at the house had nothing to do with horror. I only went to the cinema to see porn films, a double bill on continuous play.

I often deliberately went down to the morgue at the end of the evening. Patients' family and visitors would have left the hospital, emergencies would have calmed down, and this calmness had a mysterious effect.

I visited the morgue to listen to the buzz of the quiet. Often, when I saw the bodies discharging water and disgusting fluids, I wondered whether the mind like the body discharged its fears, its secrets, and its memories. It discharged them as whisperings embraced and circulated by the silence.

I was certain about it. I was hearing the discharging of souls and minds, not something carried on the wind, as some people liked to say commenting on such a situation.

Minds and souls emptied themselves so they could ascend to Heaven free of earthly cares.

When I reflected on the state of the corpses, I went beyond the bounds of logic, and imagined minds and souls at the moment of death ejecting their contents and secrets, in the way that a typewriter ejects the sheet of paper once the words have been typed. The contents and the secrets were written on sequential sheets coming out of the earholes, or the mouth, being a larger orifice. Papers to be cherished by the closest person to the departed, even though he, or anyone else, would never read them unless the deceased left instructions in a will to go through them and sort them out because of their public utility.

It was an injustice against humanity for the contents of the mind and the secrets of the soul to die with the death of the body. Assuming this plan could be put into practice, who knows what riches would fill human history and the numerous achievements that the distant future would see.

All the scientists who died, taking their theories with them.

All the poets who passed away with dozens of poems they had no chance to write down.

All the lovers who met their Maker with so many words in their hearts to their lovers unsaid.

All the mothers taken by illness, whose maternal love was still fertile and who could fill the world with tenderness.

These and other thoughts assailed me in the morgue, and kept me company.

I had not previously been enamoured of philosophical contemplation. All my life I disliked the dryness of philosophy and had no sympathy with its proponents. Our philosophy teacher at school who, in our final year drummed the theories of Socrates, Plato, Aristotle, Ibn Sina, al-Farabi, and so on into us, was fun. He often made jokes about philosophers, ancient and modern, to attract our adolescent minds, but we listened to the jokes, not the lesson. For us, the sum of philosophy lay in a smile from the girl next door, and in the shiver that went through us at a glance from a student at the girls' high school.

In the morgue I found myself philosophising.

The daily confrontation with death spurred me to think.

I did not say a word to anyone about my musings.

They were reflections that appeared and disappeared of their own accord. In the gap between their appearance and their disappearance, my soul would soar above their entanglements into the riddles of existence.

When he heard me talking about the murmurings of souls and stifled voices, Abu Moussa said he was worried about me, and advised me not to stay too long in the morgue after my shift.

Andretti did not comment.

Ghobbas, who never smiled even when tickled, laughed a lot.

Since then, I have kept my thoughts to myself, which has deepened my love for solitude. The morgue became the only place I felt warm and safe. The dead became the companions of my solitude. They listened to my ideas in their profound silence. I did not speak to them or express my fears out loud, but they heard me.

I felt that my words settled in their souls that had yet to separate from their bodies, or had separated but were still hovering close to them. These feelings made my isolation open to the world, as though these corpses were just windows for me to look out of and see Heaven.

* * *

I did not seek a new way of making money after they changed the lock on the drawer and I lost the income from the gas and oxygen cylinders, but once again luck compensated me, taking away with one hand and giving with the other.

I was shaving the chin of the corpse of a man in his sixties. Two of his relatives were waiting for me to finish, to collect the body.

I do not know why, but I opened his mouth, which had not yet stiffened shut, and saw three gold teeth inside. I had the idea of pulling them out, keeping them, and then selling them. I tried and failed to pull out the first tooth. There was not enough time to fetch something metal to use to pry it out – the two men waiting outside were impatient, and my absence, even for a few minutes, was not on.

I took my watch off my wrist and with the prong on the strap I worked away at the tooth until it came out. In the same way, I took out the other two teeth, and then hid them all in the pocket of my apron. To ensure nobody discovered what I had done, I bound the corpse's head vertically and horizontally with a length of gauze so that the mouth could only be opened if absolutely necessary. We often used that trick when the jaws could not be shut with the usual adhesive.

At the end of my shift, I went up to the room and took the gold crowns off the teeth. I wrapped them in the corner of a blanket, and stamped on them a few times with my heel to change their shape.

I went to an Armenian goldsmith. When he saw the three pieces of gold, he said the gold was high quality and used to make dental crowns. I was taken aback, and nearly picked up the pieces and left. Perhaps he knew where I had brought them from, and wanted to scare me into selling them cheap. I avoided asking him the questions his deduction had prompted.

Staring at them and turning them over in his fingers, he said he would pay thirty liras, that was ten lira a tooth. I told him I just wanted a valuation and did not want to sell.

I did not sell them, not because of the price, but because I wanted to show them to other jewellers, one of whom might pay more. I wrapped the crowns in a piece of paper and hid the paper in a sock bag. I decided to sell them once I had amassed ten. Over the following days, I opened the mouth of each corpse while I was preparing it. I learned that people over forty tended to have their teeth capped in gold so as not to lose them.

I did not come across a gold-capped tooth in the mouth of anyone younger than that, so my interest focused on the elderly.

From time to time, however, I would inspect the mouth of a young person's corpse to silence any doubts I had that I might find what I was looking for. More than once I got lucky, and that persuaded me not to exclude any corpse, as long as the effort cost me nothing. As I washed a corpse, I would open the mouth and inspect the upper and lower jaw. If I spotted a crown, I took a sharp implement like a knife blade without a point and prized it out.

The extraction only took a few seconds.

With the fingers of my left hand I stopped the jaws from closing, and with my right hand I worked at the cap with the instrument.

Very often, when the crown was well implanted, the extraction took longer, and I had to stick the blade right into the gum to lever out the crown. There was no worry about bleeding, however deep the gash. The dead do not bleed when cut, just a little water comes out. The blood coagulates in the veins once the heart stops pumping.

Gently and slowly, I would apply myself to a difficult case, so as not to repeat an earlier mistake.

That day, an upper wisdom tooth fell right out as a result of decay to the jaw from neglect and age. As soon as I applied pressure on the crown with the blade, the tooth fell out. I hid it straightaway in my trouser pocket and then went to the bathroom where I removed the crown and threw the tooth down the toilet.

I had done it as quickly as possible.

I was afraid Robert would see me and set his sights on a money-spinner that I still could not believe he had not worked out.

Barely a day went by without my bagging a crown, sometimes more. Whenever I had enough to justify action, I would go to a goldsmith I had befriended and become used to dealing with. To avoid his becoming too suspicious, I amended my story and did not deny that the bits of gold came out of people's mouths. Not, of course, the mouths of the dead, but the living.

I told him my uncle was a dentist, who kept the gold crowns he extracted in a box dedicated to the purpose. When there was a sufficient number, he would call me, and I would sell them. He donated the proceeds to poor families, or to help fund building a church. He was embarrassed to sell them himself, lest it be said he was selling the gold out of the mouths of his patients, and his reputation get ruined.

To confuse things and disguise my tracks, I explained to the goldsmith that there was a material, called "composite" in English, that replaced the crown and preserved the patient's tooth for longer.

During my explanation, I hinted that my uncle was not stealing a crown, as the person concerned did not ask what happened to it once it was removed. Perhaps they did not ask because they believed they had benefited from it for a few years, and now the time had come to lose it, even if fitting it had been expensive. They preferred to gain a tooth and lose the crown, not the other way round.

The goldsmith believed the story and commended my uncle's behaviour, and so he expected me to show up once a month.

He said he gave the pieces he bought from me to the workshop, and after a few days got them back as earrings, bracelets, chains, rings, or icons of saints.

I imagined the emotional reaction of a lady or young woman if they knew that the chain adorning their neck, or the saint's image on their chest, had come from the mouths of the dead. An experience I had been through in my own way with every crown I pulled out.

Whenever I touched or remembered a crown in my pocket before adding it to its counterparts, the face of its owner would appear to me. I even recalled what the inside of his mouth looked like. Those feelings faded when I counted the crowns, which, after crumpling their edges, all looked alike. Then, it was hard to tell whose crown was whose, and out of which jaw I had extracted it.

The strange guy, who once whispered to me "The morgue is a tap running gold", was right.

Published by Difaf Publications, Beirut, Lebanon, 2015

Check out the winner from 26 April 2016 on
www.arabicfiction.org

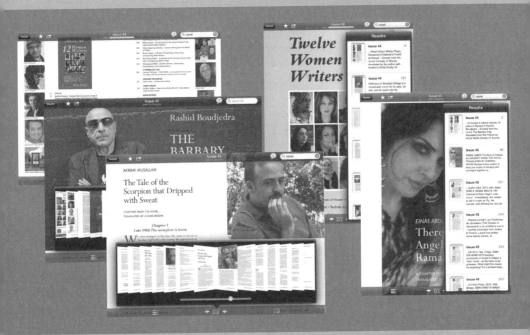
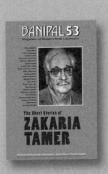

Gretchen McCullough reviews
A Portal in Space
by Mahmoud Saeed

Translated by William M Hutchins

University of Texas Press, 2015, Modern Middle East Literatures in Translation Series.
ISBN: 978-1477308103, pbk, 150pp. £16.99 / $24.95.

Living with war

Every day we are bombarded by disturbing images of war and violence in the Middle East. We think we know what it is like to live through wars. In truth, we do not. In his novel, *A Portal in Space*, set during the Iran-Iraq War, 1980-1988, Mahmoud Saeed describes the visceral, terrifying atmosphere of war and offers a deep, emotional insight into the lives of one close-knit family. Despite the daily bombings and the threat of sudden death, people still appreciate the beauty of nature, help their neighbors and yearn for enjoyment and pleasure. Imprisoned six times in Iraq, Mahmoud Saeed, has witnessed and suffered from both, the beasts of war and harsh, oppressive regimes. Even though many of his books have been censored or even destroyed, he has authored over twenty novels and short story collections. Those translated into English are *Saddam City*, (2004), *The World Through the Eyes of Angels* (2011) *Ben Barka Lane* (2013) and the book under review. Other translations of his work have appeared in *World Literature Today*, *Words Without Borders*, *Banipal* and *The Brooklyn Rail*. Saeed left Iraq in 1985 and worked in Dubai. In 1999, he applied for political asylum to the United States, and since then has lived in Chicago.

Not surprisingly, the desire for flight and freedom are a prominent theme in the novel *A Portal in Space*. Images of birds recur frequently throughout the book. In the opening scene, the family is sitting in the garden, making jokes about the bombardment, which are happening in their very neighborhood. Nur, the college-age daughter points out the zeita, the national bird of Iraq, a beautiful bird that no one has mentioned in any school text or in any scientific descrip-

tions. Nur is intellectually curious and gifted at languages while her mother is a traditional housewife, focused completely on her family and the household. Nur writes an article for National Geographic about the zeita, immerses herself in the study of English and dreams of a career in literature and translation. Much to her father's disappointment, Nur, whose name means light, marries hurriedly and flies from the nest to escape from her bitter mother, at the time he most needs support.

Other images of birds in the novel reflect the idea of domesticity. The mother sees herself as a mother hen, fiercely guarding her chicks. In the same opening scene, Nur jokes that her mother loves Anwar, the son. Her mother denies it, saying, "No, I love you both equally." However, the joke turns sour when Anwar, drafted into the war, disappears. When the mother and father go to Baghdad to check the lists of prisoners of war posted at the UN, the mother is scornful of the woman, Zahra, whom they meet there, telling her, "How can anyone who has lost a chick smile?" She surrenders to her grief and rage and continues to clean the cages of her son's lovebirds, still hoping he will return from the front. Later, when she has recovered from her depression, the mother releases the lovebirds into the open sky.

William Hutchins' natural, idiomatic English translation reflects the spontaneous banter and jokes that are so difficult to lasso when moving from Arabic to English. An attractive, engaging aspect of Arabic culture is the emotional fluidity and the humor — and one grasps it, if visiting or living in the region for a long time. But that spontaneity can also be grasped through the gift of artful translation. William Hutchins, a distinguished literary translator of many prominent writers, is best known for his translation of Naguib Mafouz's *Cairo Trilogy*. His understanding of the Arab tradition of oral storytelling is obvious in his nimble translations of exchanges between family members — and that sharing is their lifeblood. For example, in the opening chapter the mother recalls a time when, early in their marriage, the father was afraid of a mouse. Anwar and Nur, now adults, demand that he tell the story of how he failed to kill the mouse and are delighted by it: "The two artists began to dance. Nur jiggled her midriff like an excellent belly dancer, and Anwar, who was clapping happily, did a Western dance, 'Daddy won't kill a mouse. Iran's bombs kill us. Hee, hee, heeee! Daddy won't kill a mouse. The neighbors' bombs kill us.'"

But war is no joke, as Saeed describes in his novel. If people do survive war physically, they often become psychologically disturbed or go mad. When the family is looking for Anwar, they visit Ali, one of Anwar's friends, who has just returned from the front. The young man is alive, but has lost his right foot. Throughout their visit, he keeps repeating, "We university graduates are to blame. We have no manners..." After the visit, Mundhir, the judge hears his sons' words, "I want a portal in space where I can feel secure and can travel safely, without being afraid to hold my head up high." There is no safe place, even within the home.

Desperate to find his son, the judge visits the front to try to find him. The general that he sees consults a long list and avoids looking him in the eye: "Your son is missing or something else ..." Mundhir guesses the truth and rushes away: "He didn't know how long he wept but the tissue dissolved in his fingers." He must suffer the con-tempt of the driver who takes him to the front and who asks him why he didn't pay a bribe to save his son: "Who would have guessed that the life of a well-educated architect is worth fifty dinars?"

It is easy to sympathize with the judge, a thoroughly likeable char-acter. Besides his honesty, he is loyal and caring, yet fun-loving. He never abuses his position to gain favors or satisfy his ambition and ego. Despite his wide experience hearing cases, he reflects: "How could an upright citizen turn into a criminal, a courageous become

NEXT ISSUE
MAHMOUD SAEED
TALKS ABOUT HIS LIVE AND WORK
IN OUR SERIES ON
LITERARY INFLUENCES

Mahmoud Saeed

a coward, a fine person become despicable, a rational person be-
come crazed, or vice versa in a few moments ..." As long as we are
alive, we keep changing and might do anything, even murder some-
one, given the right circumstances. When the judge asks a man why
he killed his wife, the man said, "Because she made my life hell."

On the judge's first visit to Baghdad to check the International
Red Cross lists of Prisons Affairs of Iran / Iraq, his wife accompanies
him. There he meets the beautiful, lively Zahra, aptly named flower,
a widow who goes to Baghdad to see if her brother-in-law is on the
prisoners' list. After this first visit, his wife blames him for the dis-
appearance of their son and retreats to her room, refusing to inter-
act with anyone.

Mundhir finds himself in a morally compromising situation. Every
week he returns to Baghdad alone and feels himself "gliding into a
relationship" with Zahra, who has the "enormous gift of good cheer"
– a relief from the tense, acrimonious atmosphere of his own home.
Zahra and Mundhir go to a restaurant on the famous Abu Nuwas
Street while waiting for the lists to be posted. It might seem callous
that some people are singing and dancing while others are dying in

the same country. On the other hand, Saeed suggests that the desire for true companionship and the spirit of joie de vivre is like an elixir and can rejuvenate a weary spirit – what Zahra does for Mundhir. And even though Zahra is a mother, she does not see herself as a mother hen: she is still sexy, vibrant and intellectually ambitious, an aspiring novelist. However, when they are having sex in the car, Mundhir remembers all the cases where love led to disaster. He is stunned when they visit a fortuneteller who guesses they are lovers and suggests they marry. Tormented by his conscience, he cannot, however, promise Zahra marriage. Soon after, the situation at home becomes much worse, and his wife almost dies. Zahra stops coming and life acquires "a new sweet taste". He started stopping at Nur and Adil's house in Baghdad, where they would eat at that same restaurant on Abu Nuwas Street. The judge's emotional flexibility is what saves him, unlike others in the novel who cannot adjust to constant change.

A Portal in Space is a poignant, realistic novel about war. While Saeed shows how the human spirit can adapt to and resist the most terrible circumstances, it is very difficult, and often not possible, to heal from the unrelenting sorrow and tragedy that war brings. Will you ever recover if you lose your entire family in a bomb strike? Probably not. Prophets and artists often live in the margins of their societies – and if they are authentic, their message does not salute the agendas and propaganda of the authorities or even bow to the niceties of middle-class conventions. When a raggedy singer is asked to perform, Mundhir is profoundly moved when he hears his voice but shocked because he expects his looks to match his voice. Saeed's voice, like the singer in his novel, is "pure, deep, resonant and authentic".

Laura Ferreri reviews

The Dust of Promises
by Ahlem Mosteghanemi

translated by Nancy Roberts
Bloomsbury Publishing, UK/USA, 2016
ISBN 9781408866269. 305pp, hbk, $18.99 /
£15.90. Kindle £15.10.

Where writing is the only choice

The novel *The Dust of Promises* is the final part of Ahlem Mosteghanemi's trilogy that includes *The Bridges of Constantine* (Bloomsbury, 2014) and *Chaos of the Senses* (Bloomsbury, 2015). With her distinctive writing style, Mosteghanemi brings to a conclusion the love story that has as its protagonists Khaled, a painter and veteran of the Algerian War of Independence, a young novelist Hayat, who is the daughter of Khaled's commander, and a journalist, whose name remains unknown.

The journalist, who is also the narrator of *The Dust of Promises*, is in Paris to receive the prize for "Best Press Photographer of the Year". While visiting art galleries in the French capital, a painting by an Algerian exile attracts his attention. He decides to find out more about the artist and soon realizes that the painter is Khaled, the protagonist of Hayat's first novel as well as her love interest. The journalist is also in love with Hayat and, in an attempt to rekindle a connection with her, he starts a tentative friendship with Khaled. Happenstance soon brings Hayat to Paris and the three of them will have to face their feelings one last time.

This trilogy tells more than a story about a love triangle: Mosteghanemi uses the characters and a deeply symbolic language to speak about her country, Algeria, and its difficult political situation. "If you're going to write, it isn't enough for someone to give

Ahlem Mosteghanemi

you pens and a note-book. Rather, some-body has to hurt you to the point where writing is the only choice you have left. I wouldn't have been able to write this book if she hadn't supplied me with the bitterness and resent-ment I needed to fuel the project. We don't write books for peo-ple, but against them," says the narra-tor of *The Dust of Promises*, words that resemble what Hayat says to Khaled in The Bridges of Constan-tine, "we write novels for no other reason than to kill off their heroes. To finish off the people whose existence has become a bur-den", and both assertions hint at the real motive behind these three novels – the need for the author to express her sadness about the Algerian political situation and the failure of the ideals of the War of Independence. A careful reader will soon understand that Hayat is the personification of Algeria, she is both guilty of greed and cor-ruption and victim of the events. Khaled and the journalist, on the other hand, represent the author, along with that part of the popu-lation who love their country and fight for it, but are filled with bit-terness and disappointment on account of the never-changing situation.

Ahlem Mosteghanemi is one of the first Algerian writers who de-cided to resume writing in Arabic in their literary works after the country's Independence from France. Her love for this language is clear in the style she adopts in her novels: the prose poem, and this

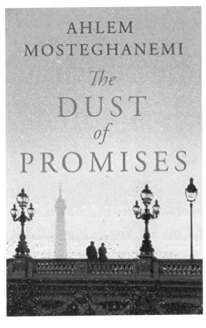

gives the reader an experience that can easily be compared to listening to music. Her language is highly lyrical and rich in symbolism and metaphors – it is a piece of art on its own. In 1998, Mosteghanemi received the Naguib Mahfouz Medal for Literature for the Arabic original of the first book of the trilogy, *The Bridges of Constantine*, in recognition of her talent. English readers will be able to appreciate this elaborate use of language in *The Dust of Promises*, thanks to the praiseworthy work of translator Nancy Roberts.

Mosteghanemi's style, however, is so distinctive that it clashes with her choice of a different narrator for each book of the trilogy. Being projected directly through the mind of each narrator, the reader would expect a different style of narration in each book, but the style remains unchanged throughout the trilogy, and it is impossible to perceive any difference from one narrator to another. However, despite this, the books are entertaining, and well able to catch the reader's attention.

The Dust of Promises will not disappoint anyone has already read the first two parts of the trilogy, and it can also be read on its own without any difficulty. However, the depth and beauty of the story can only be fully appreciated by reading all three works.

Follow us on twitter @BanipalMagazine
https://www.twitter.com/BanipalMagazine

KHALED HROUB

Mernissi: The Sindbad of Fes travels against the Cowboy

In memory of the writer, sociologist and novelist Fatema Mernissi who died on 30 November 2015 – a great friend with joyful and roving spirit that kept travelling but never left us

Who is the winner in globalisation, Sindbad the Sailor or The Cowboy? Such was Fatema Mernissi's question and title of her talk that rainy Frankfurtian evening back in October, 2004. Mernissi's inclusion of "Sindbad" in a discussion about globalisation took me off guard. Where, why and how could this fictional sailor of 11th century Baghdad featured in the legendary book *One Thousand and One Nights* relate to the globalisation of modern times?

***

My friendship with Fatema took us on a journey that kept unfolding in time, space and occasions forming lasting snapshots in my memory: This one is Asturias in the Spanish north where Fatema transported us to explore Ibn Hazm and his splendid thoughts on the limitless faces of love; Amsterdam, where we accompanied Fatema to receive her Erasmus award; Al-Muharrq in Bahrain, where we followed Fatema through the enchanting alleys of the ancient neighbourhood, searching the history of Dilmun. This one is Seville, where we sat on an old Andalusian rug channeling Averroes debating contemplations and hermeneutics with his disciples. Yet another one is the Harhoura seafront near Rabat where Fatema used

Fatema Mernissi and Khaled Hroub, Granada, November 2006

to rent a small house overlooking the Atlantic, and invite us to watch the sunset while listening to the prose and memoirs of the Moroccan poet and long-life political prisoner Abed Al-Latif al-Lu'bi. And, the snapshot that is Frankfurt, where it all started with me, witnessing Fatema running a race between Sindbad and the Cowboy.

***

Fatema Mernissi is a faithful contemporary example of her own metaphor, Sindbad. The sailor, who never rested on land or sea, trans-illuminated his soul in Fatema's spirit and way of life. A transcendent and constant traveller, Fatema spirit remains roving around in our present, defying total death. Fatema's sudden yet incomplete departure is a reminder of one desperate human victory against death. Death, now and then, fails to take the loved ones totally and entirely. Their Sindbadian spirit stays alive, refusing to leave. My following remarks are meant to honour such a spirit and the lasting hold of Fatema's presence. And, to rekindle some little thoughts inspired by that insightful metaphor of her global race between Sindbad and the Cowboy.

***

On globalisation, Fatema followed the pace of history and framed out the debate between brutal and human globalizations in her own way: in a race between the Sindbad and the Cowboy. She travels back and forth between the present and the past, tying up and knitting together her stories and discoveries, then transferring them into the spotlight. Such was Fatema's approach with other ideas and research, a combination of brave encounter, curiosity of details and historical contextualization of the given issue or locality.

With this approach she examined the endless questions of Moroccan and Arab women, as well as cultures of patriarchy that she herself lived in and witnessed. Perhaps other Arab writers had preceded Fatema in observing some of what she observed and wrote about. Yet, they lacked the courage to break into "scandalous taboos", and opted for the false warmth of collective apology. It is never easy to publicly expose the ills and disgraces of one's own society in times of weakness and failure. This is what distinguished Fatema in her famous book *Are You Protected Against Women*, challenging masculine dominance in the East, and seeking to free the Harem. If the masculine mind in the West was temporarily saved from a similar exposure in that book, a following one *Scheherazade Goes West* directly steered the brunt against that Western masculine mind, championing the freedom of the Western Harem. These two books combined dragged all patriarchal and masculine established patterns of society out into the open, from the East and the West. All was thrown out under the sun, naked and shamed. How did she accomplish the double intellectual exercise of advocating the liberation of liberation the Harem in both the East and the West?

For Fatema, as she explained in the first of these two exciting books, woman in the East is imprisoned within the bounds of physical space, whereas woman in the West is imprisoned within the shrinking limits of time/age. Arabian Khadija starts weak, dominated and kept. Her male guardian rules over her, claiming to protect her in a well-demarcated space, fearing that her beauty and youth will lead her and others lured by her astray to the path of lust. As her beauty and youth fade gradually, turning first into a mother and then a grandmother, Khadija becomes strong, liberated and elevated in society. Revered and loved, she occupies the heart of familial circles and authority. Khadija starts her life enslaved because of beauty, youth and space, but ends up liberated and bestowed with wisdom and status.

***

Again, it is Sindbad that took Fatema travelling into the worlds and histories of globalization. Sailing besides him in all directions and times she landed among us in that Frankfurtian evening to tell us that today's globalization belongs to the Cowboy, and this globalization is indeed not only undesirable but also dangerous. But what on earth did Sindbad have to do with globalization? My smug overconfidence lasted less than fifteen minutes — the time that it took for Fatema to give her presentation. It was as if she had unleashed in my face her Sindbad who was now laughing out loud over all that I thought I knew about globalization.

***

Fatema's Sindbad travels eternally and ... gently! He races with nobody. He stops at destinations, wanders around, talks to people, learns hidden wisdoms, then either stays longer or continues travelling. At one of his mystic Sufi stops Sindbad meets Fatema, incarnating his passion for learning, travel and wonder in her spirit. He conveys to her some golden words coined by the 9th century great Syrian poet Abu Tammam: "travel to be renewed". Fatema embraces these words and adds to them the commandment of the 11th century Iraqi/Egyptian poet Ibn Wakee' Al-Tanisi: "Travel for there are five rewards in voyaging: refreshing of the soul; pursuit of means of living; acquiring knowledge; gaining literature; and enjoying the company of noble men." This is the essence of a fleeting Sindbadian globalization that Fatema belonged to, admired and promoted. We can read much in this. Travelling in a Sindbadian spirit is a circular move that goes on without a destination — a global Sufi dance. The treasure of travel is knowledge. Perhaps with or without knowing Sindbad's tale, the great Mughulian emperor Humayun of 16th century India, was a great universal Sindbadian. Embedded with his ancestors' lust for travel, he used to take his books with him wherever he travelled, because he believed that one takes their most precious treasure with them in travelling. No less great Sindbad was Adelard of Bath, who left the comfort of his family and English city in early 12th century onto a magnificent Eastward knowledge-seeking journey. Years passed on with Adelard travelling across Europe, the Mediterranean and the Arab region; paving the way for his return to England as a pioneer of intellect and science combining Greek, Hindu and Arab knowledge.

***

At the heart of Mernissi's globalization is her global Sindbad who is essentially a communicator, unlike the global Cowboy who is essentially a dominator. This communicating Sindbad is thirsty for knowledge, literature and exploration; the dominating Cowboy is driven by hegemony, control and profit. While Fatema makes sharp this contrast, she surprises us by throwing out a new idea: a present day Sindbad exists, in fact, in trans-border media broadcasting. This media enjoys most of those characteristics that our ancient and beloved Sindbad used to have: adventurer, transcending borders, reaching out to the other, inter-communicating on an open field and being open up to uncharted futures and limitless possibilities. Zooming into the case of this modern Sindbad across the Arab region, Fatema applauds the impact of pan-Arab TV-broadcasting. She argues that the around the clock media transmission enriches layers of unprecedented communication among and between groups, individuals and societies. This is, as Fatema depicts, a process where Sindbad is reproduced and reborn in a new modern form. Fatema refers to her astonishment during the travels she made across the Moroccan Rif into remote villages where she found illiterate housewives following programs and talk shows on Al-Jazeera, Al-arabiya, Abu-Dhabi TV and others. They knew by heart, Fatema said, names of poets, thinkers and presenters who were based at the other end of the Arab world, and talked about them and the subjects of their programs as if they were friends or family. Fatema admired the investigative aspect of this trans-border media broadcasting, which for the sake of information and knowledge this media travels the world. Presenters of news coverage, reports of field stories, producers of revealing documentaries or even makers of mere touristic shows are seen by Fatema as various shades of a modern Sindbad. As I was listening to Fatema, her words were falling on my ears like pure music since I had for some time been someone who happened to work and appear on Al-Jazeera as a presenter and producer of a book-review talk show. In those days, criticism of Arab broadcasting media never waned; and hearing Fatema's insights was indeed refreshing balm and reassuring.

***

Today, the Cowboy and the Sindbad present in the West itself fight against each other, to promote an aggressive globalization or a human-faced one. Removing the Cowboy and the Sindbad from any fixated geographical boundaries, East / West imposed binaries or rigid conceptual theories, is what these thoughts are attempting to suggest. Today, one could say it is in fact a Western globalized Sindbad who leads the most ferocious fight against the cruelties of a Western globalized Cowboy. A long list of universalized Sindbadian agents and bodies, either originally founded in the West or which enjoy non-governmental Western support, are spread around the globe challenging the aggressiveness of the Cowboy. These Sindbadians include anti-racist, ant-capitalist, anti-war and all other anti-dehumanising humans movements; spanning human rights bodies, green and environment organizations, eradication of poverty campaigns and all the way to politically driven groups that advocate justice and freedom for the oppressed and indigenous peoples. All stand against the devastating effects of bulldozering globalization and its cold-blooded Cowboy. Today's Western Sindbad is the strongest ally to the Eastern Sindbad; they smuggle to each other the knowledge and expertise to fight back a common brutal enemy. It is within and in the shadow of a mighty Cowboyian globalization that a globalized Sindbad has grown and became stronger.

***

At the heart of the globalization of the Cowboy, the Sindbad of Fes, our Fatema, led an uprising that defied and penetrated time, space, cultures and loyalties. She called upon all those Sindbads who shared the same spirit, gathered them to march on and occupy all cracks and uncharted areas of globalization. In those cracks Fatema stood firmly, spreading her arms and legs against the walls forcing the cracks outward for ever more space. Other Sindbads followed her in a universal dance against the narrow gaps, pushing back and creating wider spaces. The continuation of this Sindbadian dance, drumming and hitting against the walls of brutal globalization is part of the great legacy that Fatema left with us.

To read the tribute in full, go to
http://www.banipal.co.uk/selections/

Paul Starkey and Youssef Rakha in conversation

Youssef Rakha, Paul Starkey, Gaby Wood and Paul Blezard at Waterstone's Piccadilly, London

BY VALENTINA VIENE

The evening after the award of the 2015 Saif Ghobash Banipal Prize for Arabic Translation, the winning translator Paul Starkey and his author Youssef Rakha were in conversation with Gaby Wood, the literary director of the Booker Prize Foundation at Waterstone's Piccadilly bookstore before a crowded and enthusiastic audience. The winning novel, *The Book of the Sultan's Seal: Strange Incidents from History in the City of Mars*, was published in Arabic by Dar El-Shorouk shortly after President Hosni Mubarak was ousted in 2011, and in English translation by Interlink Books in Spring last year.

The translator has been praised for his audacity and ability to work on a complex text that presents a series of challenges, the main one being Rakha's complex language. Youssef Rakha was inspired by the

Waterstone's Piccadilly, London

Egyptian historiographer Abdel Rahman al-Jabarti who decided to experiment with the Arabic language, following the footsteps of Mameluk historiographers. Rakha attempts to recreate what could be described as a modern version of Jabarti's language or a medieval-inspired middle Arabic, where linguistic registers are used without respecting canonical rules. Whoever has translated any Arabic fiction, however short, will know that most narrative will be written in fus-ha, classical Arabic, whereas dialogue can, but not always, employ a local dialect. This is not the case for Rakha's book: in *The Book of the Sultan's Seal* a sentence can start in *fus-ha* and end in dialect.

Paul Starkey, Emeritus Professor of Arabic at the University of Durham, said that the first challenge posed by the book was to pitch its tone. "You've got prose poems [...], you've got this wonderful Turkish sultan speaking in this sort of Ottomanized Arabic, in a very formal sort of expression [...]." In addition to that, the author's Introduction tells the reader that the novel's language will be "imitating speech in all its variety", mistakes will be kept willingly and foreign idioms will be included without even being highlighted in a different font because they have become part of the spoken language. To add to the complexity, some of the book's players are Arab, some Turkish, and their names reflect that in the translation with the name of the protagonist, Çorbacı, though Egyptian, being spelled in the Turkish way.

Margaret Obank announces the
Saif Ghobash Banipal Lecture

Paul Starkey's Afterword explains many of his stylistic choices for dealing with the challenges and is, in fact, just as interesting as the novel itself.

Paul Starkey and Youssef Rakha spoke about how they worked harmoniously together on the translation. Starkey described it as straightforward process, facilitated by the author being contemporary and speaking very good English, and complemented by the great work of copy-editor Hilary Plum. Rakha added: "Paul was really wonderful because he stayed completely neutral" towards the text, and allowed the translation to take its own shape. He also joked that for him to translate his own book would have been a real "kamikaze act".

It would have been fascinating to learn more about the experience of a senior translator, like Starkey, with other books and authors where the scenario might be completely different. For example, the author might be dead or not know any English. There are other occasions where the relationship between author and translator becomes tense or delicate, especially if the author thinks that the translator has made the wrong choices. Translator Jonathan Wright, who received the judges' Commendation for his translation of Amjad Nasser's novel *Land of No Rain*, explained that he had spent several hours with the author, asking him no less than 250 questions. He stressed how important it was for him to be in continuous

YOUSSEF RAKHA

talks to **Valentina Viene** about *The Book of the Sultan's Seal* and "rediscovering and reanimating the Arabic language"

Available online at:
www.banipal.co.uk/selections

For all information about the Saif Ghobash Banipal Prize for Arabic Literary Translation go to: **www.banipaltrust.org.uk**

conversation with the author to avoid making wrong assumptions, which would then result in a bad translation. The success of his translation was determined without doubt by this joint effort of translator and author – with this way of working strongly supported by Paul Starkey.

Margaret Obank, who administers the Banipal Trust and is Banipal's publisher, made a special announcement that the Trust and the prize's sponsor, Omar Saif Ghobash and his family, have agreed to mark the tenth award of the prize in a way that will celebrate even more the essential role of literary translation in enabling human beings to talk to and understand each other, especially in the case of Arabic literary translation. In addition to the prize, there will now be a Saif Ghobash Banipal Prize Annual Lecture on literary translation, the inaugural lecture to be held in London later this year.

Leila Aboulela was born in 1964 in Cairo and grew up in Khartoum. She has a BA in Economics from Khartoum University and an MA in Statistics from the London School of Economics. She is the author of four novels, a collection of short stories and a number of radio plays. Several stories are published in anthologies and broadcast on radio,. "The Museum" won the inaugural Caine Prize for African Writing in 2000. She lives between Abu Dhabi and Aberdeen.

Mohammad Jamil Ahmad is a Sudanese poet, writer and journalist, born in 1967 in Port Sudan. Educated in Sudan, he writes on literary matters and thought for various Arab newspapers and magazines and has published poetry collections, critical works and a novel. He lives and works in Riyadh, Saudi Arabia.

Adil Babikir is a Sudanese translator into and out of English & Arabic, living now in Abu Dhabi. He has translated *Mansi: a Rare Man in his Own Way* by Tayeb Salih and two novels by Abdelaziz Baraka Sakin. Other translations include two anthologies – of poetry and short stories.

Tareq Bakari was born in Missour, eastern Morocco, in 1988. He graduated with a BA in Arabic Literature from Mohamed Bin Abdullah University, Fes, in 2010 and obtained a diploma from the Meknes Teacher Training College in 2011. Since then, he has worked as an Arabic language teacher in Meknes. He has published many articles and creative writing, in print and online. *Numedia* (2015) is his first novel.

Emad Blake is a Sudanese novelist and critic, born in 1972. He studied architecture at Khartoum University, but became a professional journalist in Sudan and Arab Gulf countries. He has six novels, the best known being *Shawarma* (2014), excerpted above. His latest novel, *Mama Merkel*, is about migration to Europe. At present he lives in Muscat, Oman, where he works as an editor for the *Oman Daily*.

Raphael Cohen is a translator based in Cairo. His translations of contemporary Arab fiction includes Mona Prince's novel *So You May See* (2011), *Status: Emo* by Eslam Mosbah (2013), three novels of Ahlem Mosteghanemi and *Butterfly Wings* by Mohamed Salmawy (2014). He is a contributing editor of *Banipal*.

Maysoon Elnigoumi is a Sudanese writer, living in Sydney, Australia. She writes poetry and articles on literature, music and arts, some of which have appeared in Sudanese newspapers.

Najlaa Osman Eltom is a Sudanese writer based in Sweden. She has been active in the Sudanese literary scene since 2000. She has two poetry collections in Arabic, Cairo 2007, and Istanbul 2016. Some of her work is translated into Swedish and English. She has also published several literary translations into English and Arabic. She has an MA in English Literature from Stockholm University (2015).

Tarek Eltayeb is a Sudanese author, born in Cairo in 1959, and living in Vienna since 1984. He currently teaches at three Austrian universities. He has published three novels, two collections of short stories, five collections of poems, a play, an autobiographical book and a collection of essays. His books have been published in German, English, Italian, French, Spanish, Macedonian, Romanian and Serbian translations.

Laura Ferreri has a BA in interpreting and translation from Trieste University, Italy, and is completing an MA in Arabic Translation at Edinburgh University with the Centre for Advanced Studies of the Arabic World (CASAW).

Stella Gaitano was born in Khartoum in 1979 into a South Sudanese family. She graduated in pharmacy from Khartoum University. She writes short stories in Arabic and has two collections, *Wilted Flowers* and *Homecoming*. She was forced to relocate to South Sudan in 2012.

Sally Gomaa was born and raised in Alexandria, Egypt,. She has a BA in English Literature from Alexandria University and a PhD in Rhetoric and Composition from Rhode Island University, USA. She is an Associate Professor of English at Salve Regina University, USA. Her publications include an English translation of Amina Zaydan's *Red Wine* (AUC Press, 2010).

Ann Harrison is Programme Director of PEN International's Writers in Prison Committee. She has worked in human rights for many years, and was previously Deputy Director of Amnesty International's Middle East and North Africa Programme.

Khaled Hroub is a professor of Middle Eastern Studies and Arab Media Studies at Northwestern University, Qatar, and a senior research fellow at the Centre of Islamic Studies of the Faculty of Asian and Middle Eastern Studies, University of Cambridge. He is the author of several books on Middle East politics and media, culture and political Islam and hosted Al-Jazeera TV's weekly book review show 2000–2006, then the only show of its kind on Arab TV screens. He writes weekly on current affairs for the Arab press, and is a trustee of the IPAF.

Nur al-Huda Mohammad Nur al-Huda: Please see interview starting on page 144.

William Maynard Hutchins has translated many contemporary Arab authors including Naguib Mahfouz. He was joint-winner of the 2013 Saif Ghobash Banipal Prize for *A Land Without Jasmine* by Wajdi al-Ahdal (Garnet, 2012) and winner of the ALTA's 2015 National Translation Award for *New Waw* by Ibrahim al-Koni.

Volker Kaminski is a German writer, living in Berlin. He contributes regularly, with reviews, interviews and short stories to literary magazines, newspapers such as *Berliner Zeitung*, and radio programmes. His latest novel *Roter Schnee* is out later this year. He teaches Creative Writing at the Alice Salomon University in Berlin.

Abdel Ghani Karamallah is a Sudanese writer from the Blue Nile area south of Khartoum. He has published several novels and collections of short stories, and eight books of children's stories. He lives in Khartoum.

Rabai al-Madhoun is a Palestinian writer, born in al-Majdal, Ashkelon, southern Palestine (now Israel), in 1945. He has worked at the Palestinian Centre for Research Studies and as a journalist and editor with many newspapers and magazines, including *Sawt al-Bilad, Al-Quds al-Arabi, Al-Hayat*, and is currently with *Al-Sharq Al-Awsat* newspaper, London. His second novel, *The Lady from Tel Aviv*, was shortlisted for the 2010 IPAF (English edition, Telegram Books, 2013).

Becki Maddock has a 1st class BA in Arabic and Spanish (Exeter University), and working knowledge of other languages including Persian and Dari. She worked for a number of years as a research analyst and translator of texts on a wide variety of subjects, including technical, scientific, military, political and legal topics, and is presently studying for an MA at SOAS, London.

Jamal Mahjoub was born in London in 1960. He spent his formative years in Khartoum before being awarded a scholarship to Atlantic College in Wales. He went on to study Geology at Sheffield University. He returned briefly to the Sudan in search of employment after which deciding to dedicate himself to writing. His work has been translated into French, Spanish, German, Italian, Dutch and Turkish.

Ahmad Al Malik is a Sudanese novelist and storyteller. He was born in 1967 in the Island of Argo in Northern Sudan. Since 1991 he has published eight novels and one collection of short stories. His novel, *The Autumn Comes with Safaa* (2003), was translated into Dutch and French, and many of his short stories have been translated into several languages. He lives in Holland.

Rania Mamoun was born in 1979 in Wad Medani in east central Sudan, and graduated from the University of Gezira. She has one collection of short stories, *The Thirteen Months of Sunrise*, the title story was published in *Banipal 30*, and two novels *Flash al-Akhdar* (Green Flash), 2006, and *Ibn Al-Shams* (Son of the Sun), 2013. She joined the 2010 IPAF writers' nadwa.

Rosie Maxton has a BA from St. Andrews University in Arabic and Medieval History. She is currently studying for an MA at the University of Cambridge.

Gretchen McCullough is an American writer and translator. She graduated from Brown University (1984) and has an MFA from the University of Alabama. She has two collections of short stories (AFAQ, Cairo, 2011, 2013). She teaches at the American University of Cairo.

Robin Moger is a translator of Arabic literature currently living in Cape Town, South Africa. He has a BA in Egyptology and Arabic from Oxford University (2001) and worked at the *Cairo Times* until it closed. His translations include novels by Hamdi Abu Golayyel, Ahmed Mourad, Nael El-toukhy, Yousef al-Mohaimeed and Youssef Rakha.

Hamed el-Nazir was born in Sudan in 1975. He currently works in the newsroom of Qatar TV and also writes for various Arab media. He has been a presenter on Sudan radio, and on Sudanese TV for the Shorouk and Blue Nile channels, and a news correspondent for MBC. His first novel, *Farij al-Murar* (2014), won the Sharjah Award for Arab Creativity. His novel *Nubuat al-Saqqa* (The Waterman's Prophecy), excerpted above, was longlisted for the 2016 IPAF.

John Peate is a translator, university teacher, academic researcher and language consultant based in the UK. He has BAs in English and in Arabic from Leeds University, an MA in Translation from SOAS, London and a PhD in Arabic Linguistics from the University of Salford.

Mohamed Rabie is an Egyptian writer, born in 1978. His first novel, *Kawkab Anbar* (2010), won first prize in the emerging writers' category of the Sawiris Cultural Award in 2012. His second novel came out in 2012, and *Mercury* in 2014, which will be published late 2016, entitled *Otared* in English translation by Robin Moger. In 2012, he took part in the IPAF nadwa.

For more information on all the authors in *Banipal 55* and all the translators, writers and reviewers, please go to:

www.banipal.co.uk/contributors/

CONTRIBUTORS

Azza Rashad is an Egyptian writer, born in the Eastern Province. She has published novels and short story collections, also literary articles in the Arab media. See *Banipal 30* for two of her short stories.

Clare Roberts has a BA in Arabic and Islamic Studies (Oxford University) and an MA in Arabic Poetry and Turkish Politics (SOAS, London). She currently works at a charity in London, and reviews for *Banipal*.

Nancy Roberts is an award-winning translator of contemporary Arabic fiction. Her recent translations include novels by Laila Aljohani, Ahlem Mosteghanemi, Ezzat el Kamhawi and Ibrahim Nasrallah. Her translation of Egyptian author Salwa Bakr's *The Man from Bashmour* was commended for the 2008 Saif Ghobash Banipal Prize. She has also translated works by Naguib Mahfouz, Mohamed el-Bisatie and Hala El-Badry, and 3 novels of Syrian author Ghada Samman.

Basil Samara was born in 1948 in Tehran, Iran, to Lebanese parents, returning to Lebanon as a young boy. He has a PhD in Statistics from the University of Florida, USA, where he lives. He was a statistical consultant, but took early retirement to concentrate on artistic inclinations.

Mahmoud Shukair is a Palestinian writer of short stories, and novels for adults and teenagers, with forty-five books, six television series, and four plays. His stories have been translated into several languages, including English, French, German, Chinese, Mongolian and Czech. In 2011, he was awarded the Mahmoud Darwish Prize for Freedom of Expression. He has spent his life between Beirut, Amman and Prague and now lives in Jerusalem.

Olivia Snaije is a journalist, based in Paris. She has covered the Middle East for the past twenty years. She co-edited the book about the Israeli wall *Keep your Eye on the Wall* (2013) with Mitchell Albert, writes for *Publishing Perspectives* and reviews for *Banipal*.

Paul Starkey is Emeritus Professor of Arabic at Durham University, Vice-President of the BRISMES and Chair of the Banipal Trust for Arab Literature. He has translated many works by contemporary Arab authors, the latest being Youssef Rakha's *The Book of the Sultan's Seal* (Interlink, 2014), for which he won the 2015 Saif Ghobash Banipal Prize.

Mansour El Souwaim was born in 1970 in Nyala, in the Darfur District of Sudan. He studied Critique Studies at the College of Music and Drama of the Sudan University of Sciences and Technology. He has published four novels, with *Dhakirat Shirrir* (2005) excerpted above. He was one of the Beirut39 young Arab authors, with work in the *Beirut39 New Writing from the Arab World* (2012).

Shahla Ujayli is a Syrian writer, born in 1976. She has a PhD in Modern Arabic Literature and Cultural Studies (Aleppo University, Syria) and currently teaches Modern Arabic Literature there and at the American University in Madaba, Jordan. She has a short story collection and two novels, and has published a number of critical studies on the novel. In 2014, she took part in the IPAF writers' workshop.

Valentina Viene is Italian by birth, now settled in the UK. She has a BA degree in Arabic and English from the University of Naples L'Orientale, and an MA in the Theory and Practice of Arabic Translation.

Jonathan Wright worked for many years as a journalist in countries across the Arab world including Tunisia, Oman, Lebanon and Egypt. Among his recent translations are the 2013 IPAF winner, *The Bamboo Stalk* by Saud Alsanousi, Amjad Nasser's *Land of No Rain*, commended for the 2015 Saif Ghobash Banipal Prize, Youssef Ziedan's *Azazeel* (2012), joint winner of the 2013 Saif Ghobash Banipal Prize, and Hassan Blasim's *The Iraqi Christ*, which won the Independent Foreign Fiction Prize.

George Yaraq is a Lebanese novelist, born in 1958. He has worked as an editor and freelance writer for several Lebanese newspapers and magazines, including *Al-Nahar, Al-Liwa', Al-Hayat, Al-Sayyad*, and *Jasad*. His first novel, *Night*, was published in 2013.

Hammour Ziada is a Sudanese writer and journalist, born in Khartoum in 1977. He has worked for charitable and civil society organisations, and as a journalist for Sudanese newspapers. He was Chief Editor of the cultural section of the Sudanese *Al-Akhbar*. He has several works of fiction. His second novel, *The Longing of the Dervish* (2014), won the Naguib Mahfouz Medal for Literature in 2014 and was shortlisted for the 2015 IPAF.

To SUBSCRIBE TO PRINT BANIPAL see page 221 or go to:
http://www.banipal.co.uk/subscribe/

To SUBSCRIBE TO DIGITAL BANIPAL or make a trial, see page 203 or go to:
http://www.exacteditions.com/browse/20700/21379